Subject to Whose Authority?

Emory Studies in Early Christianity

General Editor
Vernon K. Robbins

Associate Editor
David B. Gowler, Chowan College

Cover Design by Gina M. Tansley
(adapted from Rick A. Robbins, *Mixed Media 1981*)

The cover design introduces an environment for disciplined creativity. The seven squares superimposed over one another represent multiple arenas for programmatic research, analysis, and interpretation. The area in the center, common to all the arenas, is like the area that provides the unity for a volume in the series. The small square in the center of the squares denotes a paragraph, page, or other unit of text. The two lines that extend out from the small square, perpendicular to one another, create an opening to territory not covered by any of the multiple squares. These lines have the potential to create yet another square of the same or different size that would be a new arena for research, analysis, and interpretation.

Subject to Whose Authority?

Multiple Readings of Romans 13

by
Jan Botha

SCHOLARS PRESS
Atlanta, Georgia

EMORY STUDIES
IN EARLY CHRISTIANITY

Subject to Whose Authority?

by
Jan Botha

Grateful acknowledgment is given to the Office of the Secretary of the University, the Graduate School of Arts and Sciences, Emory College, and the Department of Religion in support of this volume.

Library of Congress Cataloging in Publication Data
Botha, Jan.
    Subject to whose authority? : multiple readings of Romans 13 / by Jan Botha.
        p.   cm. — (Emory studies in early Christianity ; 4)
    Includes bibliographical references.
    ISBN 1-55540-922-9
    1. Bible. N.T. Romans XIII—Criticism, interpretation, etc.
I. Title. II. Series: Emory studies in early Christianity ; vol. 4.
BS2665.2.B68   1993
227'.106—dc20   93-39944
                                                 CIP

Published by Scholars Press
for
Emory University

Previous titles in the series published by Peter Lang Publishing

Publication of this volume
was made possible by a gift
by Isabella Lewis
in honor of Clay Lewis

For Carools Reinecke

TABLE OF CONTENTS

EDITORIAL FOREWORD

This volume in *Emory Studies in Early Christianity* moves a decisive step forward in the interdisciplinary context of New Testament studies as it has developed during the last two decades. The first volume in this series by David B. Gowler effects an interdisciplinary merger between narratology and social-scientific criticism (Gowler 1991). The current volume by Jan Botha merges linguistic, literary, rhetorical and social-scientific criticism in an interdisplinary mode.

It is the nature of an interdisciplinary mode of analysis to bring disciplinary strategies and results into dialogue with one another. There are two major alternative approaches in New Testament studies at present. Disciplinary analysis and investigation, which was the nature of New Testament studies until the 1970s, establishes one discipline in a hierarchical position and uses strategies and results from other disciplines in a subdisciplinary manner. This means that the interpreter uses strategies and results from other disciplines on the terms of the discipline they are holding in a dominant position, rather than on the terms of the discipline which has developed the strategies and results. Eclectic or multidisciplinary studies have been the alternative to disciplinary studies. In these studies, interpreters select strategies and results from various disciplines and use them in combinations that, in one way or another, contribute toward the goals of the interpreter.

Five approaches to New Testament texts have attempted to attain disciplinary status during the last two decades: structuralism, literary criticism, linguistic criticism, rhetorical criticism, and social-scientific criticism. At this point, literary and social-scientific criticism have become powerful disciplinary approaches alongside historical criticism. Rhetorical criticism is a powerful discipline in epistolary studies, but its influence is more diffuse in analysis of the Gospels, Acts, and Revelation. Structuralism and linguistic studies have widespread influence, but their "super"-disciplinary nature has limited the domain of their acceptance in New Testament studies.

These new disciplines have arisen in an environment where New Testament studies has changed from a disciplinary to an interdisciplinary field of study. Structuralism, linguistic criticism, and rhetorical criticism are by nature interdisciplinary, using extensive resources from both textual and social disciplines of study. Literary criticism and social-scientific criticism also are interdisciplines. The irony, perhaps, is that literary and social-scientific critics have taken these approaches into the mainstream of biblical studies by functioning in a "disciplinary" manner. Yet Michel Foucault has taught us that disciplinary investigation and power go hand in hand. People establish a discipline by focusing on a limited range of phenomena with a particular set of strategies. Anyone who investigates the same phenomena with other strategies is outside the boundaries ("out of bounds"), as well as anyone who uses the same strategies on different phenomena. In this manner, a discipline establishes the boundaries for its work and operates as a power structure that challenges other power structures in the field of study. Meanwhile, the phenomena themselves stand in relationships to other phenomena in a manner that transcends any disciplinary approach to them.

The time has come, in our opinion, for truly interdisciplinary study to "take the field." This will demand, first, that every New Testament interpreter develop at least two "disciplinary specialties." But it will demand, second, that interpreters learn the skill of negotiating disciplinary results in a manner that maintains the integrity of the insights from each discipline.

Botha's analysis of Romans 13:1-7 begins to show us the way. First, he performs linguistic analysis of the passage in a disciplinary manner; second, literary analysis; third, rhetorical analysis; and fourth, social-scientific analysis. In each instance, he takes the disciplinary nature of each approach seriously and applies it to the text in the manner in which that discipline "demands" it. He argues, however, that any one discipline, on its own, cannot fulfill the task of a "responsible reading."

The ethics of responsible reading requires that interpreters work first fully into the "world of the text." Linguistics makes the interpreter aware that syntactic, semantic, narratorial and argumentative analysis, if performed simply at the level of the "sense" of the text, is an incomplete reading that may present or contribute to a highly irresponsible interpretation. The interpreter must use the strategies of rhetorical and social-scientific criticism to investigate the "historical world" both of the text and of the interpreter. With the aid of rhetorical criticism, interpreters distinguish between historical situations — which are expansive and indefinite — and rhetorical situations — which are the specific situations constituted in all discourse, including textual discourse. With the aid of social-scientific criticism, interpreters distinguish between the nature of the world in which the text was produced and the nature of the world in which interpreters perform their investigations and draw their conclusions. In Botha's terms, a social-scientific reading must precede the drawing of historical conclusions for the present; or, in alternative terms, it must precede inferences about the relation of the world of the text to the historical world.

As Botha's study advances our understanding of the interdisciplinary nature of "responsible reading," it makes us aware that some of the most important insights into New Testament studies are coming from South Africa. New Testament interpreters have been accustomed to a dominance of German biblical scholarship during the last two centuries. For some years now, some interpreters have been pointing to Latin and South America as regions of special importance for biblical studies. More and more, new initiatives have come from North America, where the Society of Biblical Literature has become a context for 5,000 biblical interpreters to gather for forums, research seminars, consultations, and publication projects. These initiatives include special interest in social and cultural environments that experience conflict, marginalization, upheaval, renewal, and reorganization. The international rather than national nature of biblical studies in North America is becoming more and more evident with the international Society of Biblical Literature meetings outside of North America and with the international cooperation of publishers. It is not accidental, then, that a study produced in the context of South African New Testament studies may show us how to do "serious" biblical interpretation in a more complete and responsible manner.

Vernon K. Robbins
Emory University
General Editor

David B. Gowler
Chowan College
Associate Editor

August 4, 1994

PREFACE

I am very grateful to Vernon Robbins, General Editor of *Emory Studies in Early Christianity*, for accepting this book for publication in his distinguished series. For his kindness and professionalism and especially his patience, I offer him a sincere word of appreciation and respect. Through his numerous publications he has deeply influenced my scholarly development through many years and especially my views on the nature of the text and its place in the interpretation of the New Testament. It was an honor to come to know him personally through the publication process of this book. As Associate Editor of the series, David Gowler has worked very hard to get the final manuscript ready for publication. For that and for the patient and friendly manner in which he supported and encouraged me to complete this work, a word of special thanks.

The majority of this study was written as a doctoral dissertation (presented to the Faculty of Theology of the University of Stellenbosch in 1992). Bernard Lategan has acted as my *Doktorvater*. I truly admire and appreciate the scholarly expertise and wisdom he put into this effort of mine. Wilhelm Wuellner was kind enough to accept me as a visiting scholar at the Graduate Theological Union in Berkeley, California, during 1988. From numerous discussions then, as well as his enthusiastic continued interest after we left Berkeley, I have benefited greatly.

I can never adequately acknowledge all my debts to those people in the scholarly community who have taught me, inspired me, introduced me to new ways of thinking, and in many ways influenced my thought, style of scholarship, and interests. The numbers involved are too large and the occasions too numerous to mention. Nevertheless, I want to mention specifically the stimuli I have received from the following South African scholars through personal contact and through discussions at various occasions: Bernard Combrink, Jan Swanepoel, Johannes Vorster, Dirk Smit, Johannes Louw, Johann Kinghorn, Fika van Rensburg, and the late Willem Vorster; as well as the following international scholars: Lauri Thurén (Turku, Finland), John Elliott (University of San Francisco), Sjef van Tilborg (Katholieke Universiteit Nijmegen), Detlev Dormeyer (Westfälische Wilhelms-Universität, Münster), James Hester (University of Redlands, California), Charles Cousar (Columbia Theological Seminary, Decatur, Georgia) and Robert Fortna (Vassar College).

Through his example of academic excellence and integrity as a biochemist, Carools Reinecke has taught me those things about the scholarly world that one does not learn from reading books. Having lost my own father at an early age I am privileged to have him as a friend who did for me down through the years many of those things that fathers usually do for their children. It is an honor to dedicate this book to him.

Lauri Thurén, Jan Swanepoel, Heilna du Plooy, Johannes Vorster, and Elma Cornelius have been kind enough to read through parts of earlier versions of this book. My sincere appreciation for their time and for their valuable comments. A word of thanks to Annette Combrink who has corrected my English, my father-in-law and Douglas Low who did the final proofreading, Karen Veldtman who compiled the subject index, and N. Clayton Croy and Sarah Melcher who assisted in the final and all-important finishing touches of this manuscript.

The support of my family has always been a source of inspiration and helped me to pull through. To my wife Louise, our children Jan Abraham and Pieter, and my parents-in-law, PW and Lulu Buys — thank you for surrounding me with the love and warmth of a deeply happy family life.

Jan Botha
Stellenbosch
Inauguration Day: May 10, 1994

INTRODUCTION

The problematic nature of Romans 13:1-7, the famous 'church-state' text, is well-known. Many examples can be cited of the use and abuse of this text in the course of the history of Christianity.[1] The following remarks by Allan Boesak and P. W. Botha confirm its prominence in the South African socio-political context during the apartheid era.

One of the most eloquent opponents of apartheid, Allan Boesak, begins his essay titled 'What belongs to Caesar? Once again Romans 13,' with the following little story (1986:138):

> On 19 October 1977, I was visited for the first time by the South African Security Police. They stayed from 3:30 A.M. till 7:00 A.M. At one point I was challenged by the Security Police captain (who assured me that he was a Christian and, in fact, an elder of the white Dutch Reformed Church), on my persistent resistance to the government. "How can you do what you are doing," he asked, "while you know what Romans Thirteen says?" In the hour-long conversation that followed, I could not convince him. For him, as for millions of other Christians in South Africa and across the world, Romans 13 is an unequivocal, unrelenting call for blind, unquestioning obedience to the state.

Addressing a gathering of a million members of the (mainly black) Zion Christian Church near Pietersburg in April 1985, the former South African State President, P. W. Botha, praised his audience as people who 'love and respect their Bishop,' who have 'a sincere and healthy lifestyle' and who 'respect law, order and authority.' Later on in his speech he said (1985:6):

> The Bible . . . has a message for the governments and governed of the world. Thus we read in Romans 13 that every person be subject to the governing authorities.

---

[1]See Wilckens (1982:43-66) for a comprehensive discussion of the *Wirkungsge-schichte* of Romans 13:1-7. He discusses the influence of Romans 13:1-7 on the stance of the martyrs toward the authorities during the age of persecution (44-46), the problem of the fusion of church and state after Constantine (45-47), the Medieval *Zwei-Schwerter* theory and Romans 13 (47-49), Luther's interpretation, especially in the light of the revolt by the farmers led by Thomas Müntzer (47-52), the struggle of other reformers like Zwingli (who himself eventually died in a political struggle), Bucer and Calvin's attempts to come to grips with Romans 13 and the consequent influence of Calvin's interpretation on all the reformed confessions (52-55), the role of this text in the 17th century church-state relationship debates in Europe and England (55-58), the significant influence of the French revolution on the reception of Romans 13:1-7 and the subsequent interpretations by Kant, Hegel and Marx (58-61), Karl Barth and the Barmen Confession in the twentieth century (62-64), the Roman Catholic theory of state since the 18th century (65-66) and finally, Romans 13:1-7 and Liberation Theology (66).

> There is no authority except from God. Rulers are not a terror to good conduct, but to bad conduct. Do what is good, and you will receive the approval of the ruler. He is God's servant for your good.

Coming from *the* symbol of an oppressive government, addressed to a black audience, spoken only three months before the first State of Emergency was announced in South Africa, these words had indeed an ominous ring.

I believe that New Testament scholars have the responsibility to attempt to propose valid interpretation(s) of this — and other — problematic passages in the Bible. A catalogue of possible ways to deal with Romans 13:1-7 by means of 'escapes' from an authoritarian reading has been compiled by Robert Fowler (see Fowler). Yet the problem remains: What shall we do with this passage? Or, to use the terminology of Victor Furnish (1985:13–25): Is Romans 13 a 'sacred cow' or a 'white elephant' in contemporary Christians ethics? According to the sacred cow approach all the ethical teachings of Paul are in fact God's commandments and are thus eternally and universally binding; according to the white elephant view Paul's ethical teaching is outmoded, irrelevant and ridiculous — an anachronism — like an antique automobile: interesting only to antiquarians, but a real menace when driven out onto a modern expressway.

In addition to the general problematic nature of the interpretation and 'application' of Paul's moral teaching in the modern world, it is clear that the interpretation of this particular passage in the South African context is highly problematic. In addition to a number of more traditional exegetical issues (aptly summarized by Reese 1973), the main problem seems to be: Does it call for obedience to the government on the part of Christians under all circumstances, or does it not? Can it be interpreted in such a way as to leave the door open for Christians to disobey and actively resist the state with a clear conscience? Stated differently, is the intended effect of Romans 13:1-7 *conformity* or *confrontation* on the part of its readers in their conduct regarding the authorities?

The aim of this study is to attempt to put us in a better position to reflect in a plausible manner on these issues and on the general problems of interpretation of Romans 13:1-7. Therefore an interpretation of Romans 13:1-7 based on some of the recent methodological developments in New Testament studies will be undertaken in this book. This is achieved by reading Romans 13:1-7 from four different perspectives: a linguistic perspective (chapter 1), a literary perspective (chapter 2), a rhetorical perspective (chapter 3) and a social-scientific perspective (chapter 4).

Recent methodological developments in New Testament Studies

During the past three decades there have been rapid methodological developments in New Testament scholarship. Consider, for example, the following remark of Mack (13–14):

> The 1970s marked a very restless scholarship. Literary critics in general were restlessly engaged in efforts to understand their literatures as social, historical, and cultural phenomena. Scholars wanted to know more about the difference a social and cultural history made on the writing of literature, and about the difference a piece of writing might in turn make on society. Old clichés about texts, canons, the history of ideas, aesthetic objects, and the priority of myth over ritual no longer seemed adequate to explain what needed to be explained. Scholars found themselves stunned by the social upheavals of the 1960s and the cultural cross fires of the 1970s. They were embarrassed because they had no theory to account for the effective differences among competing ideologies and political programs. Semantic battles raged over the proper description of world views and social programs, and what to call a given proposal: a myth, an ideal, a system of values, an ideology, a religion, a mystery, or the raving of a tormented soul? . . . New Testament scholars took to these rapids with amazing alacrity and most managed to ride them out with some sense of exhilaration.

One of the outstanding characteristics of New Testament interpretation during the last three decades is its interaction with other disciplines (see Combrink 1986; Lategan 1978, 1984; Dormeyer). Insights, methods and procedures derived from disciplines such as linguistics, literary theory, social sciences (such as anthropology, sociology and psychology) and philosophy have changed the landscape of New Testament interpretation. The question whether New Testament scholarship has indeed moved into a new paradigm (in the Kuhnian sense) or whether the full consequences of the historical paradigm are only now being taken seriously is still being debated vigorously from a number of different viewpoints (see, for example, Martin; W. S. Vorster 1988; Lategan 1988; Van Aarde).

The awareness of the multi-dimensional nature of textual communication stimulated the urge for an all-encompassing model. Lategan (1988:69) confirms this need (see also Lategan 1985b:5–6):

> The three basic features of the text are its historical, structural and theological or conceptual aspects . . . A convincing exegetical paradigm has to account adequately for all these dimensions. Traditionally, methods of a historical nature usually dealt best with the historical aspects, insights from structuralism were mainly responsible for the progress made with the structural aspects, while different forms of theological exegesis tried to deal with the theological dimension. Attempts to integrate these aspects in a single paradigm were less successful. Neither the existence, nor the importance of other dimensions were denied by the different approaches, but an all-encompassing paradigm seems to elude exegetes.

A new methodology for New Testament interpretation which does justice to the many new insights from the many different scientific disciplines, and which enjoys general acceptance by the guild, is thus still lacking. This study does *not* intend the difficult task of developing such a new paradigm nor to map out an all-encompassing new method of interpretation within such a paradigm. However important the search for methodological integration on a higher level might be — and significant progress in this regard has been made recently (see, for example, Lategan; Robbins 1992a, 1992b, 1992c, 1994) — that is not the aim of this study. This investigation does not attempt to integrate the four methods as a comprehensive exegetical or hermeneutical model for interpreting Romans 13:1–7. I do hope that these approaches present a plausible exegesis of the passage and that, taken together, they perform most of the important tasks of a scientific interpretation of an ancient text.

The choice of perspectives and an ethics of interpretation

The four approaches used here to interpret Romans 13:1–7 — namely linguistics, literary studies, rhetoric and social-science — are but four of many possibilities. This is not to deny insights from historical studies, psychology, anthropology, archaeology and many other perspectives. I do believe, however, that these four are essential steps in a responsible act of interpretation. My choice of these four methods, as well as the sequence in which I deal with them, is the result not only of a specific view on the nature of language, of texts and of interpretation but also a particular concept of an 'ethics of interpretation.' Although an elusive concept, one aspect of an ethics of interpretation is the insistence that people should take responsibility and accept public accountability for their acts of reading and interpretation. It calls for an interpretation with a view to life. It also provides for different modes and methods of reading demanding methodological sophistication and rigor in accordance with the best of what is available on the scientific market. The method of reading as such is not ethical or unethical. Only *people* can act ethically or unethically. The interpretative acts of people, or how people use methods of interpretation, therefore, are subject to ethical reflection. If an interpretive community uses methods of interpretation in such a way that it remains an esoteric 'pure' academic endeavor, isolated from life, or if an interpretive community tolerates such practices, it becomes an ethical problem. Thus, the ethics of interpretation asks (i) *who* (that is, which individual or group) reads (ii) *which Bible* (that is, what view of the text does the interpretive community hold, what authority does it grant the text) (iii) *how* (that is, using which methods) and (iv) *why* (that is, whose interests are at stake, what does the interpretive community want to achieve with their acts of interpretation)?

In the context of biblical scholarship these questions were most pertinently asked by Elizabeth Schüssler Fiorenza (1988) in her presidential address at the Annual Meeting of the Society of Biblical Literature in Boston in December 1987. The thrust of her argument is that the dominant 'scientist' ethos of biblical scholarship should be decentered in the scholarly community of the SBL and recentered to become a critical interpretive praxis for liberation. Interpretive communities such as the SBL are not 'just' scholarly investigative communities but also authoritative communities: 'They possess the power to ostracize or to embrace, to foster or to restrict membership, to recognize and to define what "true scholarship" entails' (1988:8). She characterizes that which is currently perceived as 'true scholarship' in the SBL as 'scientist.'

The question of power, therefore, becomes central to the interpretive task: Whose interests does the interpretation serve? What kind of worlds does it envision? What roles, duties and values does it advocate? These questions, Schüssler Fiorenza (1988:14-15) maintains, require a double ethics — an ethics of historical reading and an ethics of accountability. A paraphrase of her wording produces the following description of each aspect of this ethics:

> An *ethics of historical reading* asks what kind of readings can do justice to the text in its historical context. It illuminates the ethico-political dimensions of the biblical texts in this context. It insists that the number of valid interpretations is limited — although it is aware of the pluralism of historical-critical and literary-critical methods and the pluralism of interpretations appropriate to the text. The diachronic reconstructions practiced by these methods of reading serve to distance us from the texts in their symbolic worlds in such a way that they relativize not only them but also us. It allows us to relativize through contextualization the values and authority claims of the biblical texts *and* to critically evaluate them. An ethics of historical reading requires that biblical studies continue its descriptive analytical work, utilizing all the critical methods available for our understanding of ancient texts and their historical location.
>
> An *ethics of accountability* holds the biblical interpreter responsible not only for the choice of theoretical interpretive models but also for the ethical consequences of the biblical text and its meanings. If biblical texts serve to nurture anti-Judaism, justify the exploitation of slavery or to promote colonial dehumanization, biblical scholars must take the responsibility to interpret them in their historical contexts *and* to evaluate the construction of their historical worlds and symbolic universes in terms of a religious scale of values. This kind of evaluation is of particular importance, given the growth of right-wing political and theological fundamentalism and biblicist literalism which feeds anti-democratic authoritarianism and fosters personal prejudice. The elucidation of the ethical consequences and political functions of biblical texts in their historical *as well as* in their contemporary socio-political settings forms part of the task of the responsible biblical scholar (see Schüssler Fiorenza 1988:14-15).

As could be expected, this ringing call of Schüssler Fiorenza has evoked a number of responses. For example, in the USA Daniel Patte and Gary Phillips have launched a project entitled 'Ethical responsibilities and practices in biblical criticisms.' With their call for an 'andro-critical liberation theological process' in order to correct the oppressive practices of the past and the present so that white male exegetes would become truly accountable in pluralistic contexts (see Patte and Phillips), their project represents a timely development and a worthy response to Schüssler Fiorenza's call for public accountability in biblical interpretation.

In South Africa the issue of an ethos of public accountability in biblical scholarship was initially addressed by Pieter de Villiers (a biblical scholar) (1988, 1989) and Dirk Smit (a systematic theologian) (1990a, 1990b, 1991). As could be expected, the debate on the ethics of interpretation in the South African context is dominated by views on apartheid and the role of the Bible in both the justification and the criticism of apartheid (for a discussion of this debate, see J. Botha 1992). This South African debate also represents an important development and a worthy reaction to Schüssler Fiorenza's presidential address.

Both the North American and the South African responses, however, seem to emphasize primarily the ethics of accountability (Schüssler Fiorenza's second category). I believe that emphasizing the *ethics of accountability* at the expense of the *ethics of historical reading*, or, as I prefer to put it, the ethics of taking the *textuality* (or linguisticality, literariness or rhetoricity) of the text seriously will result in another form of unethical interpretive praxis.

On the one hand I fully support the view that reading the Bible in terms of the scientist ethos in a political or social vacuum is not ethically responsible. I believe it is ethically unacceptable to hide behind structural analyses and all kinds of literary-aesthetic modes of reading Biblical texts and never dare to draw consequences for contemporary contexts from these interpretational activities, or not to realize that the practice of such modes of reading is of necessity a reflection of the social context and ideology of the interpreter. This may happen (and does indeed happen) when a scientist ethos of biblical scholarship continues to dominate New Testament scholarship.

On the other hand, claiming all sorts of ethical implications for biblical texts and for interpretations of these texts without taking the textuality of the text — in all its complexity — seriously will result in yet another set of ethically unacceptable acts of interpretation. Therefore it would also be a seriously irresponsible act of interpretation to treat the text lightly and to over-simplify the reading process only to make all sorts of claims about possible implications of biblical material for our current social and ecclesiastical contexts.

Therefore, under an ethics of New Testament interpretation I understand that the text must be read seriously and with all possible methodological sophistication and rigor. In this study, I propose that an ethically responsible reading of Romans 13:1–7 must at least consist of a reading of this text from four different perspectives, perspectives which take the linguisticality, literariness, rhetoricity and social nature of the text seriously. This is not a renewed New Critical call for close reading. The nature of language and the reading process of necessity involve the text, the reader and the society, giving a certain status and role to all (see Du Plooy 5–6, 8). This 'ethics of *reading*,' therefore, does not exclude an 'ethics of historical reading' nor does it stop short of an 'ethics of public accountability.'

With this ideal in mind, this study is partly informed by the following statement by Tracy (95–96):

> Amid the often conflicting strategies for rethinking our situation and thereby rethinking our pluralistic and ambiguous heritage, contemporary hermeneutics can prove of some aid. From the exposés of the illusions of modern conscious rationality by Freud, Marx and Nietzsche through contemporary feminist theory, modernity has been forced to rethink its Enlightenment heritage on both reason and the self in increasingly radical — that is, postmodern — de-centering forms . . . . In every case of serious postmodern thought, radical hermeneutical thinking recurs. Little wonder that the most marginalized groups of our heritage — mystics, hysterics, the mad, fools, apocalyptic groups, dissenters of all kinds, avant-garde artists — now gain the attention of many postmodern searchers for an alternative version of a usable past. The emergence of a hermeneutical consciousness is clearly a part of this cultural shift. *For hermeneutics lives or dies by its ability to take history and language seriously, to give the other (whether person, event or text) our attention as other, not as a projection of our present fears, hopes and desires* [my italics]. The deceptively simple hermeneutical model of dialogue is one attempt to be faithful to this shift from modern self to postmodern other. For however often the word is bandied about, dialogue remains a rare phenomenon in anyone's experience. Dialogue demands the intellectual, moral and, at the limit, religious ability to struggle to hear another and to respond — to respond critically, and even suspiciously when necessary, but only in dialogical relationship to a real, not a projected, other.

I submit that 'taking language seriously' implies that the text should be read with the full sophistication offered by modern strategies of reading and that such an act of reading needs to *precede* any claims about text-extrinsic relations made on the basis of the text. One could also call it an awareness of the *primacy of the text*.

Miller (1989:82) formulates this notion of the primacy of the text (or, perhaps one can specify it by calling it the 'textuality' or 'linguisticality' or 'literariness' or 'rhetoricity' of the text) as follows:

> In order to understand how a certain kind of language would make history happen, it is necessary first to understand what it means to speak of a given text as a textual allegory with a high level of rhetorical complexity. It is necessary, that is, to *read*

the *Social Contract* or whatever other text is our concern (no easy matter, nor one that happens as often as one would like) BEFORE [emphasis mine] going on to study with confidence those extrinsic relations.

A study of literature that respects the textuality of the text (as it manifests itself in its linguisticality, its literariness, its rhetoricity and its nature as social phenomenon) through a serious *reading* of the text needs to precede any claims about text-external matters — be they ancient or modern day matters of history, society or the self. Yet this preference does not imply that the New Testament scholar can remain oblivious to such text-external phenomena. If New Testament scholars (always) stop short of facing the realities of modern-day ecclesiastical and societal issues, the criticism of unethical acts of interpretation will be justified. Such a 'premature' stop is characteristic of a scientist ethos of biblical scholarship. Nevertheless, without a preceding study of the text, allowing for and trying to understand its nature, how it works, and what it can do, we cannot understand the role that the New Testament literature may have in society, history, the church, and individual life. An ethos of responsible interpretation of the New Testament implies that reading must be taken seriously — not only as understood by Schüssler Fiorenza with her notion of an 'ethics of *historical* reading' but also in her sense of an 'ethics of *reading*.'

Against this background an important delimitation of the focus of this study has to be explicated: contrary to the expectation which might have been raised by the introductory remarks regarding Romans 13 and the South African situation, elaborate discussion of this issue — as well as any other text-external issue relating to Romans 13 — will not form part of this study. The goal of the present study is to attempt to read Romans 13:1–7 in a responsible manner, utilizing the best of what is currently available on the scientific market in terms of methodology.

Delimitations and focus of the different readings

Each of the four disciplines this study uses to interpret Romans 13:1–7 contains a number of sub-disciplines and methods. For instance, linguistics contains the following sub-disciplines: phonology, morphology, syntax, semantics and historical and comparative linguistics. In the sub-discipline *syntax* it is possible to distinguish at least three main approaches: structuralism, functionalism and transformational-generativism. At least four different approaches can be distinguished in semantics: referential, mentalistic, behavioristic and pragmatic theories of meaning.

This complexity also holds true for literary criticism, rhetorical criticism and social-scientific criticism of the New Testament. Therefore, in the introductory section of the respective chapters interpreting Romans 13:1-7, I will necessarily narrow and limit the approach to a specific focus. Considerable effort will have to be spent on defining categories and setting up the necessary delimitations, for example, between a reading of Romans 13:1-7 from a linguistic perspective and a reading from a literary perspective, and, for example, as part of a linguistic reading, between meaning on word-level and other levels, or, to distinguish between an epistolary situation in a literary reading and a rhetorical situation in a rhetorical reading, and so forth. However, these demarcations are not an end in themselves and are intended simply to serve the main purpose of the study.

All four chapters follow basically the same pattern. First the nature of each particular perspective and methodology is introduced in a general and theoretical manner. This is followed by a historical overview of the impact of each approach on the study of the New Testament. Against this background the study then presents a reading of the text of Romans 13:1-7. Depending on a particular reader's interest, this book could be read in different ways. Those interested in methodological issues might find it unnecessary to read the applications in the latter half of each chapter in detail. On the other hand, those interested in the text of Romans 13:1-7 itself might find it unnecessary to read the methodological sections in detail.

CHAPTER 1

READING ROMANS 13:1-7 FROM A LINGUISTIC PERSPECTIVE

1. Introduction

The aim of this chapter is to propose a reading of Romans 13:1-7 from a linguistic perspective. Since the term 'linguistics' refers to a whole academic discipline, an interpreter has to make certain choices and give clarifications and definitions at the outset. To attempt an 'exhaustive' linguistic analysis of the passage in question — giving full attention to all possible aspects of linguistic analysis and doing it from the perspective of all possible linguistic models available — would go well beyond what is accomplishable and relevant for the problem on which this study focuses.

After the chapter clarifies some concepts and makes and supports certain choices, it will demonstrate the relevance of a reading of the text of the New Testament from a linguistic perspective. In order to accomplish this, there will be a brief discussion of the use and influence of concepts, theories and models of modern linguistics in New Testament interpretation during the past thirty years. Although it has the nature of a historical overview, this discussion also serves as an introduction of important concepts that form the background for the actual linguistic reading of Romans 13:1-7 in the final section. The actual reading of Romans 13:1-7 from a linguistic-*semantic* perspective consists of two main sections: (i) determining meaning on word-level and (ii) determining meaning on the level of the sentence and the discourse.

2. Linguistics: Definitions and focus

Generally speaking, linguistics can be defined as the scientific study of language (Lyons 1972:1). The task of the linguist is understanding and describing the nature of language. Since 'language' is a very complex phenomenon, the view of the nature of language one holds influences one's definitions of language and the study of language. From Von Humboldt in the previous century, through De Saussure at the beginning of this century, through the prominent exponents of twentieth century linguistics like Bloomfield, Sapir, Whorf, Pike, Harris, Chomsky, Fillmore, Halliday, and others, conceptions of the focus and boundaries of the discipline, 'the study of language,' have been changing continuously and significantly (see Lyons 1981a:216–237). Any definition of 'linguistics' therefore stands against the background of some other theory (for example, historicism, structuralism, functionalism, generativism) or school of linguistics (for example, tagmemic, stratificational, generative-transformational).

When interpreters view linguistics as a system of signs, it falls under the rubric of the 'science of signs,' namely, semiotics. Jakobson (352) defines semiotics as follows:

> Every message is made of signs; correspondingly, the science of signs termed *semiotics* deals with those general principles which underlie the structure of all signs whatever, and with the character of their utilization within messages, as well as with the specifics of the various signing systems, and of the diverse messages using those different kinds of signs.

Not all signs are linguistic signs, and not all linguistic elements are necessarily regarded as signs. Therefore the study of extra-linguistic and meta-linguistic signs, which also contributes very significantly to the total communicative effect of Romans 13:1–7, does not fall within the focus of this chapter.

A distinction between natural language and artificially contrived language is also important for linguistic analysis and interpretation. Since Romans 13:1–7 was (and is) part of an actual communication event situated in time and history, the focus of this chapter is on natural language, although a scientific meta-language is needed to analyze it. My discussion uses the convention among some linguists whereby the term *utterance* refers to sequences of natural (or real) language (whether oral or written). Understanding Romans 13:1–7 as an utterance requires, among other things, some measure of understanding of the *text*, that is, the actual words and sentences in Romans 13:1–7; the *co-text*, that is, the sentences, paragraphs and chapters surrounding the text and related to it (for example, Romans 1–12; 12:1–21; 13:8 – 16:27); and the *context*, that is, the social and historical setting of the text. Other chapters will treat contextual matters such as the social and historical setting of Romans 13:1–7. This chapter focuses on *text* and *co-text* from a linguistic-*semantic* perspective.

Since Saussurean linguistics has provided the major motivation for the emergence of modern linguistics in the field of New Testament interpretation (Vorster 1982:128), I take my definition of linguistics from this paradigm. Working within a Saussurean/Chomskyan paradigm, Bartsch (5, 8) distinguishes between (i) a general theory of grammar and (ii) a general theory of grammar change. A general theory of grammar focuses on a specification of the principles according to which linguistic signs in all languages are constituted, have meaning, and are used (that is, synchronic linguistics). A theory of grammar change focuses on a specification of the principles according to which the constitution, the meaning and the use of linguistic signs have changed over time (that is, diachronic linguistics). 'Linguistics,' according to him, has as its task the construction of these two theories and as such it focuses on an area narrower than that of the totality of language science. Language science in a broad sense is more than linguistics. It is primarily this focus on linguistic signs themselves which sets linguistics proper apart from neighboring disciplines such as neurology, mathematics, information sciences, logic, philosophy of language, epistemology, social history, theory of literature and philology (see Bartsch).

Linguistic signs consist of a whole range of units. A discourse is composed of individual utterances of a sentential nature. Sentences are composed of phrases which, in turn, consist of words. Words are composed of morphemes. Morphemes are composed of speech sounds, which are composed of phonological features. A network of relations between these different units exists in any given utterance. Different sub-disciplines of linguistics concentrate on the study of linguistic signs on different levels and in different combinations (for example, phonology, morphology, syntax and semantics). The complicated networks of relations between the linguistic units on different levels make it impossible to focus exclusively on any one of these sub-categories in the study of an utterance. Extensive scientific debates have been waged on, for example, the delimitation of syntax from semantics (see Louw 1979:1-31). With that said, and while recognizing the coherence of all levels and combinations of linguistic signs, a specific focus of investigation in a sensible scientific study is nevertheless necessary. In the present investigation into linguistic features of Romans 13:1-7, our focus will be on semantics on the levels of the word, sentence and paragraph.

It is the task of *pragmatics* to characterize and present the ways in which the form and function of a linguistic sign depend on the context in which it is uttered. The difference between semantics and pragmatics can perhaps best be understood from the suggestion by Leech (6) that semantics answers questions of the form: 'What does X mean?,' while pragmatics asks questions of the form: 'What did you mean by X?' Within this framework the difference between a linguistic approach to discourse analysis and a rhetorical approach appears. In a linguistic analysis of discourse, the aim is to identify the constituent elements in the semantic content of a language segment for the purpose of restating the argument in terms of its taxonomic hierarchy (Louw 1979:4). A linguistic discourse analysis is therefore concerned with semantics. A rhetorical analysis of discourse, on the other hand, is concerned with pragmatics. Whereas linguistic discourse analysis is concerned with the taxonomic structuring of an argument, rhetorical criticism is concerned with the question of why an argument could be deemed appropriate within a certain context (Vorster 1991:23; see also chapter 3). In a pragmatic approach, therefore, we attempt to 'read between the lines.' But before that can be done, a perhaps equally complicated task awaits the interpreter of the New Testament, namely, 'to read the lines.' In order to be able to read between the lines, we have to read and understand the lines themselves. Therefore a semantic analysis has to precede a pragmatic analysis. At the same time, however, it should be stressed that it is an illusion to think that we understand the meaning of a linguistic message solely on the basis of the words and structure of the sentence(s) used to convey that message. It is in fact largely due to factors other than merely the sense of sentences and words that we understand a discourse. Lexical semantics clarifies word sense, discourse analysis illuminates the development of the argument of a passage and pragmatics elucidates the mechanisms involved in our perception of implicature (Cotterell & Turner 102). In recent years the idea that a linguistic unit (word or string) can be fully analyzed without taking 'context' into account has been seriously questioned. If someone practicing lexical semantics or sentence grammar wishes to make claims about the 'acceptability' of a sentence, he/she is implicitly appealing to contextual considerations (Brown & Yule 25, 26). For practical purposes and especially because it was the practice of South African New Testament scholars during the seventies, I limit myself in this chapter to lexical semantics and a more or less 'context-less' form of word and discourse analysis.

This chapter also needs to limit the scope of the semantic investigation that the interpretation will attempt. The smallest potentially independent unit of meaning in a text or discourse is, arguably, the concept. At the other end of the scale, the largest unit of meaning is the *whole* discourse, whether a novel, a play or a scientific monograph trying to prove some particular thesis, or, as in the case of the Letter to the Romans, a long letter. Each of these may be called a unit of meaning because it (hopefully) has coherence. Therefore a magazine would not normally be regarded as a unit. Between the concept and the complete discourse lies a whole hierarchy of units of meaning (Cotterell & Turner 193, 194). As was said earlier, the focus in this chapter will be on meaning at the levels of the word, the sentence and the paragraph.

To summarize the choices and delimitations, then, this chapter focuses on:

* the linguistic signs of Romans 13:1–7 (it is not a comprehensive semiotic study of the text);
* Romans 13:1–7 as an utterance of natural language and not as an artificially contrived piece of language;
* the text and co-text of Romans 13:1–7 and not its context;
* semantics and not phonology, morphology and syntax;

* semantics and not pragmatics;
* meaning on the levels of the word, the sentence and the paragraph, taking the co-text of the letter into account, but then from the perspective of a semantic discourse analysis and not from the perspective of a literary genre, namely, a letter;
* 'modern linguistics' in the tradition of Saussurean linguistics, as it has been adapted and applied in the scholarly interpretation of New Testament texts.

3. Modern linguistics and New Testament interpretation

Major shifts have taken place in the study of language during the twentieth century (see Ivič 1970) which the famous linguist Anton Reichling labelled a 'Copernican revolution' (see Vorster 1971:145). Therefore the term 'modern linguistics' refers to the *synchronic structuralist* methods for the study of language, in contrast to the historicist, atomistic and relativistic conceptions of the previous century (see Vorster 1971:144; De Groot 403ff). Because of the dominance of classical philology[1] (Louw 1967) and the relative isolation from other scientific disciplines in which New Testament interpreters performed their work, modern linguistics faced a major task to make inroads into the study of the New Testament. Literature from the sixties and early seventies presents a clear picture of the extensive argumentation and even pathos with which advocates of modern linguistic approaches to the study of the New Testament have had to argue their case (see, for example, Louw 1967; Güttgemanns 1969:87–88; 1970:48ff; 1971; Nida 1972).

Although the application of principles of modern linguistics is at this stage no longer a primary focus in New Testament interpretation (as it was in certain circles during the sixties and seventies), the value of the use of these principles and insights is generally accepted by most New Testament scholars.[2] Yet, Erickson (257–263) still found it necessary to bemoan the way in which so much work in New Testament studies is being done without taking modern linguistic insights into account. Cotterell and Turner (31) suggest that a study of linguistics may afford new precision, system and depth to older disciplines, such as word study, and also provide new criteria for analyzing whole discourses. Yet, they aptly warn against making claims for linguistics that go beyond its competence: 'Neither linguistics, nor any other discipline, can provide certainty in interpretation' (32). In his discussion of

---

[1] Where philology is concerned chiefly with particular texts and documents of literary value, and with their content, linguistics deals rather with language, not as used in particular texts, but as illustrative of what can be and is used in all verbal communication, thus language generally as a structured, social phenomenon (Nida 1972:73–7; Erickson 5).

[2] Louw (1990) gives a valuable overview and catalogue of work done in this regard. See also Silva (1990).

the major developments of the modern study of the New Testament, Lategan (1982:56–67) distinguishes in broad terms between a historical phase, an existential phase and a structural (or text-immanent) phase.   Although 'structuralism' is a concept covering a wide area of meaning,[3] linguistics has been one of the most important areas through which structuralism has entered New Testament interpretation (Lategan 1982:66), or stated the other way around, the methods for structural analysis of New Testament texts were derived from modern generative and structuralist linguistics.

3.1 Modern linguistics

'Modern linguistics,' as the term functioned in New Testament interpretation during the sixties and seventies, could refer solely to the synchronic-structuralist view of the nature of language (Vorster 1971:144).   This idea goes back to a number of fundamental distinctions made by Ferdinand de Saussure in his book *Cours de linguistique générale*, published posthumously in 1916.   With the well-known distinctions between signifier and signified,[4] system, 'langue' and 'parole,'[5] synchronic and diachronic,[6] and paradigmatic

---

[3]It can refer to De Saussure's approach to language, namely that every language is a unique structure or system, and that the units derive their essence and existence purely from their relationships to other units in the same language system.   It can also be used to refer to a particular approach to literature by, among others, A. J. Greimas and R. Barthes, based on the social anthropology of Claude Lévi-Strauss.   He formalized a framework of contrasts, oppositions, similarities and identities by which the significance of any activity might allegedly be measured (Cotterell & Turner 29, 30; see also Vorster 1982:131–132; Jacobson 280–296 and Den Heyer 1978:76–82; 1979:91ff).

[4]De Saussure distinguished between *signifié* (signifier) as written or spoken unit and the *signifiant* (signified).   He stressed that an arbitrary relationship exists between signifier and signified (and therefore between 'word' and 'meaning').   This relationship is the result of the convention of the users of a specific language and is not due to some inherent quality of either the signifier or the signified.

[5]Because of the arbitrariness of the relation between *signifié* and *signifiant*, linguistic signs are able to generate meaning because of the contrasts between the signs themselves. The set of contrasts, i.e. the system of relationships between linguistic signs, should be studied in order to be able to understand the meaning of a particular linguistic sign.   De Saussure uses the term 'langue' to refer to the system of conventions or the underlying structure which makes the actual usage of language possible.   He uses the term 'parole' to refer to the actual use of language.

[6]De Saussure uses the term 'diachronic' to refer to the study of language from the point of view of its historical evolution over a period of time.   With 'synchronic' linguistics he means 'the relations of co-existing things . . . from which the intervention of time is excluded . . . the science of *language-states (états de langue)* . . . .   Synchrony and diachrony designate respectively a language-state and an evolutionary phase' (De Saussure 1966:80–81).   Since these two approaches are fundamentally different, they should be kept apart.   Synchronic linguistics has priority both in importance and in sequence of application.

and syntagmatic,[7] De Saussure introduced to linguistics what would later be called and further developed as 'structuralism' (see Lyons 1981a:218–223; Jacobson 280–281; for a more extensive discussion of the Saussurean distinctions, see Erickson 1–68).

In New Testament studies these insights were the cause of radical criticism against the way in which interpreters handled the study of grammar and especially the meaning of words. The principal figure in the introduction of modern linguistics to New Testament interpretation was James Barr. Thiselton (1979:79–89) illustrates how fundamentally the linguistic principles developed by De Saussure have influenced Barr. Barr's pioneering work was developed and applied to New Testament interpretation by, among many others, people like E. van N. Goetchius, Margaret Thrall, Bertha Siertsema, E. A. Nida, W. Powers, D. D. Schmidt, D. Kiefer, R. Erickson, E. Güttgemanns, J. P. Louw, M. Silva, D. A. Carson, P. W. Brennan, S. Wong, D. Black, Fika van Rensburg, A. H. Snyman, P. Cotterell and M. Turner (see Louw 1990 for a discussion of the contributions of the authors listed here).

3.2 James Barr and the biblical semantics debate

The publication of James Barr's seminal book *Semantics of Biblical Language* in 1961 was the major breakthrough of modern linguistics into New Testament scholarship. It has become a kind of historical watershed for biblical studies, rendering obsolete much in preceding biblical scholarship and setting the pace and tone of much of what has followed (Erickson 1980:14). It was a trumpet blast against the 'monstrous regiment of shoddy linguistics' (Silva 1983:18).

Barr criticized the *Theologisches Wörterbuch zum Neuen Testament* edited by G. Kittel and G. Friedrich on fundamental issues, for example, on the supposed contrast between Hebrew and Greek ways of thinking (Barr 1961:15) and the idea of a correlation of language structure and thought structure. Whatever one may think of the correlation between language and mentality (which is indeed a vexed problem), Barr claimed that the *linguistic* arguments of biblical scholars to support such a contrast are 'unsystematic and haphazard' (1961:21). Related to this problem, but on another level, the *TWNT* fails to distinguish consistently between words as linguistic phenomena and the concepts associated with them. The *TWNT* can therefore be labelled

---

[7]A linguistic unit is in two distinct ways related to the rest of the system within which it functions. The linear relationship with other words or units with which it is chained together is called the set of syntagmatic relationships. The paradigmatic relationship is an associative relationship. This is the relation between the word/linguistic unit and another such unit that is not present in the specific utterance.

a 'concept-history' arranged alphabetically in terms of words (1961:207). In connection with this confusion of word and concept, two of his best known phrases were coined (1961:218): *illegitimate identity transfer* (= when two words referring to the same object or event are for that reason taken to be semantic equals anywhere they might occur) and *illegitimate totality transfer* (= ignoring the phenomenon of polysemy). Related to the word-concept confusion there was, according to Barr, also confusion of word and reality in biblical word studies: 'you are never sure when you are dealing with the New Testament words and when you are dealing with the realities signified by them' (1961:211). (See the discussion of *sense* and *reference* below §4.6.) On the basis of De Saussure's synchronic-diachronic distinction, Barr repudiated the idea that any word has an 'original' or 'etymological' meaning which is somehow the proper one and that any proper discussion of the semantics of a word will necessarily begin with this so-called 'original' meaning (1961:107ff). Related to this etymologizing is what Barr called the 'root fallacy,' i.e. the opinion that there is a 'root meaning' which forms part of the semantic value of any variation to that (abstracted) root, and that any word can suggest meanings for other words containing the same root (1961:100).

Cotterell and Turner (120) use a very instructive metaphor to typify Barr's criticism of Hermann Cremer's idea of an 'internal' or 'theological' lexicography: 'Reference to "*internal*" lexicography is thus apt to suggest that words are like transporters, crammed with theological-conceptual freight, which they dump into the otherwise featureless field of the sentence and the wider semantically barren landscape of the discourse context.'   Barr (1961:263) reacted against the misuse of ordinary linguistic evidence of the Bible in the interests of discovering in it the outlines of a 'theological' lexicology and stressed that:

> It is the sentence (and of course the still larger literary complex such as the complete speech or poem) which is the linguistic bearer of the usual theological statement, and not the word (the lexical unit) or the morphological and syntactical connection.

The last point is the theoretical basis for another of Barr's repeated complaints, namely, that biblical theological linguists all too frequently neglected to study their data in the contexts (or, more specifically, the co-texts)[8] from where they are taken.   This observation paved the way for later developments, like the structural analysis of larger linguistic units of biblical texts.

---

[8]Working within the historical-critical paradigm, many of the contributors to the *TWNT*, such as G. Delling, R. Bultmann, H. Schlier, J. Jeremias, and others, did indeed pay much attention to matters of context in the sense of the extra-textual context (historical and social).   It is the way in which they handled the co-texts of the words they discussed which was, justifiedly, criticized by Barr.

In the so-called 'biblical semantics debate'[9] which followed the publication of Barr's book, interpreters attempted to identify the philosophical and linguistic backgrounds from which Barr raised his criticisms (Tångberg; Thiselton 1979; Güttgemanns 1969:94) and to clarify his use of the term 'biblical theology' (Boman 195; Friedrich 1969:813-4). There was general appreciation of Barr's caution against genuine misuses of etymology (even from Friedrich 1969:811) and wide-ranging support for Barr's discussion of the relation of word and sentence and larger units as bearers of meaning (see Tångberg; Nida 1972). The most significant issue in this debate, however, was the relationship between language and thought and between a word and the reality indicated by it. Interpreters accused Barr of arbitrarily selecting one approach to the problem and rejecting the other (Boman 200-204; Hill 8-10, 294; Friedrich 1969:805-807). He had chosen an empirical structuralist approach (in the wake of De Saussure) and rejected the idealistic approach (in the wake of Von Humboldt, Sapir, Whorf). The 'structuralist' approach (strongly advocated by Siertsema) understands language as an arbitrary conventional system of semantic markers and a logically haphazard relationship between thought and reality. The 'idealistic' or 'mentalistic' approach sees a strong correlation between the structures of a language and the ethnic peculiarities of its speakers as well as between those linguistic structures and both the mental conceptions of people and the extra-linguistic realities which are thought and talked about (see Sapir 26-27;[10] Whorf 265-266; Lotman & Uspenski 211-232;[11] and Bassnett-McGuire 13-14).[12]

This is indeed a very complex problem and in the final instance a matter of philosophical choice. Although much of what follows in this chapter enacts a 'structuralist' view of the nature of language (since this view was most influential in linguistic studies of New Testament material), I am more inclined to the 'idealistic' view — a position which will be developed further

---

[9]For an elaborate discussion of the biblical semantic debate, see Erickson (40-51).

[10]'No two languages are ever sufficiently similar to be considered as representing the same social reality. The worlds in which different societies live are distinct worlds, not merely the same world with different labels attached' (Sapir 27).

[11]'No language can exist unless it is steeped in the context of culture; and no culture can exist which does not have at its centre, the structure of natural language' (Lotman & Uspenski 212)

[12]'The classification of objects in terms of the words used to denote them differs from language to language. The words of a language often reflect not so much the reality of the world, but the interests of the people who speak it. This is clear enough if we look at cultures different from our own. The Trobriand Islanders have names for things that are useful to them in their life that do not correspond to words in English. The Eskimo has four words for 'snow' — 'snow' on the ground, 'falling snow,' 'drifting snow' and 'snowdrift,' while the Hopi Indians have only one word to denote a 'flier' — an aeroplane, an insect, or a pilot' (Bassnett-McGuire 13).

in the chapter on reading Romans 13:1-7 from a social-scientific perspective (chapter 4). The implication of a choice in this matter is particularly relevant in the context of a reflection on the ethics of the respective methods of interpretation. I would argue that a structuralist approach tends to be further away from real life and specific contexts. The consistent practice of a structuralist approach makes it easier for scholarship to remain incarcerated in the proverbial ivory tower. On the other hand, 'serious reading' makes an earnest attempt to define word-meanings on a sound linguistic basis indispensable.

In conclusion, New Testament interpreters have developed especially two aspects of Barr's work: (i) a semantic domain approach to the lexical semantics of the New Testament, and (ii) an emphasis on the broader linguistic units (such as the sentence and the paragraph) as bearers of meaning. Barr (1961:235) suggested that a dictionary should progress from the linguistic detail to the theological thought in order to overcome some of the faulty methodology in biblical word studies which he criticized so severely:

> This procedure would be to group the words in groups, each representing a related semantic field, e.g. the "holy" group with its chief representatives in ἅγιος, ἀμνός, and ἱερός.[13] Within a general field thus loosely defined an attempt would be made to mark off the semantic oppositions between one word and another as precisely as possible; and from this to proceed to special contexts and word-combinations in which each word occurred — bringing in, of course, the words from outside the loosely defined field freely.

This ideal for a linguistically sound treatment of word-meaning (in terms of a structuralist approach) was further developed and refined by Eugene Nida and Johannes Louw and resulted in the *Greek-English Lexicon of the New Testament based on Semantic Domains* (see §8). Barr's emphasis on broader linguistic units than the single word as bearers of meaning resulted in the application of methods of discourse analysis to New Testament texts (see §9).

3.3 The contribution of E. A. Nida and J. P. Louw to linguistics and New Testament interpretation

Interest in the scientific study of the languages of the New Testament from the perspective of structural linguistics and semantics is most notable among Bible translators. Periodicals like *The Bible Translator* (United Bible Societies) and *Notes on Translations* (Summer Institute of Linguistics), as

---

[13]Typographical note: Double quotation marks indicate the sense of words or expressions; single quotation marks — unless they indicate direct quotations or simply give emphasis to a word — present both the form and meaning of words and expressions.

well as numerous monographs from people associated with these periodicals are ample proof of this, although other people as well have taken an active interest in this area.   This short overview focuses on two of the main exponents, namely E. A. Nida and J. P. Louw, whose work has greatly influenced the ethos of New Testament scholarship in South Africa.

Through his work as Bible Translation Consultant E. A. Nida has made an enormous contribution to the application of modern linguistic insights to New Testament interpretation.   In 1969 he co-authored the book *The Theory and Practice of Translation* in which he proposes a dynamic-equivalent approach to translation (Nida & Taber 1974).   This book is a gold-mine for the New Testament scholar.   Nida advocates an approach which depends heavily on modern linguistic insights, especially structuralism and generative-transformationalism (for instance his proposed principles for the transformations of Greek surface structure sentences as part of the translation process) (see §9.2).   In 1972 he published an important article, 'Implications of contemporary linguistics for biblical scholarship,' illustrating how linguistics may provide new insights into textual criticism, matters of authorship, exegesis in general, language teaching and Bible translation.   Nida himself has translated many of these ideals into practice (see Nida 1975b for a list of his publications).   Most significant and influential are *Exploring Semantic Structures* (1975a) and *Componential Analysis of Meaning* (1979).   In the latter he gives, among other things, an exposition of the possible relations between different sets of meaning (1979:68–150) and proposes a procedure for the analysis of lexical meaning in terms of semantic domains (1979:151–193).

For most of his academic career (from the fifties until the early nineties) Johannes Louw, a Greek scholar, was involved in the study of modern linguistics.   In addition to numerous articles, his *Semantics of New Testament Greek* (1982) and *A Semantic Discourse Analysis of Romans* (1979) are of particular significance.   The former is generally regarded as a standard work on the subject (see Cotterell & Turner; Black).   Louw treats semantics on three levels, namely the word, the sentence and the paragraph.   For meaning on word-level he follows De Saussure's and Barr's fundamental distinctions and categories, adding numerous examples from the New Testament (1982:1–66).   A major part of the book is devoted to meaning on broader levels, namely the sentence (1982:67–89) and larger sections of discourse (1982:90–158).   From this pioneering work of Louw, the method for textual analysis called 'The South African Discourse Analysis' resulted and was practiced enthusiastically in South Africa during the seventies and early eighties.

J. P. Louw spearheaded the development of what came to be known as 'South African discourse analysis' in the circle of the New Testament Society of South Africa (NTSSA) (Vorster 1982:136–137). With this method, interpreters analyze the surface structure of the Greek text on the basis of the *colon* — a syntactical unit regarded as the smallest semantic unit (Louw 1982:95ff). In order to 'map' out the progression of the discourse, the interpreter analyzes the relations between the different *cola* and groups or clusters of *cola* on the basis of formal categories. Using this method, Louw (1979) analyzed the whole letter to the Romans. The NTSSA devoted its 1974 Annual Congress to the topic 'Modern linguistics and New Testament interpretation' (see *Neotestamentica* 8) and two further annual congresses (1977 and 1982) (see *Neotestamentica* 11 and 16) to a discourse analysis of the Gospel of Matthew. Criticism of the positivistic tendencies in this approach (Deist 1978) served to temper the over-optimism which characterized the work of some of the proponents of this method during the seventies. The enthusiasm with which this approach was practiced during those years was characteristic of the scientist ethos of New Testament scholarship in South Africa at its climax.

In a later development in the book *Style and Discourse* (co-authored by, among others, Nida and Louw) the *nuclear structure* — a unit determined on semantic rather than syntactic grounds — replaced the *colon* as basic unit for analysis. The categories in terms of which the relations between these units of analysis can be described were also formalized to a greater extent (Nida *et al.* 1983:101ff).

Although this type of linguistic-structural analysis still plays an important role, it is no longer in the center of developments in the theory and practice of New Testament interpretation in South Africa, and many criticize it on a number of fundamental points. As Du Toit (1981) puts it, the value of the contribution of this type of analysis is too great for scholars to leave it and return to older methods of interpretation. It is used in most institutions that teach New Testament exegesis in South Africa. Within the context of my appeal for 'serious reading' as an ethical responsibility for New Testament scholarship, I believe that linguistic-structural analysis of the text of the New Testament has an important place. On the other hand, to *end* the interpretational activity with this type of analysis as if this is all there is to be done, results in another form of ethically unacceptable interpretation.

Louw and Nida's biggest contribution to the application of modern linguistics in New Testament interpretation is on the level of lexical semantics. After almost twenty years of research, their *Greek-English Lexicon of the New Testament Based on Semantic Domains* was published in 1988. This book is generally heralded as a watershed in New Testament scholarship, and it was very favorably received by the scholarly community (see Silva 1988; Reese 1988; Boers). In a fairly extensive introduction, the editors set out the theory used for the lexicon (Louw & Nida I:vi–xxiii). This theory is based on the work of De Saussure and Barr, although it has in many ways been refined by taking into account later developments in lexical semantics. Regarding its underlying view of the nature of language, it clearly works against the background of the 'structuralist' and not the 'idealistic' view (see §3.2). In the accompanying publication to the *Lexicon*, Louw (1985a:113) rejects the 'idealistic' view (which would imply a categorizing of the New Testament vocabulary in such a manner that it would fit the worldview of the New Testament) as an approach based on dogmatic instead of linguistic considerations.

The reading of Romans 13:1–7 in this chapter follows, as far as meaning at word-level is concerned, the semantic domain-approach of Louw and Nida, while for meaning on sentence and discourse level, it uses the South African Discourse Analysis. But first it is necessary to make certain fundamental semantic distinctions in order to define the nature of this analysis of the text. Then a discussion of the word-meanings encountered in traditional interpretations of Romans 13:1–7 will demonstrate the relevance and the importance of these distinctions.

4. Dimensions and types of meaning

4.1 Meaning

'Meaning' is one of those everyday concepts which is, in fact, very complex when one tries to define it scientifically. For instance, Hofmann (7–16) distinguishes between eighteen major categories of meaning with a number of sub-categories in each case (for example, lexical meaning, figurative meaning, referential meaning, connotative or emotive meaning, grammatical meaning, encyclopedic meaning, logical meaning and linguistic meaning). The meanings (or senses) of the verb 'to mean' and the noun 'meaning' exhibit a network of similarities and differences which are in many different ways related to each other. Following Lyons (1977:5), I will use the term 'meaning' in an ordinary-language, or everyday, sense; that is to say, in an intuitive, pre-theoretical sense.

In the intensive research into synchronically oriented semantics during the past three decades, a number of basic perspectives and even more or less established principles have surfaced (Silva 1983:101).[14] The most fundamen-

---

[14]Cruse (xiii) makes an interesting observation when he typifies the approach of his book on lexical semantics: 'My aim has been an exploration of the semantic behaviour of words which, methodologically, is located in the middle reaches of the continuum stretching from mere anecdotalism to fully integrated formal theory — an exploration disciplined

tal distinction goes back to the famous triangle proposed in 1923 by Ogden and Richards (11; for a critical discussion of the triangle and further reflection on the idea, see Lyons 1977:95ff).

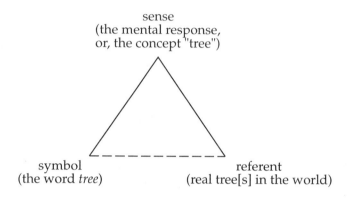

sense
(the mental response,
or, the concept "tree")

symbol
(the word *tree*)

referent
(real tree[s] in the world)

The term *symbol* refers to the word in its phonetic or written form, *sense* refers to the mental content called up by the symbol, and *referent* refers to the extra-linguistic thing denoted.   The purpose of the triangle is to stress the *indirect* relationship between a word and that to which it refers.   Although the symbol is usually a single word (for example, *tree*), it may also be composed of two or more words that constitute a single lexical unit (for example, idioms like *to kick the bucket*).   Therefore the meanings (senses) of verbal symbols (for example, words) are not the referents or the entities in the practical world.   They are concepts of distinctive features relating to the entities (Louw 1982:55).

Silva (1983:103) points out that lexical meaning may be approached in three different ways on the basis of this triangle: (i) focus on the relationship between symbol and referent which consists primarily of an analysis of the referent itself, (ii) focus on the relationship between symbol and sense in individual words and (iii) focus on the relationship between the senses of different words.   The latter results in a study of semantic domains as a basis for determining lexical sense.   This will be the approach followed in our attempt to determine the sense of certain lexical units in Romans 13:1-7.

---

by a consistent method of approach, and by a predilection for systematic, recurrent, and generalisable facts rather than for particularity and idiosyncrasy.'   From this we can infer that fundamental and generally recognizable semantic distinctions are indeed observable, although one should be careful not to speak of hard 'facts' in semantic theory (which, of course, is true of all scientific disciplines).   The categories and distinctions discussed in §§4.1 – 4.10 should also be assessed in this spirit.

4.2 Concepts

The concept 'tree' is a mental construct, part of the tapestry of mental constructs that we arrive at by segmenting our understanding of our world into identifiable and communicable portions. Yet *concept* is not identical with *sense*. The concept 'tree' could be taken in a broad sense to mean one's understanding of the nature of trees (how they grow, how and what they contribute to the ecology and the role of trees in human society). It could also be taken in a minimal sense to denote 'the bundle of elements of meaning which are necessarily or conventionally entailed' by the use of the word 'tree' (such as 'plant,' 'upright,' 'with a stem' et cetera) (see Cotterell & Turner 117). This second (minimized) type of concept is closely related to what is otherwise called the 'sense' of a word. Cotterell and Turner (117) refer to this type of concept as a *lexical concept*. This should be carefully distinguished from the broader usage of 'concept.' One's concept of 'tree' in the more general usage may include a wide range of features and functions and usages, none of which are *linguistically* linked to the word 'tree' as such. Usually these other features are treated under the rubric of 'encyclopedic meaning' (see §4.9).

There is no consensus on the precise nature of the relations between words, senses, concepts and referents/denotations. Nonetheless, for the purpose of this study, it is important to distinguish them as carefully as possible and to keep these distinctions in mind in the analysis of word-meanings in a text.

4.3 Words, forms, lexemes

Interpreters have proposed different definitions of *word*. To give a few examples:

* A *word* is the smallest cluster of sounds repeatedly employed in a language which may be surrounded by a pause, or juncture or silence (Cotterell & Turner 21).

* A word is no more than a token, a sign, available for use in the communication process, and given meaning by the context and co-text within which it appears (Cotterell & Turner 190).

* A *word* is the smallest speech unit capable of functioning as a complete utterance (Palmer 1981:33).

* Limited to written language, a word is any sequence of letters which, in normal typographical practice, is bounded on either side by a space (Lyons 1977:18).

Since each of these definitions sheds light on different aspects, which are all important, it is not necessary to choose any particular one of them to serve as basis for the argument in this chapter.

The distinction between a word and a lexeme, however, should be carefully noted. The basic root form of any set of related words is called a *lexeme* (Palmer 1981:34). For example ὑποτασσέσθω and ὑποτάσσεσθε are different forms of the same lexeme, ὑποτάσσομαι. The derived forms of the lexeme are called *word-forms* (Lyons 1977:18, 19). It is important to distinguish between 'lexemes' and 'forms' to be able to account, for instance, for the phenomenon of homonymy (that is, two lexemes which have the same form but differ in meaning).

4.4 Sense

The 'sense' of a word can be defined (in structuralist vein) as 'how that word (or expression) relates in meaning to other words or expressions in language' (Cotterell & Turner 78). Yet, we do not only speak of the sense of words or expressions, but also of the sense of sentences and paragraphs. The sense of the sentence and the paragraph lies not merely in the individual propositions or word-senses, but also in the relationships of those words and propositions to each other (Cotterell & Turner 79, 82; Louw 1982:68).

Most words in a language do not have a single sense but a whole range of senses. Words occupy a *domain* of meanings and only rarely have a single meaning. The fact that one word has a multiplicity of senses allows for considerable economy in language. For example, the Louw and Nida *Lexicon* works with 25,000 senses for the 5,000 words which can be found in the New Testament (Louw & Nida I:vi). The phenomenon of two or more lexemes having the same spelling (lexical form) and pronunciation is called *homonymy*, and the phenomenon of a single lexeme having a multiplicity of senses is called *polysemy*. Polysemy accounts for the fact that the different senses of a lexeme like ἀρχή can be classified in as many as seven distinct semantic domains (Louw & Nida II:35). In order to keep a balance between homonymy swallowing up polysemy or *vice versa*, Cotterell and Turner (137) propose a middle position: homonymy is used where we have to do with two distinct and apparently unrelated senses, while polysemy is used to refer to occasions of multiple related senses (for a discussion of sense relations, see §6.4). In this chapter, however, no attempt will be made to distinguish the senses of the words in Romans 13:1–7 in such detail. For the present purpose it will be enough to call the phenomenon that a lexeme can function in different semantic domains 'polysemy.'

Since etymology does not provide an original meaning that acts as the basis for every other sense of a word, most linguists warn against the idea of a 'single basic' or a 'core' sense for polysemous words (see Barr 1961; Louw 1982:33ff; Cotterell & Turner 138). Usually the most used or 'unmarked' sense of a word accounts for what is felt to be the 'general' sense of a particular lexeme, or it is a common component of meaning shared by the different senses of a particular lexeme. *Unmarked meaning* (or sense) is understood as that meaning (sense) 'which would be readily applied in a minimum context where there is little or nothing to help the receptor in determining the meaning' (Louw 1982:34). *Lexical meaning* is the range of senses of a word that may be counted on as established in the public domain. Since not all contextual senses and usages are actually lexical meanings, Cotterell and Turner (140) suggest that we need to distinguish between usages that are conventional (at least to a group) and so an established 'sense' of a word (for that group, or more widely), and those which are not.

In practice it is not always possible to separate lexical meanings from mere usages, especially in the case of 'dead' languages such as New Testament Greek (see for example Louw's [1982:51] discussion of βοήθεια having the lexical meaning "help" but being used in Acts 27:17 to refer to 'the kind of help(s) with which a ship was reinforced in those times, probably ropes or cables'). This distinction is similar to the one Louw (1982:56) proposes between 'figurative meaning' (that is, conventionalized figurative expressions) and 'figurative usage' (that is, unique and personal, a feature of imaginative style). Since, in the case of the New Testament, we have only written texts to work with, the only way to determine whether a word or expression has an established (or conventional) sense is to look for places in other texts which use the same sense of a particular word or expression. That leaves us with the phenomenon *hapax legomenon* as a possible example of *idiolectical sense*. But even that does not help much, since only a fraction of written texts from antiquity have survived, and interpreters obtain from written texts only a limited perspective on the way in which the language was actually spoken in everyday and natural usage. Therefore, although this distinction of Cotterell and Turner may be helpful and valuable when working with modern spoken languages, and although we have to accept that the principle is valid also for *Koine*-Greek, we are not *in practice* in a position to reach any conclusion in this regard as far as New Testament words are concerned. On the other hand, this does not imply that there is no such thing as a personal style of a particular author, although style is an exceedingly complex phenomenon to analyze and describe, even in the case of contemporary authors and speakers (see Silva 1983:114ff; Botha 1989:45–67).

Usually interpreters use two different approaches to elucidate the meaning of 'sense,' namely a *concept-oriented* and a *field-oriented* approach. The more traditional concept-oriented approach consists of defining the sense of a lexeme by working out a definition that encompasses all its characteristic and distinctive features. There are, however, a number of fundamental problems with this approach. It works best when applied to concrete nouns, although this immediately causes the danger that sense and encyclopedic information will be mixed up (that is, confusing the lexical sense of a word with some broader concept present in a context, see §14.9). With events and abstract nouns, this becomes very problematic since concepts as mental objects are hardly accessible for precise empirical analysis. Cotterell and Turner (152) introduce a valuable distinction between *lexical concepts* and *discourse concepts* to account for the difference between the lexical sense of the expressions involved and the lexical sense *as well as* germane elements of meaning contributed by the context. The main problem with concept-approaches to 'sense' is, however, the difficulty of deciding which components of the variety of discourse concepts are properly part of the *lexical concept* (or sense) of an expression.

On the other hand, when we understand 'concept' as 'a verbal description of a set of related elements of meaning which forms a coherent and discrete abstraction, accessible to scrutiny on the basis of diagnostic senses,' we are in fact moving closer toward a field-approach to sense. One of the fundamental insights of modern linguistics has been that we understand words in relation to other words (see §3.1). In terms of this insight, *sense* can be defined in terms of a set of contrasts and similarities, or the sense-relations (see §4.11.4) between words (Lyons 1977:204–206; Lyons 1981b:58). In terms of this approach, a word has to be related to other available comparable and contrasting terms (that is, other words in the same semantic field) in order to determine its sense. The field-approach forms the basis of the methodology of the Louw and Nida *Lexicon*, and it will also be used here in determining the sense of important words in Romans 13:1–7.

The main criticism against a field-approach to 'sense' is that theoretically we cannot know the sense of a word until we know all the other words in the associated lexical field and have a rough idea of their senses too (Cotterell & Turner 162). This criticism has to a certain extent been answered to by the availability of the Louw and Nida *Lexicon* which did just this: listing related meanings of words within semantic fields. More substantial criticism is raised by Silva (1988:166): the field-oriented approach works well in the case of single words or more or less clearly defined linguistic entities such as idioms, but since word combinations also contribute significantly to the sense of a sentence or discourse, such 'collocations' (that is, the unique syntactical patterns in which words are used) need to be taken into account also — something which was not done in the Louw and Nida *Lexicon*. For instance, a noun like νόμος gets a specific, almost technical sense when used with certain prepositions, like ὑπό or διά (for a study of this kind of 'formulaic language,' see Lategan 1991a; Van Rensburg 1990). My study will treat this aspect of meaning when I perform a discourse analysis of Romans 13:1-7 (see §9.3).

To recapitulate, I will follow Cotterell and Turner's (164) suggestion and use the term 'lexical sense' to indicate a descriptive meaning of a lexeme where it fulfills the following conditions: (i) it can be embodied in a verbal definition that includes both the essential and the prototypical elements of the quality, event, object or concept potentially signified by the lexeme and (ii) it is possible to specify its sense relations to closely related lexemes. The aim of §8 of this chapter will be to define the lexical sense of a number of important words in Romans 13:1-7. In order to do these things, however, it is also necessary to distinguish carefully 'sense,' from 'denotation,' 'reference,' 'significance,' 'implication,' 'encyclopedic information' and 'translation equivalent.'

4.5 Denotation

Denotation is the term interpreters use for the *relationship* that exists between words and corresponding entities in the world, for example between words like 'statue' and the objects we denote as statues, and between words like 'sculpting' and the activity in the world which we recognize to be sculpting (Cotterell & Turner 83). The association of a particular linguistic unit with a particular denotation is largely arbitrary, a matter of convention.

One of the specific problems in the New Testament that Cotterell and Turner (83) identify concerns entities that should be included in the denotation of the language of principalities and powers (just existential forces? political powers? planetary powers?). Although this chapter contains an analysis of the lexical sense of a number of important words in Romans 13:1-7 (see §§8.2 - 8.6), this particular problem of denotation does not fall within the bounds set for this chapter. An interpreter needs historical, social and literary information to address and determine this issue.

4.6 Reference

Denotation is not identical to reference. It may be possible to know the sense and possible denotation of all the words in a discourse and still not be able to understand the meaning of the discourse. Silva (1983:107) distinguishes between different levels of referentiality on a gliding scale, namely (i) fully referential (for example, a proper name like *Plato*), mostly referential (for example, a word such as *law*), partly referential (*cold*) and non-referential (*beautiful*). In the first two cases it may to some extent be possible to speak of denotation instead of reference since proper names are supposed to have only direct reference or denotation. But the further we move down the scale, the more context-determined the reference becomes and the term 'denotation' becomes less useful. It is therefore necessary to note the difference between 'sense' and 'denotation' on the one hand and 'sense' and 'reference' on the other hand.

The *sense* of a word consists of the set of distinctive features which makes possible certain types of reference, while the *reference* itself is the process of designating some entity, event, et cetera by means of a particular symbol (Nida 1975a:15). The referent of a word or expression is the 'thing' in the world which is intentionally (or rather, contextually determinedly) signified by that word or expression. The 'thing' in question may be an object or an event or a process. Reference is therefore entirely a property of utterances. A context-free sentence like an example produced to illustrate a point in grammar ('The cat sleeps on the mat'), does not have contextually determined reference. The referent is the extra-linguistic entity about which something is asserted, while the sense is the linguistic meaning of the assertion itself (Cotterell & Turner 84, 89).

Two examples may serve to clarify this important distinction: in John 1:29 (Ἴδε ὁ ἀμνὸς τοῦ θεοῦ), ἀμνὸς *refers* to Jesus, but the lexical meaning or *sense* of the word is "the young of sheep." In 2 Tim 3:16 (πᾶσα γραφή θεόπνευστος), γραφὴ refers to the Septuagint but the lexical sense of the word is "a portion or unit of written discourse." Louw and Nida (I:xvi-xvii) are very careful to keep this distinction in mind in their *Lexicon*.

4.7 Significance

The notion of signification is commonly used to describe the meaning of linguistic expressions in the following sense: words and other expressions are held to be signs which, in some sense, signify, or stand for, other things (i.e. the *significatum*). Lyons (1977:95–99) calls attention to the different ways in which people like Ogden and Richards, Peirce, Miller, Morris and Cherry have defined the distinction between sign (or symbol), concept (or sense) and significatum (or referent). Thus there is no single standard interpretation of these terms. Since there is considerable disagreement about the details of the triadic analysis of signification, this sense of signification will not be used in this study.

The term 'significance' is also used in another sense. Significance is a relation of meaning between the sense of an utterance and some person's world, or at least part of that world. A discourse may have significance for the speaker and (another) significance for the hearer or reader. Significance is always meaning-*for*-someone. The significance an utterance has for any hearer or reader depends not only on the sense of what is spoken or written and on the shared presupposition pool of speaker/writer and hearer/reader, but also on presuppositions held by the hearer not shared with the speaker/writer (Cotterell & Turner 1989:93, 94). This idea of 'significance' is in accordance with the hermeneutical theory of Hirsch and is at odds with the hermeneutical tradition associated with Heidegger, Gadamer and Habermas (see Bleicher; Palmer 1969). These philosophers rightly protested against a separation of the processes of determining discourse meaning[15] of a text (= the bringing to expression of an interpreter's understanding of an author's intended meaning) and the interpreting of the text (= the inter- preter's understanding of the significance of the text for his own world of the discourse meaning of the text). According to the Heidegger-Gadamerian tradition in hermeneutics, to which I subscribe, these two processes are inseparable. Therefore this distinction, as well as the technical term 'significance,' will not be used in this study.

4.8 Implication

Sense and implication are often confused with each other. Louw (1982:52) uses the expression ὁ λόγος ηὔξανεν in Acts 6:7 to explain the difference: the implication of the expression 'the word grew' in this context is 'the numbers of the church increased,' but its meaning is only that "the message spread." Implication needs to be determined carefully in context and is thus only a feature of utterances. Implicature is a phenomenon investigated by pragmatics (see Leech; Levinson; Du Plessis 1988:311–313).

4.9 Encyclopedic information

Encyclopedic information is anything that can be said about something, but adding all encyclopedic information about a thing does not amount to a defini- tion of the sense of the word(s) used to refer to that thing. Encyclopedic information is *more* than the diagnostic features needed to define a sense, for

---

[15]Cotterell and Turner (69) use the term 'discourse meaning' to protect themselves against 'the misunderstanding that a text means precisely and only what the author meant' (so qualifying Hirsch), and on the other hand 'to stave off the view that we can really speak of "text meaning" as though the text were autonomous.' Although critical of Hirsch on a number of smaller points, in general they find themselves in agreement with Hirsch's hermeneutical sentiments.

example, features such as 'vehicle,' 'two wheels,' 'propelled physically by the driver' et cetera are diagnostic elements by which the sense of 'bicycle' can be defined. Supplementary information like the color, size of wheels, gears, types of handles, et cetera, of the bicycle amounts to what is known as encyclopedic information and needs to be distinguished from a definition of the sense of a word or expression.[16] Dictionaries such as the *TWNT* and *The New International Dictionary of New Testament Theology* (edited by C. Brown) are very valuable with regard to encyclopedic information on the words they discuss (Louw 1985a:115).

4.10 Translation equivalents

Usually dictionaries are concerned with translation equivalents rather than meaning. In semantics the concern should be with meaning (or sense) rather than words, for words only partially overlap between languages (Louw 1982:43ff). The meaning (or sense) of a word or expression is not identical with possible translation equivalents of that word or expression in another language. In the Louw and Nida *Lexicon* a clear distinction is made between the definition of the meaning of a word and possible glosses with which it can be translated; for example, the meaning of λιμός is defined as "a widespread lack of food over a considerable period of time and resulting in hunger for many people," and 'famine' or 'hunger' is given as possible glosses or translation equivalents for this meaning. Another example is the word αὐλή: although it can perhaps be translated as 'house' in English, this translation is rather vague and problematic since our modern-day concept of 'house' differs from the ancient courtyard or dwelling — not everything understood by the English term 'house' is also understood for αὐλή (see Louw 1982:43). Meaning is not merely a gloss (that is, another word). Meaning or sense can only be expressed by means of a definition stating the semantic features of meaning (Louw 1985b:160).

5.   Confusion of categories in the description of word-meanings in Romans 13:1-7

The importance of the semantic distinctions discussed in §§4.1 – 4.8 becomes clear when we consider the discussion of ἄρχοντες in Romans 13:1-7 by, for

---

[16]See for example Louw and Nida (I:45, Domain 4.44) for a discussion of the encyclopedic information in ancient zoology regarding the nature of doves and how that added to the connotative meaning of περιστερά and τρυγών in the New Testament.

example, Webster. Regarding the 'meaning' and 'relevance' of this word, he writes: 'The translation "rulers" for οἱ ἄρχοντες in 3.3 is generally accepted, but who are these rulers?' (266). He continues by discussing a number of possible *references* of these words (Demonic angels or spirits arranged hierarchically in the cosmos? The devil as ruler of this age? Jewish authorities? Pagan officials?) and concludes that 'it is likely that ἄρχοντες as used in Romans 13.3 evolved from secular usage in Hellenistic Judaism or possibly from pagan governments themselves.'

Webster ignores a number of semantic distinctions and confuses categories such as sense and translation equivalent (see §4.10), sense and reference (see §4.4 and §4.6), and synchronic and diachronic descriptions of meaning (see §3.1). He treats the *sense* of the word briefly by proposing a *translation equivalent* or gloss (that is, a single word as translation equivalent instead of a definition of the sense of the word in terms of semantic components). He discusses several possible *referents* for the word although it is clear from his introductory sentence that he intends to consider that to be the '*meaning and relevance*' of the word. He concludes with a statement about the possible origin of the word which is an observation about the diachronic development of the use of this word. This is irrelevant when an interpreter is interested in defining the synchronic sense of the word in the context of Romans 13:1-7.

In his discussion of ἐξουσία Webster (270-272) similarly fails to distinguish clearly between sense and reference. He briefly discusses elements of the long history of conflicting interpretations of this word which he calls 'certainly the most controversial term in the passage,' giving attention to (i) the Gnostic interpretation of ἐξουσία as 'cosmic spirit-beings who rule the inferior material world' and (ii) to Cullmann's interpretation that ἐξουσία has 'a subtle implicit dual reference to the visible political authorities *and* the invisible demonic beings who, as reluctant instruments of the reign of the resurrected Christ, *stand behind the powers of the world*.' Webster rejects these 'demonological interpretations' and opts for meanings used by Josephus, Philo and the LXX where, according to him, ἐξουσία 'enjoys a strictly secular usage, as a reference to "authoritative position" or "office holders."' He concludes with the following statement:

> . . . in Rm 13:1ff ἐξουσία(ι) simply *denotes* the secular political authorities. In contrast to 1 Pt 2:13, where βασιλεῖ apparently specifies the Roman emperor, the authorities in Rm 1:1ff are not sharply defined. In view of the alternative expressions discussed above, the term *originally* may have *referred* either to secular or religious Jewish authorities or to pagan officials or to both. The present context,

however, suggests that Paul has in mind the pagan government and its many officials
of whatever bureaucratic level (Webster 272) [my italics].[17]

It is clear that Webster uses technical terms and loaded expressions such as
'reference' (see §4.6), 'denotes' (see §4.5) and 'what Paul has in mind' (confusion of semantics and pragmatics) (see §1) in imprecise and confusing
ways. I have argued that in a linguistic analysis of meaning on word-level,
these and other semantic distinctions (see §§4.1 – 4.10) should always be kept
in mind. To take the argument one step further, I would argue that *before* the
reference, denotation, translation equivalents and encyclopedic information of
a word can be considered, one should first attempt to define its *lexical meaning* or *sense* clearly (preferably in terms of a semantic domain approach).
Furthermore, reading our passage consistently from a proper *linguistic* perspective (as it was defined in the beginning of this chapter) rules out a discussion of encyclopedic information of the words in question. Such information
will only become available if we read the passage from a social-scientific or a
historical perspective. With this observation, I do not mean to dismiss or
diminish the importance of trying to identify the reference of words. In any
interpretation this will always be of utmost importance. I simply want to
work consistently within the limitations and focus set for this chapter.

I also do not mean to suggest that Webster's analysis and interpretation
make no contributions to this study. In his discussion Webster (267–268)
defines the sense of συνείδησις, as '. . . the universal presence of a divine
summons to moral sensitivity and righteousness.' For Christians, however,
συνείδησις has peculiar implications. Therefore συνείδησις in Romans 13:6
'entails the obligation resulting from the specific knowledge that one shares
with his fellow Christians in view of Romans 13:1-2 that the governing
authorities are servants of God and executors of his divine will.' With this
definition Webster moves toward the ideal of defining the lexical sense of the
word and pointing out its implications in the specific context of Romans
13:1-7.

6.   *Important concepts and distinctions for a semantic domain approach to meaning*

Before commencing with my own analysis of meaning at the word-level in
Romans 13:1-7 in terms of the semantic domain-approach based on Louw

---

[17]Numerous other examples of the confusion of sense and reference in the treatment
of ἐξουσία can also be cited: for example Strobel's (1956:75–79) definition of the meaning of ἐξουσία as "obrigkeitlichen Ämter des umfangreichen Staatsapparates des
römischen Weltreiches" which is widely accepted (see, for example, Wilckens 1982:32).

and Nida, I need to introduce briefly certain concepts and distinctions of this approach. The following concepts and distinctions are of particular importance for a semantic domain approach to lexical semantics.

6.1 Primary distinctions in the classification of meanings

Louw and Nida (I:vi) base their *Lexicon* on three categories which they regard as primary distinctions in the classification of meaning:

* *Unique referents* — these are usually proper names, although even their reference can be significant on levels wider than direct reference (see Cotterell & Turner 32).

* *Class referents* — these are the so-called common words which are usually described in terms of three semantic classes (see §6.2).

* *Markers* — these are usually prepositions and particles which serve primarily to mark the relations between content words, phrases and clauses. 'Markers' are also called 'Function Words,' where the term 'function' is understood in a linguistic sense.

6.2 Semantic classes

Three basic semantic categories of class referents can be distinguished (Nida & Taber 37–38), namely:

* *Objects* — the semantic class which designates things or entities which normally participate in events, for example, house, dog, man, sun, stick, water, spirit.

* *Events* — the semantic class which designates actions, processes, happenings, for example, run, jump, kill, speak, shine, die, grow.

* *Abstracts* — the semantic class of expressions which have as their referents the qualities, quantities, and degrees of objects, events and other abstracts, for example, red, quickly, twice, many.

Nida and Taber (38) distinguish a fourth category, namely *Relations* (that is, the expressions of the meaningful connections between other kinds of terms). Nida and Louw (vi) later decided to drop this fourth category and to treat relations under the heading of abstracts.

6.3 Classes of semantic features

The lexical sense of words in terms of a semantic domain approach is based on contrasts, for, according to Nida (1979:32) there is no meaning (or sense) apart from significant differences: 'If all the universe were blue, there would be no blueness, since there would be nothing to contrast with blue.' To be able to describe the contrasts, they distinguish three major classes of semantic features (or types of semantic components) (Nida 1979:32–39):

* *Shared* features — those elements of the meaning of lexical items which are held in common by a set of lexical items;

* *Distinctive* features — those features which separate meanings from one another;

* *Supplementary* features — those features which may be relevant in certain contexts or may play a primarily connotative or associative role.

6.4 Sense relations

An interpreter can distinguish two basic types of sense relationships: paradigmatic (substitutional) and syntagmatic (collocational) (Cotterell & Turner 155–159). The study of collocational sense relations is a relatively new field in which interpreters have not done much work (see Silva 1988:166). The results of such studies have also been less productive than those of paradigmatic relations in the determination of sense relations of words. In this study these aspects of meaning will come under consideration in the section on nuclear structures and the sense relations between nuclear structures (see §9.2).

Paradigmatic sense relations can also be divided into two categories: (i) the relations between different meanings of the same lexical unit and (ii) the relations between related meanings of different lexical units in the same semantic domain. For example, the lexical item ἐξουσία is, according to Louw and Nida (II:92), used for four different meanings in the New Testament. Therefore it is treated in four different semantic domains, namely, 'Control, Rule,' 'Power, Force,' 'Supernatural Beings and Powers' and 'Think'). Within each of these different domains, there are a number of other words, such as (in the semantic domain 'Control, Rule') ἐπιταγή ("the right or authority to command") and κτίσις ("an instituted authority, with the implication that such an authority has been created or formed") (Louw & Nida I:477), which are closely related semantically.

These two categories can, in their turn, be divided into a number of subcategories. Since these classifications give us the terminology to conceptualize the sense relations with which we work in semantic domains, I need to consider them briefly.

6.4.1 Relations between different senses of the same lexical unit

Nida (1979:121–131) distinguishes between four principal types of relations which may exist between different senses of the same lexical unit (excluding, of course, homonyms): (i) *derivation* (all the essential components of an underlying base are incorporated into another sense, belonging to a distinctly different semantic domain), (ii) *replacement* (the substitution of at least one component which alters the meaning but does not involve a shift in semantic domain), (iii) *figurative extension* (a radical shift in semantic domains in which the semantic relations between the two senses depend upon either a supplementary component or a reinterpreted diagnostic component, and (iv) *peripheral clustering* (linked sets of diagnostic components which form a semantic chain binding a series together). In my analysis of word meanings in §8, I will indicate the different sense of the same lexical unit with a letter of the alphabet in superscript, for example, ἐξουσία[a], ἐξουσία[b], et cetera.

6.4.2 Relations between related senses of different lexical units

The four possible relations between related senses of different lexical units are (i) incompatible sets of meaning, (ii) contiguous sets of meaning (improper synonymy), (iii) included sets of meaning (hyponymy, hierarchical meaning), (iv) overlapping sets of meaning (proper synonymy) and (v) complementary sets of meaning (opposites or antonymy) (Nida 1979:698–110; Silva 1983:119–132; Louw 1982:60–66; Cotterell & Turner 156–161).

Cotterell and Turner (158) use the sentence 'Blood began to ooze from the wound' to illustrate these relations. 'Blood' and, say, a word such as 'ceiling' are incompatible. 'Ooze' and a word such as 'pour' are in a contiguous relation. 'Ooze' and 'trickle' are in an overlapping relation. 'Blood' is included in the sense of a word such as 'fluid,' and 'ooze' and 'seep' are so closely related (or overlapping) that they may be regarded as near synonyms. Louw and Nida (I:xv) insist that there are no synonyms in a language in the sense that 'no two lexical items ever have completely the same meanings in all of the contexts in which they might occur. Even very close synonyms are distinguishable because of differences in connotative or associative features.' Cruse (265ff) talks about a scale of synonymity since some pairs of synonyms seem to be 'more synonymous' than others.

Contiguous relations are those which exist between lexical units which, while sharing some semantic features, cannot ever be exchanged (for example, 'ooze' and 'pour'), while lexical units related in an overlapping set of relations, may be interchanged in some contexts (for example, 'ooze' and 'trickle'). A very significant set of relations in this category are opposites, which can be divided into (i) complementaries and antonyms and (ii) directional oppositions (Cruse 197–243).

7. *Procedures to determine the lexical sense of important words in Romans 13:1–7*

An important principle for the description of lexical sense in terms of a semantic domain-approach is to work with *contrasts* since sense is defined by a set of distinctive features (or diagnostic components). Since only one sense of a lexical unit is normally used within a given utterance,[18] it should first be decided which sense is at stake in Romans 13. This will also be a safeguard against the pitfall of illegitimate totality transfer. In order to define the lexical sense of a word within a given context, it is more important, however, to determine the relationships between the related senses of different words than the different senses of the same word. Therefore there is not much benefit in contrasting the different senses of the same word and describing the nature of the relationship between them. However, the relations between different words in the same semantic domains will be carefully described in terms of a set of common and distinctive features. These features are identified through a process of contrasting neighboring semantic domains, neighboring sub-domains within a particular domain, and finally, neighboring words within a particular sub-domain. A number of shared features of meaning can be determined by contrasting the semantic domains and the sub-domains among their immediately neighboring domains and sub-domains and a number of distinctive features of meaning can be identified by contrasting the different items within the sub-domain.

Although Louw and Nida (I:xviii) emphasize that the relationships between different sets of meaning tend to be multidimensional and only rarely orthogonal, the classification of the semantic domains themselves, as well as the classification of the items within the domains, was done in terms of a generic-specific order, with the most generic term at the beginning and the most specific term at the end. This implies that meanings listed in later domains are generally included under the meanings of the directly preceding domains. Similarly, the meanings listed within a particular sub-domain are arranged according to a hierarchical pattern. Even if an inclusive sense rela-

---

[18]Although there might be instances of intentional ambiguity or the use of multiple senses in a word in a given utterance — such as the use of ἄνωθεν in John 3:3 meaning both "again" and "from above" — these cases are the exception rather than the rule. Such a play on different senses of a word is usually marked by the context (see Cotterell & Turner 175; see, however, Wendland 1990 on what he calls 'semantic density').

tion does not exist between two successive domains, sub-domains or items, certain specific contrasts between them can always be identified, because it is precisely because of these contrasts that they are listed in different domains and sub-domains.

The following procedure will therefore be followed in order to define the lexical sense of a number of important words in Romans 13:1-7:

*   The different senses of the word in the New Testament will be determined on the basis of the data given in the Louw and Nida *Lexicon*;

*   The specific sense used in the context of Romans 13:1-7 will be determined and substantiated;

*   A set of shared and distinctive features (or components) of meaning in terms of which the related meanings of the different words in the specific semantic domain can be contrasted will be identified;

*   The lexical sense of the word will be defined in terms of these components of meaning.

8. Meaning on word level (Lexical Semantics) in Romans 13:1-7

8.1 Criteria for determining which lexemes/words/linguistic units to study

Since it is not the purpose of this section to compile a lexicon of word meanings in Romans 13:1-7 or to write a commentary on the passage, it is not necessary to define the lexical sense of *all* the words in the passage. The aim of this section is to put in practice the theory of the description of meaning at the word-level discussed above. This is done in order to provide a practical example of this particular method of interpretation, which can serve as a basis for our consideration of the ethics of this method of reading. When an interpreter selects only certain words for analysis, however, this requires certain criteria. A practical criterion would be to concentrate on those words which are controversial in the interpretation of Romans 13:1-7.

Many exegetes give particular attention to the meaning of class referents such as ἐξουσίαι, ἄρχοντες, ὑπερέχουσαι, ὑποτάσσεσθαι ('. . . quite clearly a key word in this section' [Cranfield 1979:660]), ἀντιτάσσεσθαι, λειτουργός, διάκονος, ὀργή, διαταγή, ἔκδικος, συνείδησις, τέλος, φόρος and the expression τὴν μάχαιραν φορεῖν (see Sanday & Headlam 366ff; Michel 398ff; Schlier 387ff; Käsemann 1969:207ff; 1980:353ff; Cranfield 1979:656; Wilckens 1982:32ff; Webster 262-273; Jüngel 12ff; Barraclough 16ff).

There are also textually determined factors influencing the selection of words for special consideration. Certain words are repeated a number of times, namely ἐξουσία, ὑποτάσσεσθαι/ἀντιτάσσεσθαι, διάκονος/λειτουργός and φόρος. Certain words feature in prominent and significant places in the discourse, namely ὑποτάσσεσθαι at the beginning (13:1) and again at the end of the theoretical section of the argument (13:5) and συνείδησις at the end of the theoretical section (13:5). For a discussion of the textual function and prominence of these positions, see §§9.2 – 9.4. As a result of textual factors, therefore, this section will consider the lexical sense of ἐξουσίαι, ἄρχοντες, ὑποτάσσεσθαι, ἀντιτάσσεσθαι and συνείδησις. Other words, such as γαρ (Rom 13:1, 3, 4, 6), διό (13:5) and διὰ τοῦτο γάρ (13:6), serve to mark the relationship between different segments of the discourse. The section dealing with meaning on sentence- and discourse-level (see §§9.2 – 9.5) will discuss the sense and function of these 'markers.'

8.2 ἐξουσία

According to Louw and Nida (I:92) ἐξουσία is used for eight different senses in the New Testament. In order to determine which sense is used in Romans 13:1, we need to distinguish carefully between these different senses. Therefore Louw and Nida's definitions of the different senses of ἐξουσία are quoted in full.

* Senses in the semantic class *objects* in the semantic domain 'Supernatural Beings and Powers':

  * ἄρχων τῆς ἐξουσίας[g] τοῦ ἀέρος: "a supernatural power having some particular role in controlling the destiny and activities of human beings" (a title for a supernatural force or power) (with 'power,' 'authority,' 'lordship,' 'ruler,' or 'wicked force' as possible translation equivalents).

* Senses in the semantic class *events* in the semantic domain 'Control, Rule':

  * In the sub-domain 'Exercise Authority':

    * ἐξουσία[a] ας f: "the right to control or govern over" (with 'authority to rule' or 'right to control' as possible translation equivalents).
    * ἐξουσία[b] ας f: "the domain or sphere over which one has authority to control or rule" (with 'jurisdiction' as a possible translation equivalent).
    * ἐξουσία[c] ας f: "means or instrument by which authority is marked or symbolized" (with 'symbol of authority' or 'symbol of subjection to authority' as possible translation equivalents).
    * ἐξουσία[d] ας f: "one who has the authority to rule or govern" (with "an authority" or "ruler" as possible translation equivalents).

* In the sub-domain 'Control, Restrain':

    * ἐξουσία^e ας f: "a state of control over someone or something" (with 'control' as possible translation equivalent).

* A sense in the semantic class *events* in the semantic domain 'Think':

    * ἐξουσία^h, ας f: "the right to judge on the basis of having the potential to evaluate" (with 'right,' 'freedom of choice,' 'freedom of action' and 'power to evaluate' as possible translation equivalents).

* Senses in the semantic class *abstracts* in the semantic domain 'Power, Force':

    * ἐξουσία^f, ας f: "the power to do something, with or without the added implication of authority" (with 'power' as possible translation equivalent).

'Εξουσία^g can be dismissed since it forms part of a fixed expression that does not occur in Romans 13:1-3.[19] 'Εξουσία^h seems to be a *derivation* of ἐξουσία^{a-d}. From the context of Romans 13:1-3 it is clear that the ἐξουσίαι have to do with the institutions that embody certain functions (that is, which cause certain events to take place or states to come into being), therefore ἐξουσία^f (which is an Abstract and not an Event) can be ruled out. 'Εξουσία^e differs from ἐξουσία^{a-d} in the sense that they are classified into two different sub-domains. The sub-domain 'Exercise authority' does not have the component of a specific negative orientation or effect as is the case with the sub-domain 'Control, Restrain.' Since positively as well as negatively oriented actions of the ἐξουσίαι are mentioned in Romans 13:3-4, ἐξουσία^e can be ruled out. That leaves us with ἐξουσία^{a-d} as possible senses of ἐξουσία in Romans 13:1-2. Therefore we can focus on the contrasts among the items in the sub-domain 'Exercise Authority' in order to define the lexical meaning of ἐξουσία in this context.

It seems as if ἐξουσία^d is the sense being used in Romans 13:1-2 since it is not the *right, domain* or *means* of control that is in focus, but the *persons* who exercise the control. The following features of meaning can be identified when we compare and contrast the items in this semantic domain and sub-domain:

---

[19]Cullmann's (193ff) interpretation of the sense and reference of ἐξουσία in Romans 13:1 as 'the invisible angelic powers that stand behind the State government' has not met with general acceptance (see Hutchinson 57-58; Cranfield 1979:657-658; Bruce 88). Cullmann was probably influenced by the sense of ἐξουσία in other contexts (to quote him: '. . . Paul, for whom this word elsewhere always designates angelic powers, thinks of them here too') (195) and has drawn those meanings and references through a process of illegitimate totality transfer into Romans 13:1-3.

* Event
* The relationship between actor and object is on a voluntary basis (Guide, Discipline, Follow)
* Minimum control on the part of the actor
* Focus upon the controlling of someone else, not of oneself
* Negative orientation toward the desired action on the part of the object: Control, Restrain
* Positive orientation toward the desired action on the part of the object: Compel, Force
* Focus on the exercising of authority
* The right or ability to exercise authority ($\dot{\epsilon}\xi o v \sigma \iota \alpha^a$)
* The domain or sphere over which one has authority ($\dot{\epsilon}\xi o v \sigma \iota \alpha^b$)
* The means or instrument by which authority is marked ($\dot{\epsilon}\xi o v \sigma \iota \alpha^c$)
* The one who has the authority to rule ($\dot{\epsilon}\xi o v \sigma \iota \alpha^d$)
* Focus on the responsibility on the part of the one in the position of authority ($o \iota \kappa o v \acute{o} \mu o \varsigma$)
* Full authority to carry out a commission ($\dot{\epsilon}\pi \iota \tau \rho o \pi \acute{\eta}$)
* The right or authority to command ($\dot{\epsilon}\pi \iota \tau \alpha \gamma \acute{\eta}$)
* An instituted authority which has been created or formed ($\kappa \tau \acute{\iota} \sigma \iota \varsigma$)
* To have the capacity to interpret the Law of Moses with authority ($\dot{\epsilon}\pi \grave{\iota} \tau \hat{\eta} \varsigma$ $M \omega \ddot{\upsilon} \sigma \acute{\epsilon} \omega \varsigma \kappa \alpha \theta \acute{\epsilon} \delta \rho \alpha \varsigma \kappa \alpha \theta \acute{\iota} \sigma \tau \eta \mu \iota$)
* To cause someone to be under the authority of someone or something else ($\delta \acute{\epsilon} \omega^d$)
* To exercise authority on the basis that it is not legitimate ($\delta \acute{\epsilon} \omega^e$)
* To exercise authority over something on the basis of its being legitimate ($\lambda \acute{\upsilon} \omega$)
* Focus on the contents or results of the action (Punish, reward)

We can now conclude our consideration of $\dot{\epsilon}\xi o v \sigma \iota \alpha$ with a final definition and description of shared and distinctive semantic features.

The lexical sense of $\dot{\epsilon}\xi o v \sigma \iota \alpha \iota$ in Romans 13:1 can be defined as "those persons who have the authority to rule or govern," with 'authorities' or 'rulers' as possible translation equivalents (Louw & Nida I:477). The focus of this sense is on the *persons* who exercise authority and not on the *right*, *domain* or *means* of authority. The persons in question are those who exercise an event taking place between two parties who do not stand in a voluntary relationship. The action(s) of a person or persons rather than its orientation (negative: 'restrain,' or positive: 'force') is in focus. Although it does not specifically focus on any one of them, one or more of the following semantic features may be included in this sense: *responsibility* on the part of the one in the position of authority (more specifically the meaning of $o \iota \kappa o v \acute{o} \mu o \varsigma$), *full authority* to act (more specifically the meaning of $\dot{\epsilon}\pi \iota \tau \rho o \pi \acute{\eta}$), or the *right* to act (more specifically the meaning of $\dot{\epsilon}\pi \iota \tau \alpha \gamma \acute{\eta}$). The *nature* of the *origin* of the authorities (created or not, such as in $\kappa \tau \acute{\iota} \sigma \iota \varsigma$) is not a semantic component included in the *lexical sense* of $\dot{\epsilon}\xi o v \sigma \iota \alpha$, although this aspect is argued in the rest of Romans 13:1–2. Whether the $\dot{\epsilon}\xi o v \sigma \iota \alpha \iota$ have the right to interpret the Law of Moses or not, whether they *cause* someone to be under authority of someone else or not, and, whether they are *legitimate* or not is not in the focus in this sense. Neither is the *nature of the basis* of the authority, the *contents* or the *results* of the event (whether punishment or reward).

8.3 ἄρχων

According to Louw and Nida (II:36), ἄρχων is used in two different senses in the New Testament, namely ἄρχων[a] in the semantic domain 'Control, Rule' (with 'ruler' as translation equivalent), and ἄρχων[b] in the semantic domain 'Courts and Legal Procedures' (with 'judge' as translation equivalent). The word is also used in two fixed expressions (ἄρχων τῶν 'Ιουδαίων — 'member of Council'; and ἄρχων τῆς ἐξουσίας τοῦ ἀέρος — 'supernatural power'), neither of which is used in Romans 13:3. Ἄρχων[a] is the most appropriate sense in this context. Although grammatically a noun, it belongs to the semantic class *events*.

The following features of meaning can be identified when we compare and contrast the items in this semantic domain and sub-domain with the neighboring domains and sub-domains (see Louw & Nida I:472, 478–481):

* Event
* The relationship between actor and object is on a voluntary basis (Guide, Discipline, Follow)
* Minimum control on the part of the actor
* Focus upon the controlling of someone else, not of oneself
* Negative orientation toward object: Control, Restrain
* Positive orientation toward object: Compel, Force
* Focus on the exercising of authority in general
* Focus on a specific occurrence of the exercising of authority, namely, rule or govern or reign (ἐξουσιάζω; κατεξουσιάζω)
* To rule over people, involving more than but not excluding judicial decisions (κρίνω[g])
* To rule or reign over, with the implication in some contexts of 'lording it over' (κυριεύω; κατακυριεύω[a])
* One who rules or exercises authority over others (κύριος[c])
* To rule or govern, with the implication of pre-eminent position and status (ἄρχω)
* The sphere of one's authority or rule (ἀρχή[d])
* One who rules or governs (ἄρχων[a])
* To rule, with the implication of direct personal involvement (ποιμαίνω[c])
* To rule over, with the implication of providing direction and leadership (ἡγέομαι[c])
* One who rules, with the implication of pre-eminent position (ἡγεμών[a])
* To be a governor, specifically a governor of a Roman province (ἡγεμονεύω)
* One who has the power to rule (δύναμις[d])
* One who holds complete power or authority over another (δεσπότης[a])

*   Specific type of rule (for example, to rule as a king, with the implication of complete authority and the possibility of being able to pass on the right to rule to one's son or near kin [βασιλεύω[a]])

*   Title or specific type of ruler (for example, Καῖσαρ, ὁ Σεβαστός, Κανδάκη, τετραάρχης, ἐθνάρχης, Ἀσιάρχης, ἡγεμών[b] (=Latin: *praefectus*), ἀνθύπατος, εὐνοῦχος, ἐπίτροπος, στρατηγός, στρατηγός τοῦ ἱεροῦ, πράκτωρ, πολιτάρχης, γραμματεύς, ἄρχων τῶν Ἰουδαίων)

*   To have the authority to communicate or act on behalf of the ruler (πρεσβεία, πρεσβεύω)

*   Focus on the contents or results of the action (Punish, reward)

Finally, the following description and definition of the lexical sense of ἄρχοντες in Romans 13:3 can be proposed: "those who rule or govern" with 'rulers' or 'governors' as possible translation equivalents (Louw & Nida I:478).   The person or persons in question are those who are responsible for a relationship between two parties where one controls the other.   The two parties are not in a voluntary relationship.   The action itself rather than its orientation (negative: 'restrain' or positive: 'force') is in focus.   It is the exercising of authority in a specific relationship (namely that in which descriptions such as 'rule' or 'govern' are applicable) and not every possible exercising of authority (for example, the related event taking place between parents and children, or teachers and pupils).   It has no specific connotation in relation to the making of judicial decisions, although such an action may be included in this sense.   It does not have the implication of 'lording it over others' (in contrast to κυριεύω and κατακυριεύω[a]).   It may include the implication of pre-eminent position or status (more specifically the sense of ἡγεμών[a]).   It focuses on those who exercise rule from such a position and not on the sphere of the authority.   Implications such as direct personal involvement between the two parties, the provision of direction or leadership, having the power to rule, having complete power to rule, or the specific type of rule or the specific type of ruler (with specific titles) may or may not be included in the sense of ἄρχοντες.   For all these nuances there are numerous other specific words available, which implies that ἄρχοντες has a more generic sense.   The contents or the results of the event (whether punishment or reward) are not in focus.

The difference between ἐξουσίαι (used twice in Romans 13:1) and ἄρχοντες (used only once in 13:3) seems to be that ἐξουσία has the more generic sense of the exercising of authority itself while ἄρχοντες has a more specific sense of the exercising of authority specifically within a relationship where words such as 'rule' or 'govern' are applicable (that is, the relationship between governors and governed).   Although 'authority' is present in the relationships between, for example, parents and children or professors and students, the sense ἄρχων[a] cannot be used for these relationships.   Both ἐξουσίαι and ἄρχοντες are generic terms, with ἄρχοντες perhaps a specification of the nature of the authority-relationship in question.

8.4 ὑποτάσσεσθαι

It has become fashionable to comment on the possible significance of words with the stem -ταγ- in Romans 13:1-7: ὑποτάσσομαι (13:1 and 5), τάσσω (13:1), ἀντιτάσσομαι (13:2) and διαταγή (13:2) (see for example Sanday & Headlam 366; Michel 398; Cranfield 1979:660; Käsemann 1980:351). Cranfield argues that ὑποτάσσομαι (and the other etymologically related words) should be understood in terms of God's τάξις or 'order' (1979:662). In terms of our approach and focus, namely, to define the *lexical sense* of the words in this context, such an argument from etymology is not viable (see §3.2). When the relations between the meanings of these words are considered diachronically, evidence for an earlier 'general' meaning having something to do with "order" may perhaps be found. But, although etymologically related, all these words feature — in terms of their synchronically delimited senses in the New Testament — in different semantic domains and have therefore to be treated separately.

According to Louw and Nida (I:468) the word ὑποτάσσομαι (although it is used frequently) is used in only one sense in the New Testament. They define this sense as "to submit to the orders or directives of someone" with 'to obey, to submit, obedience, submission' as possible translation equivalents. This meaning is listed in the semantic domain 'Guide, Discipline, Follow.'

The following features of meaning can be identified when we compare and contrast the items in this semantic domain and sub-domain with the neighboring domains and sub-domains (Louw & Nida I:465-471):

* Event
* Help, Care for
* Guide, Lead — focus on the subject of the action
* Discipline, Train — focus on the object of the action
* A willingness on the part of others to be led
* A minimum of control on the part of the one guiding or leading
* Obey, Disobey — focus on the subject of the action
* Follow, Be a Disciple — focus on the object of the action
* Voluntary action on the part of the object
* To submit to authority or reason by obeying (πείθομαι[a], πειθαρχέω)
* To obey, with the implication of awe and reverence (εὐλαβέομαι[b])
* To listen or pay attention to a person, with resulting conformity to what is advised or commanded (ἀκούω[e], ἐπιδέχομαι[b])
* To obey on the basis of having paid attention to (ὑπακούω[a])

* To conform to some standard as a means of demonstrating its purpose (ἀναπληρόω[e])
* To submit to the orders or directives of someone (ὑποτάσσομαι)
* To continue to obey orders or commands (φυλάσσω[b], τηρέω[c])
* To obey as a means of fulfilling the purpose of a rule or standard (τηρέω[d])
* To conform to rules and regulations (δογματίζομαι)
* To conform to righteous, just commands (δικαιόω[e])
* Unwillingness or refusal to comply with the demands of some authority (ἀπειθέω[a])
* Pertaining to being rebelliously disobedient (ἀνυπότακτος[a])
* To refuse to listen to and hence to disobey (παρακούω[a], παραιτέομαι[e])

The following definition and description of the lexical sense of ὑποτάσσομαι in Romans 13:1 can be proposed: "to submit to the orders or directives of someone." It is an event taking place between two parties which focuses on the action on the part of party B (in contrast to 'guide,' 'lead,' 'discipline' or 'train' which focuses on the action of party A). It does not have specifically the semantic feature of a voluntary action (in contrast to 'follow' or 'be a disciple'). The act of obedience indicated by ὑποτάσσομαι is less generic than that indicated by πείθομαι[a], though more generic than senses which also include connotations of the *basis*, *nature* (righteous or not) or *duration* of the obedience. It does not have the implications of awe or reverence. It is not obedience that serves to fulfill the purpose of a rule or standard. It is not a means of conforming to rules and regulations. It has the specific semantic feature of a positive orientation with regard to the directions given by party A (in contrast to disobey which has a negative orientation). The nature of the relationship between the two parties is not in focus (whether parent-child, master-slave, governor-governed, et cetera). The word ὑποτάσσομαι is used twice in Romans 13:1-7 (13:1, 5), having the same sense in both cases.

8.5 ἀντιτάσσομαι

According to Louw and Nida (I:492) ἀντιτάσσομαι is used in only one sense in the New Testament, which they define as "to oppose someone, involving not only a psychological attitude but also a corresponding behavior" with 'to oppose,' 'to be hostile toward' or 'to show hostility' as possible translation equivalents.[20] This sense is listed in the semantic domain 'Hostility, Strife.' The domain involves a number of forms of interpersonal conflict, including

---

[20]Louw and Nida (I:492) indicate that there may probably be certain significant distinctions in meaning between ἀντιτάσσομαι, ἀθίστημι, ἀντίκειμαι, ἀντιδιατίθεμαι and ἐναντιόομαι, but that it is not possible to determine these distinctions precisely on the basis of New Testament usage alone.

not only generalized opposition and division, but also overt forms of strife, persecution, attack and conquering (although those meanings which involve actual military operations are not included in this domain). The domain overlaps to a considerable extent with the domain 'Attitudes and Emotions' although it differs in the sense that it also involves overt forms of behavior (Louw & Nida I:492).

It is significant that ἀντιτάσσομαι is the first of sixty one items listed in this domain, which indicates that Louw and Nida regard this sense as the most generic in this domain. From this we may infer that the meanings listed consecutively in the other sub-domains (Division, Resistance, Yielding, Struggle, Revenge, Rebellion, Riot, Persecution, Attack, Ambush, Conquer) may all be included in the general sense of "Opposition, Hostility," for which ἀντιτάσσομαι is the most generic term. This, however, does not imply that any of these senses should in fact be read into or included in the sense of ἀντιτάσσομαι in Romans 13:2. The *generality* of the event is in focus in this sense. The same holds true for all the other meanings listed in the sub-domain 'Opposition, Hostility': all of them may be included in the sense of ἀντιτάσσομαι but are not in fact included in the case of the usage in Romans 13:2.

We can therefore define and describe the sense of ἀντιτάσσομαι in Romans 13:2 as an event taking place between two parties consisting of hostility from the side of one party (usually the subordinate party). The *nature* of the act of hostility, whether it is actual war against the other party (ἀντιστρατεύομαι), the *duration* of the hostility (ἐνέχω[b] — "to maintain a state of antagonism or hostility"), the *degree* of the hostility (τάραχος[a]) and the numerous other possible specifications of the event of opposition or hostility, are not in focus in this sense. It is precisely the generality of the sense that makes it significant in the context of Romans 13:1-7: *any form* of opposition, psychological as well as in actual behavior (excluding military operations), against the ἐξουσίαι/ἄρχοντες is considered as opposition or hostility against a διαταγὴ τοῦ θεοῦ.

Three forms of the lexeme ἀντιτάσσομαι are used in Romans 13:2, namely the present participial form (ἀντιτασσόμενος), the perfect indicative form (ἀνθέστηκεν), and the perfect participial form (ἀνθεστηκότες). Although these different forms indicate a significant difference in grammatical meaning, the lexical sense of the word is similar in all three instances.

8.6 συνείδησις

Louw and Nida (II:234) have identified two different senses and one fixed expression for which the word συνείδησις is used in the New Testament as well as the expression καυστηριάζομαι τὴν συνείδησιν ('be insensitive to'). There is a significant contrast between the two meanings of συνείδησις: συνείδησις[a] means "to be aware of information about something" in the semantic domain 'Know,' with 'to know,' 'to be conscious of' or 'to be aware of' as possible translation equivalents; συνείδησις[b] means "the psychological faculty which can distinguish between right and wrong" in the semantic domain 'Psychological Faculties' with 'moral sensitivity' or 'conscience' as possible translation equivalents. It is clear that συνείδησις[b] is the sense being used in Romans 13:5.

Louw and Nida (I:320–325) list sixteen items in the semantic domain 'Psychological faculties.' When these items are contrasted, the following shared and distinctive semantic features can be distinguished:

* Event
* Physiological processes and states
* Sensory events and states
* Attitudes and emotions
* Psychological faculties
* Learn
* Know
* Psychological faculty, including intellectual, emotional and spiritual aspects, in contrast to the purely physical aspects of human existence [ὁ ἔσω (ἄνθρωπος); ὁ ἐν τῷ κρυπτῷ (ἄνθρωπος)]
* The inner being of a person as the source or agent of thought or behavior (ἔσωθεν)
* The causative source of a person's psychological life in its various aspects (καρδία[a])
* The essence of life in terms of thinking, willing and feeling (ψυχή[a])
* The psychological aspect of human nature that contrasts with the spiritual nature, in other words, that aspect of human nature that is characterized by or reflects typical human reasoning and desires in contrast with those aspects of human thought and behavior that relate to God and spiritual life (σάρξ[f])
* The non-material psychological faculty that is potentially sensitive and responsive to God (πνεῦμα[e])
* The psychological faculty of desire, intent, and feeling (σπλάγχνα[b])
* The psychological faculty of will and impulse (ὁρμή)
* The psychological faculty that can distinguish between right and wrong (συνείδησις[b])
* The psychological faculty of understanding, reasoning, thinking and deciding (νοῦς[a])
* To employ one's faculty for thoughtful planning, with emphasis upon the underlying disposition or attitude (φρονέω[a])

In the light of this set of semantic features, the following definition and description of the lexical sense of συνείδησις in Romans 13:5 can be proposed: "the psychological faculty that can distinguish between right and wrong." It is an event not pertaining to the physiological processes and states, sensory events and states, or the attitudes and emotions of being human. It might include the intellectual, emotional and spiritual aspects of human existence, although none of these aspects is specifically in focus. It might serve as the source or agent of thought or behavior or as the causative source of a person's psychological life in its various aspects, but again, none of these features is specifically in focus. Although closely related, elements such as the essence of life in terms of thinking, willing and feeling, or typical *human* reasoning and desires (in contrast with those aspects of human thought and behavior that relate to God and the spiritual life) are not in focus. It is an event not pertaining to human behavior influenced or caused by any specific relationship to God. Semantic features such as will, impulse, understanding, reasoning, thinking and deciding or thoughtful planning, with emphasis upon the underlying disposition or attitude, are all very closely related and may even be included in the sense of συνείδησις, but none of them is specifically in focus.

Συνείδησις pertains specifically to the human psychological faculty or ability to decide between right and wrong. The source of this faculty (whether exclusively or typically human, or from God), the criteria on which the decision between right and wrong is based, the intensity of the event (whether an impulse or thoughtful reasoning), is not specifically at issue. Συνείδησις is that human faculty that makes ethical reflection on ethical choices possible.

Although there are a number of other important words in Romans 13:1–7, we conclude our discussion of meaning at the word-level with the five words that have been analyzed. These analyses give a clear indication of the procedures and the results of this mode of reading at this level. In the next section, meaning at larger levels is considered.

9. *Meaning at the sentence and the discourse level in Romans 13:1-7*

As I have argued earlier (see §2), a whole hierarchy of units of meaning lies between the single concept and the complete discourse. In the previous section meaning at the level of the single lexical unit was discussed. In this section we focus on meaning at the level of the sentence and the discourse.

Cotterell and Turner (194) argue that at each level of meaning (whether concept, sentence, paragraph, chapter or whole book), the unit concerned will display both internal coherence and the 'law of principality.' According to this law, one component is usually more marked or prominent among the various components of meaning. The rest is subsidiary and/or delimiting. Usually it is the marked element and its relation to the rest that gives the required coherence to the unit of meaning. On the level of the simple sentence, the most prominent element is usually the verb. Similarly, one sentence usually dominates in a paragraph and gives coherence to the rest and in a longer discourse there have to be a few prominent points to which the rest are subordinated. If everything is equally marked or emphasized, little or nothing is communicated.

9.1 Analysis of the nuclear structures of Romans 13:1-2

The analysis of meaning at the broader levels of meaning will be performed in three phases: first an in-depth analysis of a smaller section of Romans 13:1-7 (§§9.1 - 9.2), then an analysis of the whole pericope (§§9.3 - 9.4), and then an analysis of the co-text of the pericope (§9.5). Since, as argued later on (see §9.4), Romans 13:1-2 is the most marked section of the passage, these two verses will be analyzed in more detail here on the basis of nuclear structures. Nuclear structures constitute the core units of propositions. In terms of the semantic classes (see §6.2), the events on the surface structure of the text (whether grammatically in verb form or in nominalized form) form the nuclei of the kernel sentences in the deep structure. The breaking down of a text into kernel sentences is followed with an elucidation of the relations between the kernels. Beckman and Callow (287 312) have worked out a fairly exhaustive system in terms of which these relations can be described. Cotterell and Turner (216) provide a diagram of the possible types of kernel relationships identified by Beekman and Callow. Neither the discussion nor the diagram need to be repeated here, but will simply be used as a basis to describe the inter-nuclear relations. Following such an elucidation, the kernel sentences can be restructured into a translation (see Nida & Taber 33ff and Nida et al. 1983:93ff for an exposition of the principles and practice of these procedures). Although Nida and Taber proposed this procedure primarily for translation purposes, it is also a very valuable interpretative tool since translation inevitably consists of interpretation.

1. Every soul should be obedient (πᾶσα ψυχὴ ὑποτασσέσθω)
2. People govern (ἐξουσίαις)
3. People exercise control (ὑπερεχούσαις). (This kernel sentence depends on another kernel sentence at an even deeper level: God put people in a position to exercise control.)
4. Nobody governs (οὐ γὰρ ἔστιν ἐξουσία)
5. God lets them govern (εἰ μὴ ὑπὸ θεοῦ — although not on the surface structure, the event is supposed in the deep structure)
6. People govern (αἱ δὲ οὖσαι)
7. God appoints them (ὑπὸ θεοῦ τεταγμέναι εἰσίν)
8. Somebody resists (ὁ ἀντιτασσόμενος)
9. People govern (τῇ ἐξουσίᾳ)

10. Somebody resists (ἀνθέστηκεν)
11. God institutes them (τῇ τοῦ θεοῦ διαταγῇ)
12. People resist (οἱ δὲ ἀνθεστηκότες)
13. They themselves will receive (ἑαυτοῖς λήμψονται)
14. God judges (κρίμα)

9.2 Relations between nuclear structures

Kernel sentence 2 qualifies the nature of the event expressed in 3: the nature of the control exercised is that of governing.

(2–3) is the object of 1.

5 is the condition for 4, (the condition is marked with the particle εἰ).

7 is the condition for 6.

Note that (4–5) and (6–7) repeat exactly the same proposition. In the first case it is negative ('nobody governs if not appointed by God') and in the second case positive ('those who govern govern, only on the condition that they are appointed by God'). These two parallel statements are linked with the particle δέ.

9 is the object of the event expressed in 8.

11 is the object of the event expressed in 10.

(10–11) is the consequence of (8–9): to resist the people who govern is to resist what God ordains. In this sense, (10–11) qualifies the nature of (8–9): It is God who ordains or institutes people to govern. Note that essentially the same proposition is once again repeated, although it was already repeated twice in (4–5) and (6–7).

13 is the contents of 12.

(13–14) is the result of 12.

(12–14) is the consequence of the condition stated in (8–11). The particle δέ marks the consequential relationship.

(8–14) is the consequence of (4–7). This relationship is not explicitly marked on the surface structure, but it is clear from the consequential semantic hierarchy in the two sets of kernel sentences: God ordains people to govern, to resist them results in God's judgment.

(4–14) serves as motivation for (1–3). This relationship is marked with the conjunction γάρ.

It is noteworthy that the discourse repeats the proposition 'God ordains people to govern' on different semantic levels as many as four times: in kernel sentences 3, 5, 7 and 11. This repetition serves as the primary motivation or ground for the basic exhortation in kernel sentence 1. The matters of resistance against those who govern and the consequential judgment of God are all subsidiary to this basic proposition. Our elucidation of the inter-nuclear relationships exhibits the important role of markers such as γάρ, εἰ and δέ. Except for the relation between (4–7) and (8–14), all the important relations are explicitly marked on the surface structure with particles or conjunctions.

The following translation reflects the kernel sentences as well as the relations between them, without all the repetition present in the actual discourse:

> Every soul should obey the people who exercise control by means of government, because God ordains people to govern. Consequently, to resist those who govern is to resist what God ordains. Consequently, God will punish those who resist the people who govern.

9.3 Colon analysis of Romans 13:1–7

The importance of meaning at the level of the single lexical unit or the nuclear structure or sentence may never be ignored, but the conviction has grown (since Barr) that the sentence cluster, or short paragraph, is the basic unit of communication in a discourse (Louw 1979:6; 1982:91ff; Cotterell and Turner 195). In order to analyze the meaning of Romans 13:1–7 on the level of the paragraph (or pericope) and its broader co-text (in §§9.4 – 9.6), I will begin with the sentence, move on to the relations between sentences and groups of sentences and proceed finally to the relations between paragraphs and groups of paragraphs. However, I will use the *colon* (and not the traditional grammatical *sentence*) as the unit of analysis (See Louw 1982:95ff and especially H. C. du Toit, for a definition and description of the *colon*). For the description of the relations between cola, I will use the model proposed by Nida (1975a:50–54) and refined by Nida *et al.* (1983:102–103). In this model, the meaningful relations between the cola and the colon-clusters can be described in terms of a set of coordinate and subordinate relations, each having a number of sub-categories. The same system will be used to describe the meaningful relations between paragraphs and groups of paragraphs.

9.4 Relations between cola and clusters

The meaningful relations between the cola and clusters may be described as:

> 2–3 — Additive equivalent (or additive different non-consequential): (2) 'authorities are from God' = (3) 'authorities are from God.' The same statement is made twice, first negative and then positive, linked by the particle δέ.
> 4–5 — Reason-result: (4) 'rebellion against the authorities is rebellion against an institution of God' is the reason (marked with δέ) for the result (5) that 'they will bring judgment on themselves.'

(2-3)-(4-5) — Basis-inference: (2-3) 'authorities are from God' is the basis for the inference (4-5) 'he who rebels against them, rebels against an institution of God and he will be punished.'

1-(2-5) — Inference-basis: the instruction in (1) that 'everyone should obey the authorities' is an inference flowing from the fact that (2-5) 'God has instituted authorities and that people rebelling against them will be punished because they are rebelling against an institution of God.'

1. Πᾶσα ψυχὴ ὑποτασσέσθω.
      ἐξουσίαις ὑπερεχούσαις
2. οὐ γὰρ ἔστιν ἐξουσία
       εἰ μὴ ὑπὸ θεοῦ,
3. αἱ δὲ οὖσαι ὑπὸ θεοῦ τεταγμέναι εἰσίν·
4. ὥστε ὁ ἀντιτασσόμενος   ἀνθέστηκεν,
      τῇ ἐξουσίᾳ   τῇ τοῦ θεοῦ διαταγῇ
5. οἱ δὲ ἀνθεστηκότες ἑαυτοῖς κρίμα λήμψονται.

               A

6. οἱ γὰρ ἄρχοντες οὐκ εἰσὶν φόβος
      τῷ ἀγαθῷ ἔργῳ
      ἀλλὰ τῷ κακῷ.
7. θέλεις δὲ μὴ φοβεῖσθαι τὴν ἐξουσίαν;
8. τὸ ἀγαθὸν ποίει,
9. καὶ ἕξεις ἔπαινον ἐξ αὐτῆς·
10. θεοῦ γὰρ διάκονός ἐστιν σοὶ εἰς τὸ ἀγαθόν.
11. ἐὰν δὲ τὸ κακὸν ποιῇς,
      φοβοῦ·
12. οὐ γὰρ εἰκῇ τὴν μάχαιραν φορεῖ·
13. θεοῦ γὰρ διάκονός ἐστιν,
      ἔκδικος εἰς ὀργὴν τῷ τὸ κακὸν πράσσοντι.
14. διὸ ἀνάγκη ὑποτάσσεσθαι,
      οὐ μόνον διὰ τὴν ὀργὴν
      ἀλλὰ καὶ διὰ τὴν συνείδησιν.

               B

15. διὰ τοῦτο γὰρ καὶ φόρους τελεῖτε,
16. λειτουργοὶ γὰρ θεοῦ εἰσιν εἰς αὐτὸ τοῦτο προσκαρτεροῦντες.
17. ἀπόδοτε πᾶσιν τὰς ὀφειλάς,
18. (ἀπόδοτε) τῷ τὸν φόρον τὸν φόρον,
19. (ἀπόδοτε) τῷ τὸ τέλος τὸ τέλος,
20. (ἀπόδοτε) τῷ τὸν φόβον τὸν φόβον,
21. (ἀπόδοτε) τῷ τὴν τιμὴν τὴν τιμήν.

               C

Cola 1-5 form a cluster (A) of which colon 1 is the most prominent element that gives coherence to this cluster.

7-8 — Condition-result: (7) 'if you do not want to fear the authorities' is the condition for (8) 'then you must do right/good.'

9-10 — Result-reason: The fact that (10) 'the authority is a servant of God which is appointed to do you good' is the reason for the result that (9) 'the authority will commend you' when you do right.

(7-8)-(9-10) — Cause-effect: Because you do right/good (7-8) the effect is that the authority will commend you (9-10).

12-13 — Result-reason: (13) 'the authority has as its duty to be a servant to punish the bad/the wrong' is the reason which has as its result that (12) 'he bears the sword.'

11-(12-13) — Effect-cause: That the authority must punish the bad/wrong and that he therefore carries the sword (12-13) is the cause which has as its effect that (11) 'you shall fear the authority when you do wrong/bad.'

(7-10)-(11-13) — Dyadic contrastive: (7-10) deals with the attitude and action of the authorities against people doing good/right and (11-13) its attitude and action against those doing wrong/bad. These two propositions are coordinate (on the same semantic level) but in contrast to each other: doing good/right and its consequences are contrasted with doing wrong/bad and its consequences. The contrast is marked by the particle δέ in 11.

6-(7-13) — Generic-specific: the generic statement in (6) that 'the authorities hold no terror for those who do right/good but for those who do wrong/bad' is specified or explained in (7-13). In this specification of the 'doing good' and 'doing bad' in (6) the sequence is maintained: (7-10) deals with the 'doing good' and (11-13) deals with the 'doing bad.' Thus, we have an important semantic parallelism in the discourse structure.

(6-13)-14 — Basis-inference: The whole argument about doing good or bad and its consequences (6-13) forms the basis for the inference made in (14) and is introduced by διό: 'it is necessary to obey the authorities, not only because of possible punishment but also because of conscience.' If one links 'punishment' to 'doing bad/wrong' and 'conscience' to 'doing right/good' we may perhaps speak of an example of ostranenie (*Verfremdung*/defamiliarization):[21] a pattern (good-bad, good-bad) is set in (6-13) and in (14) it is reversed ('punishment' is named first and then 'conscience'). A certain expectation is created and then it is frustrated.[22]

Cola 6-14 forms a cluster (B) of which colon 14 is, in terms of the law of principality, the most marked element. Colon 14 repeats essentially the proposition made in colon 1, including, however, the elements of ὀργή and συνείδησις which serve as summary statements for the argument in the second cluster.

---

[21]See Cronjé (214-227) for a description of these terms and for an application to Galatians.

[22]Venter (91-92) uses the typification of the ἐξουσία as διάκονος τοῦ θεοῦ (colon 10) and λειτουργοὶ τοῦ θεοῦ (colon 16) as the basis for his demarcation of cluster A as consisting of cola 1-9, cluster B consisting of cola 10-16 and cluster C consisting of cola 17-21. This demarcation, however, ignores the significant good-bad good-bad bad-good pattern, and, more importantly, the significance of the marker διό in 13:5 is overlooked. Although I differ from this demarcation, I want to emphasize that there is no such a thing as *the* (correct) structure of Romans 13:1-7. Such an idea is a positivistic notion that is sometimes associated with this kind of structural analysis (see Deist 1978).

15-16 — Result-reason: (15) 'you (must) pay taxes' is the result of the reason (16) 'for authorities are God's servants who are committed to just this (= receive taxes).'

18-19-20-21 — Additive equivalent: the same instruction is given four times: 'pay up!'

17-(18-21) — Generic-specific: the generic term ὀφειλάς (the things that you owe other people/institutions) in (17) is specified with regard to four things to be paid: taxes, revenue, respect, honor.

Cola 15-21 form a cluster (C) with colon 15 as the most marked element.

Finally, the semantic relationship between the clusters will be discussed. In cluster A a generic statement is made which is specified in the other two clusters. In cluster B the principle stated in A is argued in terms of general ethical values (good and bad behavior), and in C this principle is illustrated concretely with the paying of taxes. Thus, cluster A's generic statement is specified in a double sense: theoretically in B and practically in C. The relationship between cluster A and cluster B is marked with the relational γάρ in colon 6. The relationship between clusters B and C is marked by the relational διά, with the whole of cluster B (and perhaps also cluster A) being the referent (in the linguistic world) of τοῦτο in colon 15. Cluster A is a generic statement, specified in cluster B. Clusters A and B as a unit serve as the basis on which the inference in cluster C is made. From this analysis of the relationships between the clusters, it becomes clear that the most marked element in the passage is the statement in colon 1: 'every soul should obey the governing authorities.' All the other elements are subsidiary to it, elaborating on it in several ways. The call for obedience to the authorities, therefore, serves to give coherence to the passage. In terms of the four patterns of structuring an argument (see Louw 1982:117) it seems that here we have an example of the so-called triangle: the basic point is made right at the beginning, and it is then elaborated, ending with a climax in which the far-reaching consequences of the basic thesis are expressed.

9.5 Romans 13:1-7 in its co-text

According to Cotterell and Turner (224), commentators on Romans have struggled with the problem of the relationship of immediately adjacent nuclear structures. They regard the commentary of Cranfield to be 'a model of how a careful attempt can be made to see how each nuclear sentence is modified by the expansions which follow and precede in the discourse.' Unfortunately, such attention is not always given to the relations between larger sections of discourse. While the description of the relations of clauses and prepositional phrases is conducted with utmost syntactic rigor, such rigor and a consistent system seem to be lacking when the relations between paragraphs are discussed. Although most commentaries on Romans give an outline of 'the structure' of the letter (see for example Käsemann 1980:ix-xi; Schlier ix-x; Michel 7-9; Wilckens 1978:15-22; Nygren 38-41; Ridderbos 21; Cranfield 1975:27-29), this is usually done on a more or less intuitive thematic basis. Cotterell and Turner (225) argue that semantic structural analysis provides a framework within which relations of meaning within a paragraph and between paragraphs may be discussed systematically. It involves the interpreter in making refined judgments on the basis of, among other things, clearly indexed linguistic features. Louw's (1979) analysis of the semantic structure of Romans is a model in this regard.

In terms of the law of principality, one element is usually the most marked or prominent in a unit of meaning, whether that unit is a concept, a nuclear structure, a colon, a cluster or a paragraph. Once this element in a paragraph has been identified, the theme of the paragraph can be formulated. On the basis of these formulated themes, the relations between paragraphs can then be elucidated. The same system that was used to elucidate semantic relations between units on other levels of meaning will again be used here. In order to determine and formulate themes for the paragraphs in the co-text of Romans 13:1-7, I have applied the procedures used in the case of Romans 13:1-7 above (§9.3 - 9.4) on all the other paragraphs in Romans 12:1 - 15:13) (namely 12:1-8; 12:9-21; 13:8-10; 13:11-14; 14:1-12; 14:13-23; 15:1-13). That need not be repeated here. Only the results of the investigation will be used.

Since Louw's (1979:143-148) analysis is based on a consistent linguistic procedure, we will take that as our point of departure. He proposes the following broad structural analysis of the letter:

1:1-17	— Introduction
1:18 - 8:39	— δικαιοσύνη ἐκ πίστεως
9:1 - 11:36	— Israel
12:1 - 15:13	— Christian behavior
15:14 - 16:27	— Conclusion

It should be noted that this demarcation of units of meaning in the letter is based on a semantic structural analysis, and markers such as epistolary formulae and forms or rhetorical units and forms do not feature very prominently in the demarcation of these units. Nevertheless, taking into account such matters (as will be done in subsequent chapters) does not necessarily result in demarcations contrary to them. On the contrary, it may provide additional grounds for these demarcations. For the analysis of the letter as a whole, however, I would argue that such factors have to play an important role and an analysis based on such grounds may be more convincing. This will be in focus in the next two chapters.

Almost all scientific studies of the letter to the Romans identify chapters 12:1 - 15:13 as a distinct unit of meaning with its own specific nature and coherence. Therefore, I will simply accept this conclusion and will proceed to elucidate the meaningful relations between the different paragraphs in this section.

1.	12:1-8	Commit yourself to the service of God. This involves commitment to serve each other.
2.	12:9-21	Rules for behavior towards one another.
3.	13:1-7	Everyone should obey the governing authorities, since God ordains people to govern.
4.	13:8-10	Love one another since love fulfils the law.
5.	13:11-14	Be alert and act accordingly, since the beginning of a new day is at hand.
6.	14:1-12	Do not play the judge by condemning your fellow believer on debatable matters.[23]
7.	14:13-23	Do not let your behavior cause your fellow-believer to stumble.[24]
8.	15:1-13	Help one another by following the example of Christ so that God may be praised.

It is noteworthy that all of these paragraphs have a command as the most marked element, with paragraph 2 (Romans 12:9-21) consisting of a whole series of loosely related commands. With the exception of paragraph 2, all the others provide argumentation in order to support the basic command. Paragraph 1 is a generic statement, setting the tone and providing the basis for all the rest that follows. This paragraph is introduced with the marker οὖν which has the whole argument of chapters 1-11 as its referent in the linguistic world. The generic nature of paragraph 1 seems to be the most important element giving coherence to paragraphs 1-8. Although paragraphs 2-8 can be divided loosely into three groups, there do not seem to be formal and closely related logical structures linking them and providing conjunctions between them. Paragraph 2, in fact, excels in its lack of explicit markers of logical relations: a series of commands is given abruptly and without supporting argumentation. Paragraph 3 (Romans 13:1-7) is similarly introduced with an abrupt command, but immediately followed by a very tightly knit logical argumentation. There seems to be no explicit linguistic marker which indicates the relation between 2 and 3, just as there are no explicit markers between the different commands given in paragraph 2. What distinguishes 2 and 3 is the lack of argumentation in 2 and the notable difference in the orientation of the commands: in 2 all commands are related to behavior towards fellow human beings on a rather inter-personal and individual basis, while the command in 3 relates to the state. The semantic relation between 2 and 3 may be typified as *additive different non-consequential.*

---

[23]The command is given in the form of rhetorical questions in 14:4 and 14:10.

[24]In 14:15 and 14:20 this command is repeated twice, serving to give even more prominence to this, the most marked element in the passage. In 14:19 essentially the same command is repeated a third time, this time, however, positively.

Paragraph 4 seems to be linked more directly to 2 than to 3, consisting of 'love one another' as a generic statement summarizing all the commands given in 2. As is the case with 2 and 3, paragraph 4 is also not linked to the previous paragraph(s) with an explicit linguistic relational marker. Between 3 and 4 there seems to be another *additive different non-consequential* semantic relation. Paragraphs 2–4 can be grouped as a unit under the rubric 'general rules for Christian behavior.' Although in itself generic in nature, this unit (2–4) is more specific than 1, which is an even more generic statement.

A more explicitly marked relation exists between 4 and 5, with 5 being introduced with the conjunction καὶ τοῦτο (13:11). On this basis the relation between 4 and 5 may be typified as *effect-cause*: the urgency of the new day that is about to break is the cause, which has as effect the command to love one another.

The relation between 6 and 7 is marked with the important conjunction οὖν (14:13), establishing a close and direct logical relation that may be typified as *basis-inference*: not acting as a judge over fellow human beings is the basis from which the command not to cause someone to stumble is inferred.

Between 7 and 8 a less subordinate relation than between 6 and 7 can be identified. This relation is marked with the particle δέ. Whereas 7 has a negative command as its most marked element, a more general, yet directly contrastive, command is given in 8. Therefore, the semantic relation between 7 and 8 can be typified as *coordinate dyadic contrastive*: do not let your behavior cause someone to stumble; you should rather help one another in a positive way.

Paragraphs 6–8 seem to form a unit that is linked to the preceding unit with the relational δέ in 14:1. Although a significant coherence and logical development of argument could be identified in these three paragraphs, there is not a similarly closely marked relation with the unit that precedes this unit. It seems as if the more or less abrupt style of introducing new commands relating to different forms of behavior that was identified in 2–4 is taken up again. In this sense 6–8 add to and specify the set of commands given in 2–4, and 5 forms an important injunction between these two bigger units. Therefore, we conclude that the same relation may be identified between 5–(6–8) as in (2–4)–5, the only difference being the order of the elements. The semantic relation between 5–(6–8) may be typified as *cause-effect*: the urgency of the new day that is about to break is the cause which has as an effect the command not to judge one another (or cause someone to stumble, but rather to help one another).

From this discussion, a clear picture of the place of Romans 13:1–7 within its co-text has emerged. It is one of a series of commands given on the basis of and specifying the general exhortation given in 12:1–8. Whereas the immediately preceding set of commands (12:9–22) seems to be supported, grounded and summarized in the general exhortation of 12:1–8 as well as the generic command to love one another in 13:8 (that is, in the paragraph directly after 13:1–7), the motivation and grounds for the command given in Romans 13:1 are given in the passage itself (Romans 13:2–7). In the development of the argument the appeal to be alert in the light of the new day that is about to dawn seems to play an important additional motivational role. Although not very closely and logically argued, a significant cohesion and progression could be identified in the development of the thought structure in the co-text of Romans 13:1–7 into which this passage also fits well.[25]

10. Summary and conclusions

The aim of this chapter was to provide a reading of Romans 13:1–7 from a linguistic perspective. The nature of the approach was explained at the outset (§2). This was followed by a brief overview of the impact of linguistics on the study of the New Testament (§3). Fairly extensive attention was given to a number of important theoretical distinctions in semantics (§4). The aim was to describe and delimit the nature and aims of the practical analyses in the last two sections and in particular to prevent the confusion of categories that is all too often the case in the study of linguistic elements of Romans 13:1–7 (§5). Before the actual study of lexical sense in Romans 13:1–7, it was necessary to introduce the terminology associated with the semantic domain approach (§6). On the basis of this theoretical discussion, specific procedures for the determination of lexical sense were spelled out (§7). Finally, in the practical application, meaning in Romans 13:1–7 was considered at a number of levels, the level of the word (§8), sentence, paragraph and discourse as a whole (§9).

The analyses presented in the last two sections illustrate how a number of important linguistic principles and procedures can be used to read a specific text. They also give an example of the type of results achieved when a text is read from this perspective. On the basis of these results, the observation already expressed by many others (for example, Nida 1972; Louw 1982; Cotterell & Turner 27–33) seems to be valid: the application of principles and methods of modern linguistics to New Testament interpretation does not necessarily lead to revolutionary new insights into the text in question. It is, however, very valuable to explicate a number of important choices that are usually made intuitively in the reading process. Theoretically grounded systems in terms of which these choices can be supported are also provided.

---

[25]On this point I concur with De Kruijf (319–326) and Moiser (571–582) who offer numerous other arguments supporting this conclusion, *contra* Käsemann (1980:352) who calls Romans 13:1–7 an 'alien body' (*Fremdkörper*) in its co-text and Kallas who regards it as an interpolation.

For this reason, I submit that taking linguistic considerations explicitly into consideration is an essential aspect of responsible reading. To read 'carefully, patiently, and scrupulously' (Miller 1987:284) requires that the text as linguistic phenomenon should be taken seriously. It is an essential aspect of the obligation to read. A serious and systematic attempt to determine the lexical sense of the words being used in the text, linked with a serious and systematic attempt to describe the semantic relations of different parts of the text and of the text in its cotext have to precede any attempt to study with confidence any extrinsic relations of the text. How else can one make any plausible claims about ethical directives to be inferred from the reading of a text or any other form of external relationship if one of the basic obligations of reading — to determine the senses of the words and sentences in the text — is ignored? How else are we going to know what the text is and says and what it can do?

This serious and systematic attempt to determine the senses of words and sentences does not take place in isolation from the act of reading itself. It is not as if the reader is inactive in this process, or as if ideological and other 'text-extrinsic' matters play no role in this process. It is not as if the reader is passive or 'empty' while this 'serious scholarly thing' (*sic!*) is going on. To say that this process must take place *before* the extrinsic relations are studied or before ethical imperatives can be inferred is not to say that this process itself has nothing to do with those extrinsic relations. As was illustrated in this chapter, this is a process characterized by a whole range of choices and delimitations at a number of levels. All those choices are made *by the interpreter*; they are not just ready-made 'out there' in the text or anywhere else.

This chapter presented one possible example of 'serious reading' done with rigor and methodological sophistication. It is one example of what it means to take the linguisticality of the text seriously. Any ethics of public accountability in biblical scholarship must of necessity be accompanied by this type of reading. The perception that this type of linguistic analysis, however, embodies *all* that needs to be done in the interpretation of New Testament texts (as was indeed the case at a certain stage among New Testament scholars in South Africa, see Deist) is a manifestation of the scientist ethos of interpretation. In a recent essay on linguistic discourse analysis Snyman (1991) is careful to point out that while discourse analysis is 'both the point of departure and the point of arrival for the text-linguist' (1991:86), discourse analysis cannot be presented as 'an exegetical method complete in itself' (1991:90). To conclude the process of interpretation with this type of linguistic analysis is a specific choice made by the interpreter. As such, therefore, it is a matter for ethical consideration.

Perhaps the point that I want to make with this chapter can best be explained with this example: if one decides to count from one to ten, one *has to* begin from one and then proceed to ten (Note the 'has to.' We are thus dealing with an ethical issue). One cannot begin with three or four, since then you are no longer counting from one to ten. What was presented in this chapter is perhaps the one and two. On the other hand, if one wants to count from one to ten you cannot begin with one and stop with two. You have to proceed beyond them to ten, otherwise, once again, you are not counting from one to ten. The decision to count from one to ten is a decision made by the person who wants to count from one to ten. The decision to interpret the New Testament is a decision of the interpreter. In order to do this counting or interpreting[26] responsibly, the person involved in this act 'has to' go through a number of processes. To read a text responsibly implies that one 'has to' honor it as a linguistic phenomenon.

In a consideration of the ethics of reading, a linguistic reading as it was performed in this chapter also requires an evaluation at a deeper level. The specific approaches used in this chapter (namely the semantic domain approach for lexical semantics and the specific types of structural analysis for broader levels of meaning) are all linked to a particular world view, a particular understanding of the nature of language and the relation between language and thought and language and culture (namely, 'idealistic' or 'structuralistic'). Evaluating the methods of reading from a linguistic perspective in these terms immediately brings matters such as 'context' and 'relevance' into consideration. Although I have argued that some sort of linguistic analysis of a text is an essential aspect of responsible interpretation, this does not imply that it should necessarily be done in terms of the methodology of a structuralist perspective on the nature of language. In New Testament scholarship methods presupposing this perspective are well-developed and have produced some of the most valuable tools which reflect modern linguistic insights, in particular the Louw and Nida *Lexicon*. As far as I am concerned, there is no need to stop practicing these methods (or to stop using this *Lexicon*). Given the particular way in which reference and context are understood within such a structuralist perspective on the text, it is, however, all the more necessary not to end the act of interpretation with such a structuralist linguistic reading. This is but one way to take the linguisticality of the text seriously. The literariness and the rhetoricity of the text ask for other modes of reading which are also essentials in the process of responsible interpretation. In the next chapter, therefore, a reading of Romans 13:1–7 will be undertaken from a literary perspective in an endeavor to take the literariness of the text seriously.

---

[26]This analogue of counting and interpreting must not be extended any further than the specific point that I want to explain with this example. Obviously, interpreting an ancient text is much more complicated than counting from one to ten.

CHAPTER 2

READING ROMANS 13:1-7 FROM A LITERARY PERSPECTIVE

1. Introduction

The aim of this chapter is to propose a reading of Romans 13:1-7 from a literary perspective. Since the terms 'literary,' 'literary studies,' 'literary theory' or 'literary criticism' have a wide-ranging field of reference, however, certain choices have to be made and clarifications and definitions are required at the outset. It needs to be emphasized again: to attempt an exhaustive literary analysis of the passage in question — giving full attention to all possible aspects of literary analysis and reading from the perspective of all possible literary models and theories available — would go well beyond what is achievable and relevant for the problem on which this study focuses, namely the ethics of the interpretation of Romans 13:1-7.

This chapter is structured in the following way: After some concepts have been clarified and certain choices supported (§2), the relevance of a reading of the text of the New Testament from a literary perspective is demonstrated by referring to the impact of concepts, theories and models of modern literary studies on New Testament interpretation (§3). Following this overview, the study of New Testament letters from a literary perspective is discussed in more detail (in §4). Major trends and developments during the last century are pointed out, with more specific attention to developments during the last thirty years. The aim is to provide a general framework to introduce a number of important concepts for a literary reading of Romans 13:1-7. This reading consists of two sections, namely, a literary reading of Romans as a letter against a formalist background (§5) and a literary reading of Romans as a letter in terms of a communicative approach (§6).

I shall argue that the attempt to take the literariness of the text seriously compels one to move beyond a formalistic literary reading to a more 'communicative' approach. To take the literariness of the text seriously implies that one cannot stop with a formal literary analysis of the text. On the other hand, formal literary features of the text cannot be ignored either.

2. A 'literary perspective': definitions and foci

For the purposes of this study 'reading a text from a literary perspective'

means to read it with the methods and approaches developed for the interpretation of 'literary' texts. Therefore, we should first try to get an idea of
the nature of what may be called 'literary texts' and then reflect on possible
literary methods or approaches suitable for the reading of such texts.

Defining 'literary texts' ties in with one's understanding of literature —
a complex problem on its own. Here one can only hope to develop a working
definition and adapt it for the present purposes. With this in mind, the point
of departure is Roman Jakobson's description of the nature of literary texts,
which can be regarded as the foundation of modern literary criticism.

Drawing on Russian Formalist insights, Jakobson proposed a popular —
though not unproblematic — way to characterize 'literary' texts and to distinguish them from 'non-literary' texts, namely to speak of the 'literariness'
of these texts (see also Visser 16). This feature involves aesthetic codes and
sets these texts apart from those that are primarily used for pragmatic communication. This does not, however, mean that texts serving primarily as
incidental media for pragmatic communication do not or cannot contain
aesthetic elements or do not manifest literariness. It also does not imply that
so-called literary texts do not and cannot serve as a medium for pragmatic
communication. This is especially true of biblical texts. Biblical texts exhibit
undoubted aesthetic elements, but they can also have a definite pragmatic
intention. I use this broad distinction merely to set the focus in this chapter
and to distinguish it from approaches reading a text from a non-literary perspective. In normal circumstances one will not, for example, analyze the
information on the back of a concert ticket with literary methods in order to
describe the aesthetic elements in such a text (although it would in principle
be possible to do that). Yet both the literary quality and the pragmatic
orientation of biblical texts justify the study of these texts by means of literary
methods. Jakobson links 'literariness' specifically with the presence of
aesthetic codes in texts. For the purposes of this chapter, the concept
'literariness' is adapted to denote any piece of language that is taken as a text
(see Miller 1989:81 for a broader explanation of this conceptualization of
'literariness'). Another deviation from Jakobson's conceptualization is that
this 'literariness' is, to my mind, not something 'out there' *in* the text. It is
rather a quality that the interpretive community ascribes to certain texts in
terms of the cultural and literary conventions of that interpretive community.

The study of literary texts finds itself in an ongoing process of develop-
ment. Among the major schools of literary criticism in our century the fol-
lowing may be mentioned: Russian Formalism, Anglo-American New
Criticism, Literary Hermeneutics, Structuralism, Semiotics, Marxist Literary
Theories, Reception Theory, Post-structuralism (including Deconstruction),
Feminist Literary Criticism and other varieties of Ideological literary

criticism, and modern Psychoanalytic criticism (see, among many others, Fokkema & Kunne-Ibsch; Ryan & Van Zyl; Ohlhoff and Jefferson & Robey for information on these various schools). Different and often incompatible methods for the study of literature or literary processes are proposed by these schools. Each method or approach presupposes a set of theoretical conceptualizations on a number of issues (for example, the nature of the object, the relationship between subject and object, the purpose of the method — see Swanepoel 1986:296–297 for a succinct and informative comparison of the different schools). Even the way in which the object of literary criticism itself is understood differs fundamentally among the proponents of the different schools. This state of affairs necessitates explicit *choices*. Such explication and clarification are of fundamental importance for the consideration of the ethics of the use of these method(s) of interpretation. Since we are making choices, we are inevitably involved in ethical/un-ethical actions.

The literary interpretation of Romans 13:1–7 in this chapter draws on elements of Formalism and Literary Communication Theory. Formalism has for many years been widely used by interpreters of the New Testament, a situation that has not altogether changed during the last thirty years, especially in the case of the interpretation of the letters of the New Testament (see Poland 1–7). More recently, aspects of literary communication have become prominent. For the actual reading of Romans 13:1–7 in this chapter, I therefore focus on the literary phenomena of the *literary genre* (letter), the *literary form* (paraenesis) and elements of the *literary communication* of Romans 13:1–7. In addition to the historical motivation for these choices (the fact that they have been so widely used in New Testament studies), I concur with Tolbert (4) that literary approaches applied to a text should be guided by goal-specific and text-specific criteria. One of the most important text-specific criteria of Romans 13:1–7 is its literary genre, since, as Aune (1987:13) puts it: 'The original significance that a literary text had for both author and reader is tied to the genre of that text, so that the meaning of the part is dependent upon the meaning of the whole.' Aune's definitions (1987:13) are also helpful to clarify the decision to concentrate on matters of genre. He defines *literary genre* as a group of texts that exhibit a coherent and recurring configuration of literary features involving form (including structure and style), content and function. Letters exhibit all these features and can therefore be regarded as a distinct literary genre. *Literary forms*, on the other hand, while exhibiting similar recurring literary features, are primarily constituent elements of the genres that frame them. Paraenesis is one example of such a literary form.[1] A. Fowler (260) emphasizes the importance of genre

---

[1]Gammie (50ff) works with the same concepts, although his terminology is just the opposite: for him a *letter* is one possible *form* in which *Paraenesis*, a sub-*genre* of the

for interpretation in no uncertain terms: '. . . the hermeneutic act has long been understood to be bound up with the identification of genre.' He (278) writes:

> Much of the tenor of this book [that is Fowler's book, *Kinds of Literature: An Introduction to the Theory of Genres and Modes*] has gone to show that while literature may move away from the old genres, it cannot move away from genre altogether *without ceasing to be literature. It would neither communicate with readers nor have leverage on existing values* [his italics].

Reading the New Testament texts from a 'literary' perspective, furthermore, needs to be distinguished from approaches reading them from, for example, a linguistic or a historical or a social-scientific perspective. In the previous chapter, Romans 13:1–7 was read from a linguistic perspective and special attention was given to the determination of the lexical meaning of words, sentences and broader textual units by means of linguistic methods. These linguistic procedures are also applicable to non-literary texts, for example a marriage contract, a record of a business deal or a testament. Literary methods that investigate the characteristics of literary forms and the peculiarities of literary communication (usually with an eye to aesthetic elements), however, are not so easily applicable to texts that are manifestly non-literary (for example, a marriage contract). This is an important respect in which the linguistic and the literary approaches used in this study differ.

One final distinction has to be mentioned briefly, namely the one between literary *criticism* (or practical criticism) and literary *theory* (or poetics). The former focuses on the study of concrete literary texts with analysis, interpretation and evaluation as its aim. The latter investigates the conditions for literary communication and the deeper processes and systems responsible for the production of texts and meaning (Swanepoel 1986:290). While the focus of this chapter is clearly on literary criticism, theoretical reflection continually plays an important role since reflection on the ethics of literary interpretation of the New Testament necessitates both these aspects.

To summarize:

* The point of departure for this chapter is that Romans 13:1–7 is a literary text and can therefore be interpreted by means of literary methods and approaches.
* The chapter focuses on the literary phenomena of *genre* (a letter) and *form* (Paraenetic Literature).[2]
* Genre and form are first dealt with in a formalist frame (§5), with its particular conceptions of the nature of the object of literary studies and of the aims of literary interpretation.

---

secondary genre, Paraenetic Literature, may be expressed (see §6).

[2]Following Gammie Paraenetic Literature is written with a capital letter when it is used to indicate the name of a (sub)genre.

*   Secondly (in §6), the contributions of Heikki Koskenniemi, Patrizia Violi and
Janet Altman on the literary genre 'letters' and the nature of literary communication by means of letters are used as a theoretical basis for the second
phase of this reading of Romans 13:1-7.

3. Modern literary theory and New Testament interpretation

3.1 The New Testament as literature

The trend during the seventies to use insights from general (or 'secular')
literary criticism for the interpretation of the New Testament raised questions
regarding the feasibility of such a project. One of the reasons for these reservations is the assumption that the Bible, perceived and used as a religious
book by the Christian community, cannot and should not be interpreted like
any other body of literature. It was maintained that this would violate the
religious or theological character of the Bible (for an exposition of this sentiment, see Longman).

For the purpose of my argument, I need not enter the well-known debate
on the relationship between the Bible and literature initiated by K. L. Schmidt
and A. Deissmann. I concur with Barr (1973) that it is not possible to make
an absolute distinction between a theological use of the Bible and its literary
'appreciation.' Thiselton (1985:79) expresses the well-balanced view that,
although biblical hermeneutics and literary theory are not coextensive, and
although biblical interpretation is not merely a sub-category within literary
theory (as if the Bible were no more than a particular example of literature
that raises no distinctive theological questions), theories of biblical and
literary interpretation have much in common. Particularly in the context of
the conceptualization of the ethics of interpretation as I have described it in
the Introduction (pp. 4-9), any distinction between 'theological' or 'literary'
interpretation is unnecessary. Taking the linguisticality, the literariness and
the rhetoricity of the text seriously in responsible interpretation, holds true
for any literary text — whether or not it is perceived as 'theological' by any
interpretive community.

3.2 Literary criticism and New Testament interpretation

The introduction of modern literary theory to the methodology of New Testament interpretation since the seventies has been accompanied by a serious
confusion in terminology, especially where the term *literary criticism* is concerned. The term 'literary criticism' is widely used within the historical

paradigm of biblical scholarship. It is usually understood as the separating out of chronologically different layers in composite works and as the history of the tradition during the period of its development in written form as distinct from its development in oral form (Barr 1973:21). Or, as Petersen (1978:10) puts it:

> . . . for most historical critics "literary criticism" refers to *source* criticism. The adjective "literary" is used principally in connection with the notion of literary history, which refers to the history of the form and style of the material used in the composition of biblical writings.

This interest in matters of origin, background and the intention of the author who produced it can be ascribed in part to similar trends in general literary theory and practice. Before the rise of New Criticism, literary criticism was practiced almost exclusively on the assumption of the literary historian that the meaning of a literary text is located in its causes — in the artistic personality, or in its causal antecedents in the political, social, or economic spheres (Poland 1985:2–3). In the historical paradigm of biblical scholarship, a whole arsenal of methods based on these assumptions was developed, namely textual criticism, source criticism, tradition criticism, form criticism and redaction criticism (see Marshall; Klijn and Hayes & Holladay for discussions of these different methods of interpretation).

In their schema summarizing and categorizing developments during the twentieth century, Fokkema and Kunne-Ibsch distinguish three major concepts of the nature of the text that characterized different approaches: (i) the *text-as-document* (that is, the text is a document of the author in the time when she or he lived), (ii) the *text as monument* (that is, the text is an independent, a-historical, synchronic system that should be studied in terms of itself), and (iii) the *text-as-sign* (that is, the text is viewed no longer in terms of its background, nor solely in terms of itself, but as a sign within a network of codes (see also Swanepoel 1989:46–49). Lategan (1984:3–4) demonstrates how these tendencies manifested themselves also in biblical hermeneutics: the focus has shifted from the *source* (historical), to the *message* (text-immanent), to the *receptor/reception* (treating the texts as acts of communication).

The use of literary theory in New Testament studies (see Combrink 1985:9; Alter; Frye) can in general be ascribed to growing dissatisfaction with the historical paradigm of biblical scholarship (Barr 1973; Petersen 1978:9–11; Macky 265–266). The work of Amos N. Wilder marked the turn away from a preoccupation with source criticism and other approaches in the historical-critical paradigm (see Wilder 1956:8; Danker 211). New Critical objections formed the basis for this break. Barr (1973:21) contrasts the definition of 'new literary criticism' in Biblical hermeneutics with the old, source-oriented definition as follows in New Critical terminology: '. . . the term "literary criticism" refers to the study of the structures and the imagery of works, their modes, symbols, and myths, their poetic, dramatic and aesthetic effect.'

The assumption that the text itself, as a whole and in its final form, is the bearer of meaning (=auto-semantic) is the major characteristic of what came to be known as a 'new literary approach' in biblical interpretation. Deliberately excluding 'antecendent' and 'external' factors from consideration, the aim was to avoid the 'genetic fallacy' and the 'referential fallacy' — both battle cries taken over from New Criticism. Numerous studies (New Critical as well as Structuralist) were undertaken, building on the work of V. Propp, A. J. Greimas, C. Lévi-Strauss, R. Barthes, C. Bremond, and others (see Lategan 1982:67; McKnight 1985:49–58; Longman 33–37). The vast amount of work based on Formalist, New Critical and Structuralist presuppositions makes it difficult to present an adequate overview (for good examples see Patte 1979; Petersen 1978; Rhoads & Michie; Van Iersel; Culpepper; Tannehill). The focus is mainly on narrative texts in the New Testament, since the new methods seem to be more directly applicable to these texts than to the argumentative and epistolary texts. Especially with regard to the parables, modern literary criticism and literary theory have fundamentally changed the ways in which they are interpreted (for an overview of the contributions of Amos N. Wilder, Norman Perrin, R. W. Funk, D. O. Via, J. D. Crossan, Susan Wittig, Paul Ricoeur, T. Aurelio, Hans Weder and Wolfgang Harnisch, see I. J. du Plessis 41–56). This is not to say, however, that the New Testament letters received no attention from structuralist criticism. In a somewhat different form from the kind of structuralist criticism applied to narrative texts, meticulous studies were made of the structure of New Testament letters.[3]

Although this process continues, valid criticism of these attempts gave rise to the emergence of yet further types of literary approaches, like reception theory (see McKnight 1985; Combrink 1988; Lategan 1991b), rhetorical criticism (see chapter 3) and post-modern literary approaches (see McKnight 1990; Van Tilborg 1986, 1991). Current literary interpretation of the New Testament displays the full range of approaches, methods, theories and practices characteristic of general literary studies.

---

[3]See Vorster 1982:135, 139 for the differences between '*structurele exegese*' and '*structurale exegese*.' See Louw 1979 for an example of '*structurele*' (structural) and Patte 1983 for an example of '*structurale*' (structuralist) exegesis of the Letter to the Romans.

Against this background, the choices made in the previous section (§2) for this reading of Romans 13:1–7 from a literary perspective should be underscored again. The analysis is undertaken in terms of the assumptions and methods of the so-called 'new literary phase' in New Testament scholarship: a genetic interest is replaced by a 'text-immanent' approach, focusing on the documents on their own terms and on the basis of how the form of these documents contributes to the creation of their meaning. Thus, I am going to read Romans 13:1–7 *as part* of *the paraenetic section* of *a letter* with the assumption that these literary forms contribute in a particular way to the meaning it may have. In its pure form a reading in terms of these assumptions is a formalist reading. That will be done in §5. To end the act of interpretation with such a formal analysis, however, is yet another manifestation of the scientist ethos of biblical scholarship.[4] That is why the second phase of this literary reading moves beyond a formalistic approach toward a more communicative approach, although still with the text itself (and not its genesis) in focus. Before we can proceed with the reading as such, however, a brief overview of how New Testament letters have been interpreted thus far is needed.

4. *The modern study of New Testament letters*

4.1 *Introduction*

According to Aune (1987:183) the study of Greco-Roman letters during the twentieth century has taken three different routes, namely formal literary analysis (including form-critical analysis specifically as it is understood in New Testament scholarship), thematic analysis and rhetorical analysis. These categories correspond broadly (although not exactly) with the schema described above (§3.2), namely text-as-document, text-as-monument, and text-as-sign. Much of the form-critical work on New Testament letters is typical of the text-as-document concept as it is practiced in the historical-critical paradigm. Many of the thematic analyses of the letters also fit under this rubric, although there has been a movement towards the text-as-monument concept. Rhetorical analyses usually presuppose the text-as-sign concept. Although the work of Adolf Deissmann fits more or less in the first category, it will be treated separately since it laid the foundation of what was to follow in twentieth century study. Heikki Koskenniemi and Stanley

---

[4]See chapter 1 (§3.3) for another variety of the scientist ethos of biblical scholarship.

Stowers were responsible for substantive advances and will therefore also be treated separately.

4.2 Adolf Deissmann

Reading Deissmann's book *Licht vom Osten* (1923), one can almost feel the excitement caused by the new discoveries of papyri from the refuse dumps of ancient, sand-covered towns in Egypt (see Turner 1967:17-53). The papyri revealed much more about everyday life than could be gleaned from the literary sources that had been available before these discoveries. Deissmann believed that these papyri provided valuable information for the interpretation of New Testament letters in a number of different areas. He did this by comparing many of these papyrus documents with New Testament language, literary conventions and its social and cultural background.

With regards to the style and genre of the papyrus letters, Deissmann believed that the language of the New Testament letters was closer to the language of the common papyri than to the classic literary language of Demosthenes and Plato. This conviction led him to distinguish real letters (like those exemplified by the common family and business papyrus letters) from epistles (exemplified by the literary letters of writers like Epicurus, Seneca, Pliny and Cicero). Letters are private, non-literary, purely occasional, warm, personal and artless documents and serve merely to convey information. Epistles are public, literary, conventional, artful and written for posterity (Deissmann 193-198). As for the New Testament, Deissmann characterized the letters of Paul as letters, and James, 1 and 2 Peter and Jude as epistles (1923:212-213). As far as the social class and context of the letter writers are concerned, Deissmann painted a romantic picture of Paul as champion of the lower classes who responded in his letters to the real-life issues in early Christian groups spontaneously and unaffected by literary conventions (Deissmann 210). Concerning the relationship of Christian language and letters to Hellenistic and Jewish cultures, Deissmann maintained that the papyri clearly demonstrated that its particular language and style were not due to Christianity's roots in Jewish culture. He argued that the language of the New Testament should not be seen as derived and adapted from Semitic, but rather as *Koine*-Greek proper (Deissmann 228-242).

Although, according to Stowers (1986:18), much of Deissmann's 'vividly illustrated portrait of early Christian letter writing has withstood the test of time,' it has been modified in important respects by subsequent critical scholarship. Because Deissmann based his observations primarily on non-literary papyri from Egypt, it was pointed out that the situation and conventions in the other great Hellenistic centers, particularly those of early

Christianity, might have been different (Meecham).   This relativizes Deissmann's claims to a certain extent.   Furthermore, his distinction between letters and epistles (although perhaps the most lasting aspect of his legacy) can be criticized in a number of ways.   Both the public/private and spontaneous/artificial contrasts on which Deissmann based this distinction rest on the views of society and literature of Deissmann's age (end of eighteenth, beginning nineteenth centuries) and not that of ancient Hellenistic times (see Stowers 1986:19).   Aune (1987:160) argues that Deissmann's distinction has obscured rather than clarified the spectrum of possibilities that separated the short personal letters from the literary letters of antiquity.   For example, none of Paul's letters, not even the letter to Philemon, are really private letters (Keck & Furnish 19).   On the other hand, it is significant that Deissmann presupposed an inter-relatedness between literary form and social context.   Later research tended to focus on the form of the letters in isolation from their social context, as will be indicated in the next section.

4.3 Historical and form-oriented studies of New Testament letters

The title of W. G. Doty's 1966 thesis is indicative of the nature of the study of New Testament letters in the period subsequent to Deissmann: *The Epistle in Late Hellenism and Early Christianity: Development, Influences, and Literary Form.*   This focus on the historical development of letters and on the historical and circumstantial influences on the formal aspects of letters is typical of the text-as-document view of literature and the nature of literary studies.   Much of the work on New Testament letters followed this approach.[5]   Schnider and Stenger provide perhaps one of the best examples of the results of this approach although they have moved beyond formalism and also consider rhetorical phenomena in the letters.

Comparing sources is an important hallmark of the historical-critical methodology.   In the study of New Testament letters, comparative work draws its material almost exclusively from the non-literary or documentary papyri (for an example of this approach, see White 1986).   It is only recently that the comparative work has been broadened to include sources from the larger world of Greco-Roman letter-writing, literature and rhetoric (see, for example, Betz 1979; Stowers 1986; Malherbe 1988).

To a great extent, New Testament epistolary research became preoccupied with the literary conventions of the *openings* and *conclusions* of Paul's

---

[5]See for example Exler, Schubert, Meecham, C. H. Kim, various studies of White (1972; 1978), Bjerkelund, Sanders, various studies of Mullins (1962; 1968; 1972; 1973; 1980; 1984) and Doty.

letters, and how the authors modified and adapted these formulae for their own purposes. White's (1972) study of the body of the letter is an exception, but only to a certain extent: his focus is still on form and formulae. Non-Pauline New Testament letters were largely neglected or dismissed as derivatives of the Pauline letter form. Aune (1987:185-192) has drawn up the following list of formulaic features which have been analyzed extensively in this type of research, which he labels the 'formal literary analysis' of letters: framing formulae, opening formulae, closing formulae, internal transitional formulae, epistolary topoi, autobiographical statements, travel plans, and concluding paraenesis. Under 'form-critical analysis' Aune (1987:192-198) lists research on liturgical forms such as benedictions, blessings, doxologies and hymns, and paraenetic forms such as vice and virtue lists and the codes of household ethics. Much of this work is directly relevant for a literary interpretation of Romans 13:1-7, provided that the view of literature presupposed by this kind of work is kept in mind: form is regarded as a bearer of meaning.

4.4 Koskenniemi: ancient epistolary theorists and characteristic features of the Greek letter

Although not specifically concerned with New Testament letters, Heikki Koskenniemi introduced an important new direction in the study of ancient letters with his book *Studien zur Idee und Phraseologie des Griechischen Briefe bis 400 n.Chr.* His concern was to investigate the relationship between the internal logic (the 'idea' of the letter) and its external expression (its phraseology) (16). He was not only interested in a formal description of the ancient epistolary formulae, but tried specifically to determine the characteristic features of letters on the basis of ancient epistolary theory (that is, the epistolary handbooks of Demetrius, Pseudo-Libanius, Julius Victor, and others). With his attention on the communicative elements on letters, Koskenniemi was ahead of his time. Dippenaar (6) maintains that Koskenniemi 'caused a breakthrough in the isolation of the common letter tradition, in that his work introduced external control, allowing for broader generalizations. It also provided a framework for all past and future research into the purely formal traits of the letters.' To this one can add that Koskenniemi's work also represents the beginnings of an attempt to move beyond pure formalism toward a more communicative approach.

From his study of Greco-Roman epistolary theorists, Koskenniemi concluded that three aspects were constitutive of the ideal letter, namely φιλοφρόνησις, παρουσία and ὁμιλία (Koskenniemi 35-47). These theoretical ideals were also reflected in the phraseology of the common letter practice.

These constitutive aspects were all three closely related to the epistolary situation. The friendship situation (φιλοφρόνησις) as reflected in the phraseology was understood as the essence of the letter and therefore it influenced all other aspects of the letter form (93). Similarly, the physical separation of the correspondents was of fundamental importance in the epistolary situation. Therefore the letter had to serve as a mode of making-the-sender-present (παρουσία). Flowing forth from the 'presence' created by the letter, the epistolary situation is constituted by a third element, namely a 'conversation' or 'interaction' (ὁμιλία) between the sender and addressee. The structure of the basic letter form reflected these elements by means of its prescript and health wish (greeting), body (conversation proper) and closing formulae (leave-taking) (1956:155). The epistolary situation is therefore created by the structural framework that identifies the writing as a letter and reinforced by the conventional phrases associated with the situation.

From this emphasis on the epistolary situation by Koskenniemi, I conclude with Dippenaar (8) that the epistolary situation serves as the basic interpretive context for the letter because it provides the letter with its unique characteristics that set it apart from other forms of communication. Therefore, in my reading of Romans *as a letter*, and specifically Romans 13:1-7 as part of a letter, particular attention will be given to the epistolary situation.

4.5 *Stowers: letters as social actions*

With his book, *Letter Writing in Greco-Roman Antiquity* (1986), Stanley K. Stowers has re-introduced an important and (since Deissmann) overlooked dimension to the study of New Testament letters, namely, the social context. The contribution of Stowers is significant in three respects: (i) his call for recognition of the influence of the ancient social context of letter-writing on the understanding of these letters (1986:16); (ii) his proposal of a new typology for ancient letters, based on insights from these contextual considerations and the work of ancient epistolary theorists (1986:49); and (iii) his call for the extension of the comparative material for the study of New Testament letters to include not only documentary papyri, but also Greco-Roman literary and rhetorical sources, for example, the letters of Seneca, Cicero, Pliny, and others (1986:23).

Stowers argues that ancient letters cannot be understood merely on their own terms (as is presupposed in general by New Testament scholarship). The hallmark of his contribution is perhaps the following statement (1986:15):

> From the modern perspective, it is natural to think about letters in terms of the information they communicate. The interpreter, however, should resist the tempta-

tion to overlook the great multiplicity of functions that letters performed and speak only of the communication of information. *It is more helpful to think of letters in terms of the actions that people performed by means of them* [my italics].

Therefore knowledge of the Greco-Roman society in which the actions were performed is indispensable for understanding these letters. Of particular importance are the three sets of social relationships which were, according to Stowers, central to that culture, namely the hierarchical relation between subordinates and superordinates (exemplified by institutions of the patron-client relationship), the relationship between equals (exemplified by the institutions of friendship) and the social relations of the household (a mixture of the other two sets of relations) (Stowers 1986:27). The role and meaning of praise and blame, and that of bestowing honor within these relationships, differ significantly from twentieth century Western culture (Stowers 1986:27).[6] Drawing on the implications of these assumptions for the study of ancient letters, Stowers (1986:49–173) proposes a typology of six epistolary types of Greco-Roman letters based on ancient epistolary theory and on the three typical social relations that provided the context for letter-writing: (1) letters of friendship, (2) family letters, (3) letters of praise and blame, (4) letters of exhortation and advice [which included paraenetic letters (exhortation and dissuasion), letters of advice, protreptic letters (exhortation to a way of life), letters of admonition, letters of rebuke, letters of reproach, letters of consolation], (5) letters of mediation and (6) accusing, apologetic, and accounting letters. Stowers illustrates these six different types of letters with material from a wide variety of sources, documentary papyri as well as literary letters, for example, letters of Epicurus, Cicero, Seneca, Pliny, the letter to Diognetos, Jerome, Julian, Basil, and others. In each case, he compares the New Testament letters with this broad body of material.

Stowers's study represents a major advance in the study of New Testament letters. Insights from the work of Stowers will therefore be used extensively in my reading of Romans as a letter, which forms the framework for a literary interpretation of Romans 13:1-7 (see §6.2). In my analysis, however, I will also move beyond Stowers's position to a more consistent text-immanent literary approach. This difference can be demonstrated as follows: Whereas the majority of studies of New Testament letters strives to analyze and describe the information (propositional content or 'theology') of the letters, or the form and structure of letters, Stowers (1986:15) contends that 'The interpreter, however, should resist the temptation to overlook the great multiplicity of functions that letters performed and to speak *only* of the communication of information' (my italics). It seems as if the 'communica-

---

[6]For more detail, see Malina 1981:25–50. See also chapter 4, §5.

tion of information' is for Stowers something different and narrower than the 'function' of letters. The latter refers to the broader question of the social functions of letters in ancient Greco-Roman society. However, Stowers does not consider the question of *how* the letters *as letters* (that is, as literary products) 'work' in order to fulfill these functions. The nature of literary communication by means of letters is not addressed by Stowers, and he clearly still works within the historical paradigm.

4.6 N. Petersen and M. C. Dippenaar: Introducing a 'new literary phase' to the interpretation of New Testament letters

During the eighties, the study of New Testament letters entered a new phase. The issue of *how* literary communication by means of letters works in terms of modern literary theory became the focus of attention. Norman Petersen (1985) and M. C. Dippenaar, among many others, made significant contributions. I limit my discussion here to their contributions. What they propose is in fact much more complex and sophisticated and moves beyond what could be perceived as a purely literary approach. Nevertheless, they also integrate insights from modern literary criticism in their study of the letters of the New Testament.

The sub-title of Petersen's book is indicative of the integration of literary insights with the sociology of knowledge: *Philemon and the Sociology of Paul's Narrative World* (1985). He maintains that letters have stories and that from these stories the narrative worlds of both the letters and their stories can be constructed (1985:43–53). As such letters exhibit 'the fundamental fictions of narrative — point of view, plot, and closure' (1985:10). Furthermore, being narratives, a distinction should be made between the 'real world' and the 'narrative world' of these letters/stories (1985:14–17). In fact, the concept of 'real world' is problematic when dealing with the *textuality* of letters. The complex issue of the relation between the 'real world' and 'the world created by/in the text' will be taken up again and again in this study (see chapter 2, §6.3.1; chapter 3, §5 and chapter 4, §2) since it lies at the heart of the understanding of the ethics of reading that I am proposing: respecting the textuality of the text implies that the 'world created by the text' cannot be simply equated with the 'real world.' This, furthermore, implies that plausible claims about the 'real world' — for example ethical directives — cannot be postulated as if there were no difference between these two worlds. For Petersen history — the 'real world' — is always *story* (1985:10–14). In his study of the letter to Philemon, he uses categories of narratology such as the distinction between poetic sequence and referential actions (plotted time and story time) (1985:69ff). With his sociological analysis of the 'narrative worlds' which he constructs by means of literary methods, Petersen moves beyond the usual limits of literary studies and integrates insights from the sociology of knowledge. Petersen's remarkable book represents a significant advance in the study of New Testament letters.

Dippenaar (8) also introduces insights from contemporary literary theory. He writes: 'Instead of starting off with questions of epistolary classification and asking what sort of letters Paul wrote, a more profitable point of departure would be to ask the more general question: What are the inherent properties of the letter qua letter?' He finds an answer to this question in Janet Altman's study, *Epistolarity. Approaches to a Form* (Dippenaar 9). Altman's (i) aim is 'to push a certain kind of formalist reading to its limits on a particularly intriguing "form,"' namely, 'the epistolary novel.' She focuses on 'those occasions, wherever they may be found, when the creation of meaning derives from the structures and potential specific to the letter form' (4). Although she develops her own methodology, she states her indebtedness to the Russian Formalists, the German and French narratologists, and even to Jacques Derrrida, who has criticized this type of formalist reading (ii).

What distinguishes the work of Petersen and Dippenaar from that of Stowers and others working in the historical paradigm is the fact that they work explicitly with the categories and insights of contemporary literary theory. This presupposes different conceptions of the nature of the text, of literature, of genre and of literary communication. One example of this difference is the distinction between the 'real world' and the so-called 'world of the text.' This distinction is fundamental in what may be called here for our purposes, a 'new literary approach.' For White, Koskenniemi and Stowers, the 'author' of the Pauline letters is the historical, empirical Paul, and the 'addressees' are the historical Roman Christians living in the late fifties of the first century. Contemporary literary theory (and rhetorical theory, see chapter 3) has a more complex concept of 'author' and 'addressees,' distinguishing between the addresser as a real person (the empirical author of the text) and the narrator as a figure of discourse (a textual abstraction inscribed in the linguistic production), and the addressees as real persons and the implied readers as a textual construction (Violi 151). I will introduce in more detail the relevant aspects of the theory behind the 'new literary approach' along with the literary interpretation of Romans 13:1–7 in section §6 of this chapter.

5. Reading Romans as a letter: a formal approach

5.1 Introduction

I have indicated that consideration of matters of form and genre is an important and indispensable element of a literary reading (see §2). Literary genres may change and literature cannot totally move away from genre without ceasing to be literature. There is more than one way to approach the study of literary genre. In this section, the *form* of the letter is analyzed. Such an analysis is an important aspect of the attempt to take the literariness of the text seriously.

5.2 A formal analysis of the Letter to the Romans

I have noted that much of the scientific study of New Testament letters has been devoted to formal analysis, and specifically, the *opening and closing* sections of the letters (see §4.3). One of the most recent analyses from this perspective is the work of Schnider and Stenger. Regarding the formal analysis of the letter *body*, the only significant study was done by White (1972).[7] My own analysis reflects aspects of the work of Schnider and Stenger and White, although I do not follow any of them exclusively. The aim is merely to identify different sections and/or forms in the letter and by doing that, to provide a formal description of the letter as a whole. Given the purpose of this formal analysis, I do not indicate in each instance whether I follow Schnider and Stenger or White or whether the particular demarcation is my own. Many pages can be written to support why a particular section ends precisely at this verse and why the next section begins at that verse and not another one. This kind of elaborate argumentation is usually not very interesting reading matter. Therefore, I will simply present the results of my own structural analysis. The possible *epistolary functions* of the different epistolary forms, and their possible bearing on the determination of the meaning of Romans 13:1-7, will be discussed in later sections (§§6.2 - 6.3). Consideration of the possible *rhetorical* or *pragmatic functions* of these forms, or any other element in the letter not determined on formalist grounds, does not form part of this chapter (see, however, chapter 3).

---

[7]Doty (34) gives four explanations why the letter-body has received least attention with respect to its formal elements: (i) the body as a formal entity has not been recognized as sufficiently unitary or consistent from letter to letter to reward formal analysis, (ii) it is difficult to identify how the 'normative' forms of the body took shape, (iii) it is difficult to define where the body begins and ends and (iv) there is confusion because of several letters in which the body seems almost entirely assimilated to the thanksgiving (for example 1 Corinthians, Philippians and 2 Thessalonians).

I. Letter-opening (1:1-7)

superscriptio	1:1	Παῦλος
intitulatio I	1:1	δοῦλος Χριστοῦ Ἰησοῦ κλητὸς ἀπόστολος
statement of office	1:1-6	ἀφωρισμένος εἰς εὐαγγέλιον θεοῦ, ὃ προεπηγγείλατο διὰ τῶν προφητῶν αὐτοῦ ἐν γραφαῖς ἁγίαις, περὶ τοῦ υἱοῦ αὐτοῦ τοῦ γενομένου ἐκ σπέρματος Δαυὶδ κατὰ σάρκα, τοῦ ὁρισθέντος υἱοῦ θεοῦ ἐν δυνάμει κατὰ πνεῦμα ἁγιωσύνης ἐξ ἀναστάσεως νεκρῶν, Ἰησοῦ Χριστοῦ τοῦ κυρίου ἡμῶν, δι᾽ οὗ ἐλάβομεν χάριν καὶ ἀποστολὴν εἰς ὑπακοὴν πίστεως ἐν πᾶσι τοῖς ἔθνεσιν ὑπὲρ τοῦ ὀνόματος αὐτοῦ, ἐν οἷς ἐστε καὶ ὑμεῖς κλητοὶ Ἰησοῦ Χριστοῦ
adscriptio I	1:7	πᾶσιν τοῖς οὖσιν ἐν Ῥώμῃ
intitulatio I	1:7	ἀγαπητοῖς θεοῦ
intitulatio II	1:7	κλητοῖς ἁγίοις
blessing	1:7	χάρις ὑμῖν καὶ εἰρήνη ἀπὸ θεοῦ πατρὸς ἡμῶν καὶ κυρίου Ἰησοῦ Χριστοῦ.

II. Thanksgiving (1:8-12)

Πρῶτον μὲν εὐχαριστῶ τῷ θεῷ μου διὰ Ἰησοῦ Χριστοῦ περὶ πάντων ὑμῶν, ὅτι ἡ πίστις ὑμῶν καταγγέλλεται ἐν ὅλῳ τῷ κόσμῳ. μάρτυς γάρ μού ἐστιν ὁ θεός, ᾧ λατρεύω ἐν τῷ πνεύματί μου ἐν τῷ εὐαγγελίῳ τοῦ υἱοῦ αὐτοῦ, ὡς ἀδιαλείπτως μνείαν ὑμῶν ποιοῦμαι πάντοτε ἐπὶ τῶν προσευχῶν μου, δεόμενος εἴ πως ἤδη ποτὲ εὐοδωθήσομαι ἐν τῷ θελήματι τοῦ θεοῦ ἐλθεῖν πρὸς ὑμᾶς. ἐπιποθῶ γὰρ ἰδεῖν ὑμᾶς, ἵνα τι μεταδῶ χάρισμα ὑμῖν πνευματικὸν εἰς τὸ στηριχθῆναι ὑμᾶς, τοῦτο δέ ἐστιν συμπαρακληθῆναι ἐν ὑμῖν διὰ τῆς ἐν ἀλλήλοις πίστεως ὑμῶν τε καὶ ἐμοῦ.

The thanksgiving is introduced by the typical formula εὐχαριστῶ τῷ θεῷ which is also found in almost all the other letters of Paul. The end of the thanksgiving is marked by the typical formula which introduces the self-recommendation section of the letter, οὐ θέλω δὲ ὑμᾶς ἀγνοεῖν in 1:13.

A number of conventional formal elements can be identified in the thanksgiving, namely, (i) the main verb of thanksgiving, εὐχαριστῶ, (ii) the customary temporal note, although the adverb πάντοτε is not used here in conjunction with the main verb, but instead the report of thanksgiving commences with πρῶτον μέν, (iii) the object of the main verb, τῷ θεῷ to which the personal pronoun μοῦ is added, (iv) the customary phrase περὶ ὑμῶν with the insertion of πάντων, (v) the expression of the ground or basis of the thanksgiving by means of the conventional causal ὅτι-clause, ὅτι ἡ πίστις ὑμῶν καταγγέλλεται ἐν ὅλῳ τῷ κόσμῳ; (vi) a report of the author's petitionary prayer, introduced by εἴ πως instead of the more conventional final clause introduced by ἵνα which ends the Pauline thanksgivings (see Schubert 10–39 and O'Brien 202–221 for more detail on the form and structure of the thanksgiving). Two elements in the thanksgiving are exceptional in terms of the Pauline convention, namely, the phrase διὰ Ἰησοῦ Χριστοῦ directly after the mentioning of the object of the main verb (1:8) and the oath μάρτυς γάρ μού ἐστιν ὁ θεός in 1:10.

III. Self-recommendation (1:13–15)

> οὐ θέλω δὲ ὑμᾶς ἀγνοεῖν, ἀδελφοί, ὅτι πολλάκις προεθέμην ἐλθεῖν πρὸς ὑμᾶς, καὶ ἐκωλύθην ἄχρι τοῦ δεῦρο, ἵνα τινὰ καρπὸν σχῶ καὶ ἐν ὑμῖν καθὼς καὶ ἐν τοῖς λοιποῖς ἔθνεσιν. Ἕλλησίν τε καὶ βαρβάροις, σοφοῖς τε καὶ ἀνοήτοις ὀφειλέτης εἰμί· οὕτως τὸ κατ' ἐμὲ πρόθυμον καὶ ὑμῖν τοῖς ἐν Ῥώμῃ εὐαγγελίσασθαι.

Two arguments corroborate the conclusion that 1:12 is the end of the thanksgiving in Romans (*contra* Schubert 10–39 and O'Brien 202 who regard 1:13–15 also as part of the thanksgiving), namely:

* The typical transitional formula in the ancient letter which introduces 1:13 which White has identified as 'the polite form of the disclosure formula': οὐ θέλω δὲ ὑμᾶς ἀγνοεῖν (see White 1972:2–5, 52).

* The change of perspective from the thanksgiving to God in which the *recipients* are in focus to a section in which the *author* (in his relationship to the recipients of the letter) is in focus. In Romans 1:13 this change of perspective is signalled by the direct and explicit address to the recipients: ἀδελφοί.

According to Schnider and Stenger (54–59) the following are typical features of the self-recommendation in New Testament letters:

* It focuses the attention of the readers on the person of the author, especially with regard to their relationship with him.
* It appeals to the recipients' emotions.
* It is a foundation of the author's authoritative position in his relationship with the recipients.
* It gives credibility to the author.

IV. Letter body (1:16 – 15:6)

The body of the letter can be analyzed in a number of ways. The main problem is the demarcation of 1:16 – 8:39 into smaller sections. With regard to the sections 9:1 – 11:36 and 12:1 – 15:13, scholars are almost unanimous in their recognition of these sections as distinct larger units.

1. Body-opening (1:13–15). For White (1972:52–53) the phrase οὐ θέλω δὲ ὑμᾶς ἀγνοεῖν, ἀδελφοί (1:13) marks a section that he calls the 'body-opening.' For Schnider and Stenger (54) this phrase serves to introduce a section which they call the 'self-recommendation' of the letter. We need not enter into a debate on the correct label here. From a formal point of view, it is clear that Romans 1:13–15 can be demarcated as a distinct form or section in the letter.

This section seems to state a motivation for the writing of the letter: Paul's desire to visit the Christians in Rome. It is an issue already touched on in the thanksgiving (1:10–12), and it is mentioned again in the body-closing (15:14–33).

2. Body-middle 1:16 – 11:36. There is wide consensus among scholars that 9:1 – 11:36 is a sub-section within the body-middle. Concerning the demarcation of 1:18 – 8:39 into two smaller sections, there are basically two positions:

* Position 1: 1:18 – 4:25 and 5:1 – 8:39; the break is at the end of chapter 4.
* Position 2: 1:18 – 5:21 and 6:1 – 8:39; the break is at the end of chapter 5.

From a survey of commentaries on Romans (of which most use arguments from content and theme as basis for demarcation), it is clear that both positions have significant support, although the first position seems to be the most popular one:[8]

Commentator	Position 1	Position 2
Godet	–	x
Moule	–	–
Sanday and Headlam	–	x
Barth	–	–
Greijdanus	x	–
Hodge	–	–
Nygren	x	–
Michel	x	–
Barrett	–	–
Ridderbos	–	x
Leenhardt	-x	-x

---

[8]*Key*: x indicates the particular commentator's choice; -x indicates that no specific choice is made.

Schmidt	x	–
Lekkerkerker	–	–
Cranfield	x	–
Schlier	x	–
Käsemann	x	–
Hendriksen	–	–
Louw	x	–
Wilckens	–	x
Pelser	x	–
Achtemeier	–	-x

A number of commentaries give no indication of how they understand the *dispositio* of Romans, while the majority prefer the first position. However, there are three influential commentaries opting for the second position, namely, Sanday and Headlam, Ridderbos and Wilckens. Wilckens even takes the end of chapter 5 as the division between the the first and second volumes of his commentary.

Contrary to these commentaries, which base their demarcation on arguments of content and theme, White (1972:52–53, 56–68) proposes the following division, based primarily on *formal* epistolographical considerations:

* Part 1: Rom 1:16 – 4:25
* Part 2: Rom 5:1 – 11:36

In 1:16 Paul states his basic argument briefly, namely that he is not ashamed of the gospel, the gospel that has two attributes (the second of which has a positive and a negative aspect):

*δύναμις
*δικαιοσύνη   * (1) justifying δικαιοσύνη
                                  * (2) condemning δικαιοσύνη (ὀργή)

These three elements are subsequently treated in reverse order in Part 1 of the letter-body:

*condemning δικαιοσύνη (ὀργή): 1:18 – 2:12
*justifying δικαιοσύνη: 2:13 – 3:22
*δύναμις: 3:22 – 4:25

It is important to remember that White supports this demarcation of subsections in the body of the letter with formal aspects, such as the use of letter-formulae, and not primarily on the basis of the propositional content. The role of the formula οὐ γάρ is significant in this demarcation of sub-sections in 1:18 – 4:25 (White 1972:58, 116):

1:16 – 2:12   <u>Οὐ γὰρ</u> ἐπαισχύνομαι τὸ εὐαγγέλιον (1:16)
                    <u>οὐ γάρ</u> ἐστιν προσωπολημψία παρὰ τῷ θεῷ (2:11)

2:13 – 3:22   οὐ γὰρ οἱ ἀκροαταὶ νόμου δίκαιοι παρὰ τῷ
              θεῷ ἀλλ᾽ οἱ ποιηταὶ νόμου δικαιωθήσονται (2:13)
              οὐ γὰρ ὁ ἐν τῷ φανερῷ ᾽Ιουδαῖός
              ἐστιν . . . (2:28)
              Τί οὖν τὸ περισσὸν τοῦ ᾽Ιουδαίου. . . (3:1)
              Τί οὖν (3:9)
              οὐ γάρ ἐστιν διαστολή (3:22)
3:22 – 4:25   οὐ γάρ ἐστιν διαστολή (3:22)
              Οὐ γὰρ διὰ νόμου ἡ ἐπαγγελία . . . (4:13)
              Οὐκ ἐγράφη δὲ δι᾽ αὐτὸν μόνον . . . (4:23) ἀλλὰ
              καὶ δι᾽ ἡμᾶς . . . , τοῖς πιστεύουσιν ἐπὶ τὸν
              ἐγείραντα ᾽Ιησοῦν τὸν κύριον ἡμῶν ἐκ
              νεκρῶν . . . (4:24).

Although these formulae are important markers, the demarcation cannot be based exclusively on them. The propositional content or subject matter has also to be taken into account.

White (1972:58) divides Part 2 of the letter-body (5:1 – 11:36) into two sub-sections:

*   5:1 – 8:39 — spiritual Israel
*   9:1 – 11:39 — Israel in the flesh

Neither of these sections opens with a distinctive transitional construction or formula. Nevertheless, White (1972:58) argues that the division of these sections may be established by other formal means, such as the exclamations in 8:31–36 and 11:33–36. Furthermore, although οὐ γάρ, ἄρα οὖν and τί οὖν are not so consistently employed as formal markers, as is οὐ γάρ in part 1, these three discrete constructions are nevertheless significantly employed (for example οὐ γάρ in 7:15b, 19; 8:15; 9:16; 10:12 and 11:25ff; ἄρα οὖν in 5:18; 7:3, 21; 8:1, 12; 9:16, 18; 10:17; and τί οὖν in 6:1, 15; 7:7, 13; 8:31; 9:14, 30; 11:1, 7, 11). For the present purposes it is sufficient to conclude that the body-middle (1:16 – 11:36) forms a unit, consisting of a tightly woven argument, which precedes the section in which I am primarily interested, namely, the paraenesis (12:1 – 15:13).

V. *Paraenesis (12:1 – 15:13)*

In his analysis of the letter-body, White ignores Romans 12:1 – 15:13 and moves directly from 11:39 (the end of the body-middle) to 15:14 (the beginning of what he calls the body-closing). According to him only 1:13 – 11:36 and 15:14–33 may be identified as body sections (White 1972:46). Therefore it seems as if he does not consider this paraenetic section to be a part of the body since it does not exhibit the 'idea' and formulae which are typical of the body of the ancient Greek letter — as this was analyzed by him in comparison with Greek documentary papyri. Whether or not the paraenesis has to be regarded as part of the letter-body seen in such a formalistic manner need not be at issue here. There is general agreement that the paraenesis forms a distinct unit in the letter, and that it is in one way or another linked with the argumentation in the preceding sections. A more detailed discussion of the paraenesis will be undertaken in the next section (§5.3).

VI. Closing (15:13 - 16:24)

Two sections can be distinguished in the 'closing' of the letter, namely, a body-closing (15:14–33) and a letter-closing (16:1–24).

1. *Body-closing (15:14–33)*. This section consists of three elements, namely, a motivation for the author's responsibility to write, a formula of confidence and the apostolic *parousia*. Each of these elements is identified by a number of formal characteristics.

a. *Motivation for writing-responsibility* (15:14–15) 'briefly reiterates the message of the body and urges appropriate response to it':

* formulaic statement of authorship — καὶ αὐτὸς ἐγώ (15:14)
* reference to the act of writing — ἔγραψα (15:15)
* reiteration of reason for writing — ὡς (15:15)

b. *Confidence formula*: affirms confidence in an appropriate response from recipients:

* emphatic use of the pronoun ἐγώ (15:14)
* perfect form of the verb πείθω in which Paul alleges his "confidence": πέπεισμαι (15:14)
* specification of the basis of confidence, defined as residing in Paul's addressees: περὶ ὑμῶν (15:14)
* explicit mention of the object concerning which Paul is confident introduced by ὅτι: ὅτι καὶ αὐτοὶ μεστοί ἐστε ἀγαθωσύνης, πεπληρωμένοι πάσης {τῆς} γνώσεως, δυνάμενοι καὶ ἀλλήλους νουθετεῖν (15:14)

c. Implementation of the apostolic *parousia*-formula:

* stating Paul's disposition or purpose (15:15–16): ἔγραψα . . . ὡς ἐπαναμιμνήσκων ὑμᾶς διὰ τὴν χάριν τὴν δοθεῖσάν μοι ὑπὸ τοῦ θεοῦ εἰς τὸ εἶναί με λειτουργὸν Χριστοῦ Ἰησοῦ εἰς τὰ ἔθνη, ἱερουργοῦντα τὸ εὐαγγέλιον τοῦ θεοῦ, ἵνα γένηται ἡ προσφορὰ τῶν ἐθνῶν εὐπρόσδεκτος, ἡγιασμένη ἐν πνεύματι ἁγίῳ.
* stating the basis of Paul's apostolic relation to the recipients (15b-21): ὡς ἐπαναμιμνήσκων ὑμᾶς διὰ τὴν χάριν τὴν δοθεῖσάν μοι ὑπὸ τοῦ θεοῦ εἰς τὸ εἶναί με λειτουργὸν Χριστοῦ Ἰησοῦ εἰς τὰ ἔθνη, ἱερουργοῦντα τὸ

εὐαγγέλιον τοῦ θεοῦ, ἵνα γένηται ἡ προσφορὰ τῶν ἐθνῶν εὐπρόσδεκτος, ἡγιασμένη ἐν πνεύματι ἁγίῳ. ἔχω οὖν {τὴν} καύχησιν ἐν Χριστῷ Ἰησοῦ τὰ πρὸς τὸν θεόν· οὐ γὰρ τολμήσω τι λαλεῖν ὧν οὐ κατειργάσατο Χριστὸς δι᾽ ἐμοῦ εἰς ὑπακοὴν ἐθνῶν, λόγῳ καὶ ἔργῳ, ἐν δυνάμει σημείων καὶ τεράτων, ἐν δυνάμει πνεύματος· ὥστε με ἀπὸ Ἰερουσαλὴμ καὶ κύκλῳ μέχρι τοῦ Ἰλλυρικοῦ πεπληρωκέναι τὸ εὐαγγέλιον τοῦ Χριστοῦ, οὕτως δὲ φιλοτιμούμενον εὐαγγελίζεσθαι οὐχ ὅπου ὠνομάσθη Χριστός, ἵνα μὴ ἐπ᾽ ἀλλότριον θεμέλιον οἰκοδομῶ, ἀλλὰ καθὼς γέγραπται, Οἷς οὐκ ἀνηγγέλη περὶ αὐτοῦ ὄψονται, καὶ οἳ οὐκ ἀκηκόασιν συνήσουσιν.

* hindrance to his coming (15:22): ἐνεκοπτόμην.
* desire, eagerness to see (come to) them (15:23b): ἐπιποθίαν δὲ ἔχων τοῦ ἐλθεῖν πρὸς ὑμᾶς ἀπὸ πολλῶν ἐτῶν.
* hope (ἐλπίζω), wish (θέλω), intention (προτίθεμαι) to see/to come to them (15:24b): ἐλπίζω γὰρ διαπορευόμενος θεάσασθαι ὑμᾶς.
* to be sent on by them (15:24c): καὶ ὑφ᾽ ὑμῶν προπεμφθῆναι ἐκεῖ.
* specific apostolic *parousia* which takes the form of an announcement or promise of a visit, or that a visit is expected, hoped or prayed for (15:28b): ἀπελεύσομαι δι᾽ ὑμῶν εἰς Σπανίαν.
* invocation of divine approval and support for the apostolic *parousia*, the prayer for his presence may be a request for prayer, their prayer, his own prayer (15:30-31): Παρακαλῶ δὲ ὑμᾶς {ἀδελφοί,} διὰ τοῦ κυρίου ἡμῶν Ἰησοῦ Χριστοῦ καὶ διὰ τῆς ἀγάπης τοῦ πνεύματος, συναγωνίσασθαί μοι ἐν ταῖς προσευχαῖς ὑπὲρ ἐμοῦ πρὸς τὸν θεόν, ἵνα ῥυσθῶ ἀπὸ τῶν ἀπειθούντων ἐν τῇ Ἰουδαίᾳ καὶ ἡ διακονία μου ἡ εἰς Ἰερουσαλὴμ εὐπρόσδεκτος τοῖς ἁγίοις γένηται.
* invocation of divine approval and support for the apostolic *parousia*, the convention "if God wills" (15:32): διὰ θελήματος θεοῦ.
* benefit from the apostolic *parousia* accruing to Paul (15:32b): συναναπαύσωμαι ὑμῖν.[9]

2. *Letter closing (16:1-27).*

Note of recommendation	16:1-2	Συνίστημι δὲ ὑμῖν Φοίβην τὴν ἀδελφὴν ἡμῶν, οὖσαν {καὶ} διάκονον τῆς ἐκκλησίας τῆς ἐν Κεγχρεαῖς, ἵνα προσδέξησθε αὐτὴν ἐν κυρίῳ ἀξίως τῶν ἁγίων, καὶ παραστῆτε αὐτῇ ἐν ᾧ ἂν ὑμῶν χρῄζῃ πράγματι, καὶ γὰρ αὐτὴ προστάτις πολλῶν ἐγενήθη καὶ ἐμοῦ αὐτοῦ.
Grussaufstrag	16:3-16a	
Holy kiss	16:16a	Ἀσπάσασθε ἀλλήλους ἐν φιλήματι ἁγίῳ

[9]For a more detailed discussion of apostolic parousia in Romans as well as in other Pauline letters, see Funk.

Grussausrichtung	16:16b	Ἀσπάζονται ὑμᾶς αἱ ἐκκλησίαι πᾶσαι τοῦ Χριστοῦ
	16:21,23	Ἀσπάζεται ὑμᾶς Τιμόθεος ὁ συνεργός μου, καὶ Λούκιος καὶ Ἰάσων καὶ Σωσίπατρος οἱ συγγενεῖς μου. ἀσπάζεται ὑμᾶς Γάϊος ὁ ξένος μου καὶ ὅλης τῆς ἐκκλησίας. ἀσπάζεται ὑμᾶς Ἔραστος ὁ οἰκονόμος τῆς πόλεως καὶ Κούαρτος ὁ ἀδελφός
Greetings from author	16:22	ἀσπάζομαι ὑμᾶς ἐγὼ Τέρτιος ὁ γράψας τὴν ἐπιστολὴν ἐν κυρίῳ.
Benediction	16:25-27	

Regarding the problem of the end of the letter to the Romans, I concur with the results of the careful study of Gamble (127–144) and the well-argued view of Vorster (1991:80–90), namely, I take chapter 16 as part of the letter (*contra* Manson and Petersen 1987).

5.3 Romans 13:1–7 as Paraenetic Literature

Regarding the modern interpretation of Pauline paraenesis,[10] Doty (37) made the following important observation:

> One of the most important projects in the history of biblical research was the reclaiming of Paul as a situational or contextualist theologian and ethicist rather than as a dogmatic moralist. Instead of visualizing Paul as an abstract thinker spinning webs of ethical and moral duties, modern interpreters see him as involved with his addressees in the process of dialogic piecing-together of concrete ethical responses in each situation.

This 'reclaiming' of Paul as 'ethicist' is characteristic of the ideals of the historical paradigm. Although this is a lofty ideal, the problem is that links between the 'ethical' (or paraenetical) sections in Paul's letters and the contexts or 'real world situation' to which they are seen as concrete responses are all too easily made, without due regard that these 'ethical' sections form part of *letters*. The implications of the letter as literary phenomenon must be taken seriously *before* any claims about the 'concrete situations' to which they

---

[10]Singular: paraenesis; plural: paraeneses or moral exhortations.

were responses can be made. To ignore this 'literariness' of the 'ethical' or 'paraenetical' sections all too easily results in a simplistic mirror-like concept of representation (see also chapter 3, §5 and chapter 4, §3). In order to be able to interpret Romans 13:1-7 against this background, the literary features of paraenesis must be examined carefully since they provide important clues for the determination and description of the meaning of this passage. In this analysis, therefore, the formal characteristics of paraenesis as literary phenomenon are analyzed. This analysis is yet another example of the important 'before' of the ethics of reading for which I am arguing in this book: the text must be *read* (also with due regard for its formal literary qualities) before we will be able to study any text-extrinsic relations (see the Introduction 3-9).

5.3.1 Paraenetic Literature as a complex secondary genre

Although the term 'paraenesis' is widely used to characterize the nature of the literary form of which Romans 12:1 - 15:13 seems to be an example (see Michel 365; Koester 55; Malherbe 1986:125), closer examination reveals that it is not that simple to get a grip on the meaning and reference of this term. From Malherbe's (1986:125) general discussion of paraenesis, from Kraftchick's (1985:4-29) survey of the meaning and reference of the term 'paraenesis' in classical rhetorical treatises, and from Gammie's (51-52) survey of the contributions of a number of writers who have during the twentieth century devoted efforts toward a definition of 'paraenesis' (inter alia Burgess, Vetchera, Dibelius, Malherbe, Perdue, Fiore and Stowers), a number of characteristics generally ascribed to paraenesis can be distilled:

* 'traditional materials' or 'precepts' are present in paraenesis

* paraenesis gives general rules which does not mean that it is not related or adapted to the settings in which it is given

* paraenesis focuses on the practical conduct of life

* paraenesis may be diverse in content and often consists of series of brief unconnected admonitions strung together

* paraenesis contains commands or summons directed to a specific type of audience, pressing them to continue a certain way of life rather than convincing them to adapt a new way of life (paraenesis is confirmation literature; see, however, §6.2)

* paraenesis sometimes refers to content (for example, traditional maxims or precepts of wisdom, especially moral wisdom)

> *   paraenesis sometimes refers to the form or process of moral teaching (that is, the process of addressing words of encouragement or discouragement about behavior to a person or persons)

Going beyond these general characteristics of paraenesis, Gammie (52) presents a thorough and systematic definition of paraenesis as a literary genre or type. The result of his study is a taxonomy of Paraenetic Literature. According to Gammie (70) paraeneses are:

> Moral exhortations which usually feature an assemblage of precepts and comprise a major division of Paraenetic Literature. Frequently paraenesis is taken to be a synonym for exhortation, or to be aimed at conforming the addressee in a given course of conduct.

Gammie's focus on paraenesis as *form* and his attempt to define Paraenetic Literature as a literary genre or type (41) is precisely that which was identified in §2 as the focus of the first part of this literary reading. His programmatic essay is therefore directly relevant for my purpose.

A number of presuppositions underpin Gammie's study of Paraenetic Literature:

> *   His aim is programmatic, to identify the most significant *formal* elements to be found in Paraenetic Literature, but he does not show how these various elements interrelate and are interwoven in specific texts (65).
>
> *   He maintains that 'modern usage of the term paraenesis should seek to show both some correspondence with and awareness of classical usage' of the term (57). His aim is to provide an *emic* treatment of the subject, that is, a study of a system from inside (in contrast to an *etic* approach which studies a system from outside).
>
> *   The purpose of genre analysis is not simply taxonomic but should also be *heuristic* (42, 66). Therefore, it must enable an exegete to be more ready to reflect on how these elements are presented and interrelated in a particular work.
>
> *   A basic procedure to provide the data and criteria in terms of which such a taxonomy can be compiled is that of *comparison*. As basis for comparison Gammie uses materials from the ancient Near Eastern worlds of Egypt, Sumeria and Babylon to the Mediterranean world of the Roman Empire (41–42). This presupposition and, specifically, the breadth and depth of the basis of comparison is in accordance with a trend in modern literary approaches to the study of New Testament letters (see §4.5).
>
> *   The taxonomy of literary forms is based on formal grammatical and syntactical considerations. Paraenesis as a social act and the social character and functions of paraenesis fall outside the scope of the formal literary description of Paraenetic Literature.

Two of these presuppositions are problematic. Regarding the emic ideal for the genre studies of ancient literature, Stowers (1986:91) writes:

> The terminology, types of literature, and traditions associated with exhortation and advice can be very confusing and require explanation. There is much overlapping

and ambiguous terminology, which is partly due to the fact that exhortation was
never systematically treated by rhetoricians.

This is undoubtedly a valid assessment of the limits of ancient genre analysis
on the basis of the work of contemporary theorists. On the other hand, this
does not mean that the views of ancient theorists may be disregarded.
Although they do not provide definitive categories and clearly defined
terminology in a systematic way, they do discuss the matter quite extensively
and distinguish a number of rhetorical (and literary) genres and forms. The
modern interpreter is thus challenged to interact creatively with the available
ancient theoretical viewpoints as well as a study of the literary phenomena of
the ancient materials itself, in order to compile a taxonomy of ancient literary
genres and forms. This is exactly what Gammie endeavors to do.

Robbins (1990:262) has also indicated the limits of the purely formalistic
criteria (grammar and syntax) used by Gammie for the compilation of his
taxonomy of Paraenetic Literature. Robbins maintains that a taxonomy
should be based on 'topics' and 'persuasive figures' rather than on syntax and
grammar since the arenas of life from which people glean topics and figures
of persuasion are social phenomena (1990:262). Taking the arenas of life
into account will result in a richer interpretation, going further into social and
anthropological issues (1990:263). Again I would agree that this is valid
criticism of Gammie's taxonomy. On the other hand, within the structure of
this study, Gammie's taxonomy and the formalist criteria he used to compile
it fall precisely within the stated focus of this chapter (see §2). Social-
scientific considerations in the interpretation of Romans 13:1-7 are indeed
relevant, but will be treated in chapter 4. This distinction is made purely for
practical reasons. Not all the relevant and necessary aspects which have to
be taken into account in a responsible interpretation can be dealt with
simultaneously (see Introduction, pp. 8–9).

One of Gammie's (48) basic propositions is that two main composite
sub-genres (divisions) of Paraenetic Literature may be identified, namely
Instructions[11] and Paraeneses (or Moral Exhortations) (with Protreptic as a
possible third category; see, however, §6.2). Both are complex genres comprised of sub-genres, although both form part of an even broader and more
complex category, namely the secondary genre Paraenetic Literature, which
in turn is a subdivision of the major literary genre, Wisdom Literature. Just
as not all Apocalyptic Literature consists of apocalypse, not all Paraenetic
Literature consists of paraenesis. To handle it in such a way is comparable to
reducing all prophetic speech to judgment speech (*Gerichtswort*) and ignoring

---

[11]Spelled with a capital letter since it indicates a specific (sub)genre. Following
Gammie (1990) Paraenesis, Precepts, Protreptic, Paraenetic Literature and Wisdom
Literature are written with capital letters for the same reason.

speech of salvation (*Heilswort*). Gammie (45) warns that a sub-genre should not be allowed to usurp the field of secondary literature. He suggests the following distinction: Wisdom Literature (a major literary genre), Paraenetic Literature (a secondary literary genre) and Paraenesis (a sub-genre), with a number of sub-genres under Paraenesis (Admonitions, Warnings, Exhortations, Biographical Examples, Precepts, Praises, Wisdom Sayings, Fables, Parables, Riddles, Didactic Tales and occasionally Diatribes) (46).

Gammie (70) defines Paraenetic Literature as 'a complex and secondary literary genre the aim of which is frequently hortatory and instructive.' This genre is broader than Paraeneses and Instructions. These two constitute the two largest divisions of Paraenetic Literature. How Protreptic fits into this system is a rather complicated matter which necessitates more extensive consideration (see §5.3.2). Romans 13:1–7 clearly falls under the rubric Paraenetic Literature. It is hortatory in nature, giving a number of specific instructions for conduct with regard to authorities:

* πᾶσα ψυχὴ ἐξουσίαις ὑπερεχούσαις ὑποτασσέσθω ('let every soul be subject to the governing authorities' 13:1),
* φόρους τελεῖτε ('pay your taxes' 13:6),
* ἀπόδοτε πᾶσιν τὰς ὀφειλάς ('pay all of them their dues' 13:7).

This general identification of Romans 13:1–7 as Paraenetic Literature, however, will be considerably refined, especially when a more detailed analysis of the passage is made in terms of the categories which Gammie provides in his taxonomy. Such an analysis will be undertaken in §5.3.3. But first it is necessary to address the question whether the literary form of Romans 13:1–7 is paraenesis or protreptic.

5.3.2 Romans 13:1–7: Paraenesis or Protreptic?

Since paraenesis and protreptic seem to be very closely related sub-genres, it is important to try to distinguish carefully between them. However, precisely what protreptic as sub-genre is supposed to be remains unclear (see Attridge 213ff). A consideration of what protreptic may be and how it differs from paraenesis can provide illuminating background information for the interpretation of Romans 13:1–7.

Burgess (230) notes that παραινέω and προτρέπω are often used interchangeably without clear definition. To this general remark, he nevertheless adds that in its specific meaning προτρεπτικὸς λόγος

> is an exhortation to some general course — philosophy, rhetoric, virtue. It gives a comprehensive view, setting forth the advantages and removing the objections . . . .

The παραίνεσις is practically without formal definition . . . . In distinction from the προτρεπτικὸς λόγος the παραίνεσις presents a series of precepts which will serve as a guide of conduct under fixed conditions . . . . The παραίνεσις as part of philosophy may have a restricted and personal application, *e.g.*, how to manage servants; or it may be more general, *e.g.*, how to live well.

For Malherbe (1986:124) paraenesis differs from protreptic in the sense that it is broader in scope, it contains useful rules for conduct in common situations and adopts a style that ranges from censure to consolation. Interestingly enough, Malherbe (1986:122) maintains that protreptic only makes its appearance in Christian literature in the second century (for example, *Epistle to Diognetos, Letter of Ptolemy to Flora*), which means that he considers no part of the New Testament to be protreptic.

In direct opposition to this view, Stowers (1986:114) emphatically states that the whole of the letter to the Romans (not only 12:1 - 15:13) is a protreptic letter (see §4.5). The most important criterion for Stowers (1986:92) to distinguish between paraenesis and protreptic is the difference in the nature of the *audience* each of these presupposed: protreptic refers to hortatory literature that calls the audience to a new and different way of life, while paraenesis refers to advice and exhortation to continue in a certain way of life.

Gammie (52–54) provides a more elaborate and systematic treatment of this issue in which he brings together a number of the insights touched on so far. He uses four criteria to distinguish between paraenesis and protreptic: (i) the role of precepts, (ii) the role of argumentation, (iii) breadth, and (iv) audience. He argues that the criterion of audience should be dropped in favor of the other three. For Gammie (54) the criterion of audience is problematic since it leaves a student of literature at a loss as to how to classify writings with dual audiences. He refers to a number of works that presumably presupposed such audiences (for example, the *Letter of Aristeas* which has both persons in Hellenistic non-Jewish communities and the Jewish community itself as its audience). More importantly and in line with the position that I will set out in more detail later on (see § 6.3.1), I want to argue that the criterion of audience presupposes a view of literature more in accordance with historical critical views than with 'new' literary views (see §3.2). Audience, in the way in which Stowers uses it, as a criterion for the characterization of either paraenesis or protreptic, seems to be a text-external phenomenon, while the considerations of the presence or absence of precepts, the role of demonstration and the breadth of topic/sharpness of focus seem to be proper text-internal phenomena. Therefore, although on different grounds than Gammie, I also opt for the exclusion of audience as a criterion for the determination of protreptic or paraenesis.

The presence of precepts and a commending of them as a way of life is for Gammie not an optional feature for paraenesis, while protreptic may or may not contain precepts. Precepts are 'sentences, usually in the indicative mood, which instruct and contain an implied or obvious directive for conduct' (Gammie 70). While Romans 13:1 is not in the indicative mood and may therefore on strict formalist grounds not be regarded to be a precept, Romans 13:5 is in the indicative mood and perfectly fits this definition of precept. More important for Gammie, however, is the observation that protreptic seeks to persuade frequently through sustained argumentation, using syllogistic argumentation, while demonstration is less systematic, organized and regular — or altogether absent — in paraenesis. On the basis of this criterion, it seems as if the series of exhortations in Romans 12:9–21, with their lack of argumentation, qualifies as paraeneses, while Romans 13:1–7 seems to be protreptic since the exhortation in 13:1 is demonstrated by means of syllogistic argumentation in 13:2–5 (see chapter 3, §7.2.4 for an analysis of the syllogisms in Romans 13:1–7). Gammie's third criterion, breadth of topics covered and/or sharpness of focus, seems to provide additional grounds for this observation. Paraenesis is broader in content than a protreptic work. Applied to the passage in question, we observe that Romans 12:9–21 touches on a number of issues (love, showing honor, zeal, hope, patience, prayer, compassion, hospitality, conduct in persecution, harmony, humbleness, revenge, conduct with enemies), while Romans 13:1–7 is devoted to one issue (obedience to the authorities). On the basis of this criterion Romans 13:1–7 seems therefore to be protreptic rather than paraenetic. For the same reasons Romans 14:1 – 15:13 qualifies to be labelled protreptic rather than paraenetic: it consists of rather elaborate argumentation, it focuses basically on one issue, namely, tolerance, although this issue has been argued with regard to diverse matters such as whether all kinds of food may be eaten (14:2) and whether certain days should be kept as special days (14:5–6) and causing others to stumble because of differences of opinion (14:13 – 15:13).

In the light of all these considerations, I conclude that Romans 13:1–7 should be regarded as protreptic rather than paraenesis. Since both paraenesis and protreptic form part of Paraenetic Literature, Romans 13:1–7 can still be regarded as Paraenetic Literature in terms of a general classification. What remains to be done is to analyze Romans 13:1–7 in terms of the component sub-genres of Paraenetic Literature, that is, sub-genres subsidiary to protreptic.

5.3.3 *The component sub-genres of Paraenetic Literature in Romans 13:1–7*

Gammie (47) presents the main divisions of Paraenetic Literature by means of the following taxonomy:

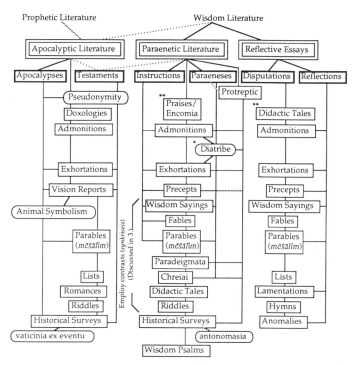

The Secondary Genres of Wisdom Literature

Legend

———	= usual component
-----	= possible component
(oval)	= device rather than sub-genre
(double box)	= Secondary Genres
(black box)	= Composite Sub-genre (Divisions)
(box)	= Sub-genre
*	= May utilize form of the letters
**	= Serve as framing sub-genres

From this taxonomy it is clear how complex and interwoven the sub-genres and further divisions (which Gammie calls 'simple genres') of Paraenetic Literature are. Most of the forms can, in fact, be classified under both Instructions and Paraeneses (and Protreptic). The distinction that Gammie (51) proposes between Instructions and Paraenesis (and Protreptic) is quite informative: just as 'hurricane' and 'typhoon' are different labels used for a similar event (a storm accompanied by torrential downpours and high winds), both Instructions and Paraeneses refer for a large part to the same phenomena in literature. But, just as the use of either 'hurricane' or 'typhoon' serves to alert one as to the locality of the storm (the Caribbean or the Pacific), so the use of either Instruction or Paraenesis serves to locate the passages in question to either ancient Egypt or ancient Greece as original models. Instructions and Paraenesis overlap therefore rather extensively. In the case of Romans 13:1-7, being part of a Hellenistic letter, the model would be ancient Greece, and therefore it would be more properly labelled Paraenesis (or Protreptic, as I have argued above).

Three of the component sub-genres of protreptic can be identified in Romans 13:1-7: 13:1 is a Major Exhortation with 13:2-5 as motivational argumentation, consisting of 13:3b as Minor Exhortation, 13:2, 3a and 5 as Precepts and 13:4b as Admonition. Rom 13:6 may be taken as a Precept (if τελεῖτε is taken as an Indicative) or Exhortation (if the verb is taken as Imperative), with 13:6b as clause of motivation for the Exhortation. Finally, 13:7 consists of a series of Exhortations. Closer examination of each of these sub-genres or forms is illuminating, especially when the differences between them are considered.

5.3.3.1 Romans 13:4b as Admonition

Gammie (50) maintains that the Admonition as sub-genre (or form) subsidiary to Paraenetic Literature aiming at dissuasion (or warning) must be distinguished from the exhortation. Admonitions and exhortations are both recognizable sub-genres of Paraenetic Literature. The exhortation invites the addressee to a given course of action, whereas the admonition warns the addressee against taking a given course of action or attitude. Admonitions are frequently mingled with exhortations. Admonitions themselves exhibit a simple and recurring pattern, namely, (i) the use of the vocative in direct address, (ii) the use of the grammatical forms of imperative, jussive or prohibitive, and (iii) the presence of clauses of motivation (Gammie 59).

Romans 13:1-7 forms part of a larger section, starting at 12:1, where the vocative ἀδελφοί is used. Thus, although a vocative is not present in 13:1-7 itself, the vocative in 12:1 may be taken as a marker that indicates that admonitions and exhortations may be present in this passage. In verse 4b an admonition, ἐὰν δὲ τὸ κακὸν ποιῇς, φοβοῦ (if you do wrong, be afraid!) is given in the imperative, φοβοῦ. The admonition is immediately followed by two clauses of motivation, οὐ γὰρ εἰκῇ τὴν μάχαιραν φορεῖ (for he does not bear the sword in vain), and θεοῦ γὰρ διάκονός ἐστιν, ἔκδικος εἰς ὀργὴν τῷ τὸ κακὸν πράσσοντι (for he is the servant of God to execute his wrath on the wrongdoer). This sentence, therefore, exhibits all three characteristics of Admonition as sub-genre of Paraenetic Literature.

5.3.3.2 Romans 13:1, 3b, 6 and 7 as Exhortations

The Exhortation, as subdivision of Protreptic, invites, encourages, directs or commands that the implied reader pursue a given course of action or adopt a given attitude (Gammie 60). Gammie (60–61) identifies three formal characteristics of Exhortations: (i) the use of vocative in direct address, (ii) the use of questions, conditional clauses, imperatives or an indicative followed by an infinitive clause to issue the exhortation, and (iii) the use of clauses of motivation. The role of the vocative, ἀδελφοί, in 12:1 has already been pointed out. The form of the verb in the exhortation in 13:1a (πᾶσα ψυχὴ ἐξουσίαις ὑπερεχούσαις ὑποτασσέσθω) is imperative. The exhortation in 13:1a is followed by a clause of motivation in 1b: οὐ γὰρ ἔστιν ἐξουσία εἰ μὴ ὑπὸ θεοῦ, αἱ δὲ οὖσαι ὑπὸ θεοῦ τεταγμέναι εἰσίν (for there is no authority except from God, and those that exist have been instituted by God). The form of the verb in the exhortation in 3b (τὸ ἀγαθὸν ποίει) is imperative, and it is followed by a clause of motivation, καὶ ἕξεις ἔπαινον ἐξ αὐτῆς (for you will receive his approval). The form of the verb in the exhortation in verse 6 (διὰ τοῦτο γὰρ καὶ φόρους τελεῖτε) may be taken as imperative, followed by a clause of motivation, λειτουργοὶ γὰρ θεοῦ εἰσιν εἰς αὐτὸ τοῦτο προσκαρτεροῦντες (for they are ministers of God, attending to this very thing). The form of the verb in the exhortation in verse 7 (ἀπόδοτε πᾶσιν τὰς ὀφειλάς) is imperative. This last exhortation, however, is not followed by a clause of motivation. Romans 13:1-7, therefore, contains four exhortations, all of which (except for the exhortation in verse 7, lacking a clause of motivation) exhibit all three formal characteristics of exhortations.

5.3.3.3 Romans 13:2, 3a and 5 as precepts

Gammie (58, 67) indicates that the precept, as recognizable sub-genre (or form) subsidiary to Paraenetic Literature, should be distinguished from the simple observation. An observation can be defined as a sentence in the indicative in which attention is drawn to an observable phenomenon without either implicitly or obviously directing the hearer to a given course of conduct (for example, 'The poor is disliked by his neighbors, but the rich has many friends,' Proverbs 21:15). A precept, on the other hand, will also usually employ the Indicative, enjoining a specific action.

Three precepts can be identified in Romans 13:1–7. Verse 2 is a sentence in the indicative that instructs and contains an implied directive for conduct: ὁ ἀντιτασσόμενος τῇ ἐξουσίᾳ τῇ τοῦ θεοῦ διαταγῇ ἀνθέστηκεν, οἱ δὲ ἀνθεστηκότες ἑαυτοῖς κρίμα λήμψονται (he who resists the authorities resists what God has appointed, and those who resist will incur judgment). The conduct advised is: do not resist. A clause of motivation forms part of the precept: God has appointed authorities. In verse 3a another precept is used: οἱ γὰρ ἄρχοντες οὐκ εἰσὶν φόβος τῷ ἀγαθῷ ἔργῳ ἀλλὰ τῷ κακῷ (rulers are not a terror to good conduct, but to bad). The implied directive is: do not conduct yourself badly. Verse 5 consists of another full precept, including a sentence in the indicative, διὸ ἀνάγκη ὑποτάσσεσθαι (it is necessary to be subject), followed by a clause of motivation, οὐ μόνον διὰ τὴν ὀργὴν ἀλλὰ καὶ διὰ τὴν συνείδησιν (not only to avoid God's wrath, but for the sake of conscience). The implied directive is: be subject to the authorities.

5.4 The ethics of reading and formal literary analysis

The first part of this analysis included a formal description of the letter to the Romans as a whole. This description identified the place of the paraenetic section within the letter. The second part contained an analysis in more detail of this paraenetic section. This analysis has revealed that Romans 13:1–7 contains one admonition, four exhortations and three precepts. These three are among the most important sub-genres of Paraenetic Literature that Gammie lists in his taxonomy. On formal grounds, we can conclude that Romans 13:1–7 is clearly an example of Paraenetic Literature, which can be more closely identified as protreptic in nature and in which three different sub-genres of Paraenetic Literature are intermingled, namely Admonition, Exhortation and Precept.

I have already indicated (§5.1) that I regard such a formal reading as one way of taking the 'literariness' of the text seriously. It does indeed have a heuristic value of some sort, although I would not evaluate its heuristic value with the same enthusiasm as Gammie did. Even though it is valuable, its value is limited. The aspect of the ethics of reading that I have been dealing with in this chapter necessitates that the 'literariness' of the text 'must' be taken seriously. The example that I have used to explain the need and limits of a linguistic reading in the previous chapter (see chapter 1, §10), may be used here again. If one wants to count from one to ten, one must begin with one and end with ten. One cannot skip any number nor stop before one has reached ten. Just as it is necessary in a responsible act of reading to honor the linguisticality of the text, in the same degree it is necessary to honor the literariness of the text. Both 'must' be done. But just as there are more ways than one to take linguisticality seriously, so there are also more ways than one to take the text's 'literariness' seriously. The formal analysis presented here is one possible way.

To disregard formal analysis altogether would result in an irresponsible act of reading. On the other hand, to end the process of interpretation with a mere formal analysis would be typical of the scientist ethos of biblical interpretation. An ethics of responsible reading calls for a 'both and' situation here: both the formal *and* the communicative aspects of the text as literary phenomenon must be studied. To end the act of interpretation with a formal analysis enables the interpreter to keep a greater distance between what he or she is doing in interpretational work and matters of life and reality. To move beyond formal analysis to a study of the intra-textual communicative aspects in the text is also a move closer to life and reality — although as textual procedure this communication must not simplistically be equated with life and reality and history. In the next section, therefore, Romans 13:1–7 is read in terms of a communicative approach to the letter as a literary phenomenon.

6. Reading Romans as a letter: a communicative approach

6.1 Introduction

This reading consists of two parts. The first part considers the letter-type and the possible social function performed by the letter. This is of utmost importance in a communicative approach to the reading of a letter. Communication always takes place within a social context. For this reason, I do not limit the discussion to the letter to the Romans itself. The possible social context and social functions considered in this section, however, are treated in general terms. They are possible social functions of the letter as literary phenomenon. In this respect, therefore, it differs from a historical and a social-scientific approach. In the second phase of this reading, I continue to work within a textual paradigm and, in this phase, no comparative work is done. I limit the discussion exclusively to the letter to the Romans, which is a prerequisite of a consistent *textual* approach. The communication to be described here is an intra-textual phenomenon.

6.2 Letter-type and social action performed by the letter

Scholars have attempted to classify Romans in terms of the categories of ancient letters. K. P. Donfried (1977a:145–147), for example, maintains that

M. L. Stirewalt's description of the 'Greek Letter-essay' in the category of the letters of Epicurus, Dionysios of Halicarnassus and selections from the works of Plutarch '[is] very suggestive' and 'may give us further insight into Romans.' For K. Berger (1984a) Romans is a 'general tractate' like those written in Hellenistic times by teachers to individual pupils or communities of pupils or even to cities.   R. Jewett (1982) characterizes Romans as an 'ambassadorial letter.'

Stowers (1986) develops their insights further. On the basis of ancient epistolary theory and ancient rhetorical handbooks, Stowers (1986:49–174) proposes and illustrates elaborately a typology of six epistolary types, namely, (1) letters of friendship, (2) family letters, (3) letters of praise and blame (functions of epideictic rhetoric), (4) hortatory letters (with seven sub-types: paraenetic letters, protreptic letters, letters of advice, admonition, rebuke, reproach and consolation), (5) letters of recommendation, and (6) accusing, apologetic, and accounting letters (functions of juridical rhetoric). All these types indicate the kinds of social actions which are performed by letters (Stowers 1988:78–79).

For Stowers (1986:114) the letter to the Romans is both in form and function a *hortatory*, and more specifically, a *protreptic* letter. He finds no specific definition of the protreptic letter in any ancient theorist or rhetorician (1986:112). However, on the basis of Aristotle's *Protreptica* and Cicero's *Hortensius*, he defines protreptic in a semi-technical way as 'those writings which fall broadly into the tradition of *protreptikoi logoi* (protreptic speeches)' (1986:113), that is, exhortations to take up the philosophical life (1986:113). Protreptic works urge the reader to convert to a way of life, to join a school or to accept a set of teachings as normative for the reader's life. Protreptic speeches can be traced back to the Sophists who tried thereby to win students to their schools and to the wisdom which they taught. According to Stowers (1986:113), protreptic writings were important to early Christianity because of their strong missionary impulse. Other examples of Christian protreptic writings are Clement of Alexandria's *Protrepticus*, Tatian's *Oration against the Greeks*, and the *Epistle to Diognetos*.

Protreptic works varied according to writers' views of human nature and the human situation. Most protreptic works attempt not only to exhort their audience/recipients to a certain way of life (exhortation) but also to turn them away from a certain way of life (admonition). According to Epictetus, (*Discourses* 3.23) the genuine protreptic work does not use the flattering invitation of epideictic rhetoric. Genuine protreptic must make the hearers realize their evil plight, cast aside self-conceit, come to their senses, and recognize their need for a teacher. Stowers (1986:113) finds this equation of the protreptic process with the achievement of self-knowledge already in the protreptic speech of Socrates in Plato's *Euthydemus*.

Stowers supports his identification of Romans as a protreptic letter as follows: in this letter Paul introduces the Romans to his gospel, and at the same time he presents himself as a master teacher. Therefore the letter serves as an introduction and invitation to the teaching Paul hopes to do in Rome. His polemic against Judaism is particularly protreptic. Furthermore, he censures, in protreptic manner, the arrogance and pretentiousness that prevent Jews and Gentiles from accepting his gospel to the Gentiles (see Rom 2:1-6, 17-24; 3:1-9; 3:27 - 4:2; 9:9-21; 11:13-32; 14:4, 10). If we accept this identification of the type of the letter to the Romans, it follows that the social action performed by Paul by means of this letter is to exhort his readers to a specific (new) way of life and to accept a set of teachings, that is, the gospel as he understood it.

There are indications in the letter that Paul envisioned some kind of teaching activity for himself in Rome. He writes that he and his recipients will be 'mutually encouraged' (συμπαρακληθῆναι) whenever they meet personally (1:12) (perhaps a polite way to refer to his envisioned teaching activity?). More directly, he foresees that he will preach the gospel to them (1:15) — which usually encompasses a teaching activity. He foresees that, although he will see them 'in passing' (διαπορευόμενος) to Spain, he will stay for some time with them (ἐὰν ὑμῶν πρῶτον ἀπὸ μέρους ἐμπλησθῶ, 15:24). He hopes to have time to engage in teaching activities. In obedience to his calling as apostle, he intends to go to Spain to preach the gospel. This does not rule out that he will also 'minister' to the Romans, that is, preach and teach the gospel to them. It is important, however, to emphasize that the teaching situation foreseen when he visits them is not identical with what he was already in fact actually doing by writing the letter (e.g., a short letter from somebody to invite you to an academic lecture is a letter of invitation, not an academic lecture).

Aune (1987:219) disagrees with the identification of the letter as protreptic. He argues that Romans was not intended to present the gospel to the recipients for the purpose of converting them to the Christian faith. The aim of the elaborate and complex presentation of the gospel (Romans 1-11) was to enable the recipients to understand more about it. Aune understands the letter as *epideictic* in intention (that is, reflection on views held by the author unconnected with the actual situation of his recipients). He refines the picture by arguing that Romans must be understood on two levels: in the epistolary situation of Romans, the presentation of the gospel (both in the 'theological' argumentation, chapters 1-11, and the paraenetic section, 12:1 - 15:13) is epideictic; in the prior setting of his ministry of preaching and teaching it was protreptic.

Aune (1987:219) maintains that the views set forth in Romans must have been developed by Paul during many years prior to the writing of the letter. With the epistolary type characterized in this way, it follows that the social action performed by the letter was to give an exposition of views held by Paul in order that the already existing Christian faith of the recipients might be encouraged and strengthened. I submit that we must go one step further: the letter does not merely intend to strengthen the existing values of the recipients; it does so with the more particular aim to ensure their cooperation for Paul's future plans to preach the gospel in Spain. This position will become clearer when we consider the epistolary situation of Romans.

At this stage, however, it is already possible to point out tentatively some of the implications of the epistolary type and social action for the interpretation of Romans 13:1-7. The exhortations with regard to the authorities are manifestations of Paul's own ethical code, rather than direct commands or appeals to the addressees to follow a certain course of action. It is in the first place an exposition of Paul's own views on Christian relations with the authorities. This does not rule out that, as a secondary goal, he also might have considered it a wise course of action for his addressees in their particular situation. This is a preliminary conclusion, to be refined when we consider the epistolary situation.

6.3   Epistolary situation of the Letter to the Romans and its implications for the interpretation of Romans 13:1-7

6.3.1   Introductory remarks: epistolary situation and historical situation

The epistolary situation must not be confused with the actual historical situation or occasion which caused the letter to be written. The epistolary situation is primarily a *text-internal, literary phenomenon*. It is the situation created by the structural framework that identifies the writing as a letter. Important elements of this structural framework are the inscribed communicative axis, represented by the role of narrator/narratee and the I-you personal deixis, and the specific characteristics of temporal and spatial deixis in a letter (see §6.3.3 below). While the epistolary situation as a literary projection does refer to a life situation characterized by spatial and temporal separation between correspondents, its primary function is to provide a framework for the interpretation of the letter and not to 'reconstruct' its historical occasion (Dippenaar 15). The distinction between the 'real world' and the 'world of the text' (which I have already introduced briefly in §4.6) now becomes directly relevant. Some of the results of the historical-critical investigation of the problem of the occasion of Romans, and particularly Romans 13:1-7, are summarized here in an *excursus* since this does not form part of our present purpose, namely, a literary reading of Romans 13:1–7. The purpose of this excursus is to illustrate the difference between a 'historical' and a 'literary' approach to the occasion and purpose of Romans.

Excursus: Historical occasion of Romans and Romans 13:1–7

It is clear from the formal analysis (§5.2) that Romans quite obviously exhibits the formal characteristics of a letter. However, there is a long tradition in the history of its interpretation which questions the assumption that it is indeed a letter. With his characterization of Romans as a *christianae religionis compendium*, that is, an abstract theological summary and not a real letter that originated in particular historical circumstances, Melanchton *(Loci communes 2.1, 7)* established a conception that has dominated the study of Romans for many generations, and that only came under fire in twentieth century historical-critical scholarship (see Donfried 1977b:x–xvii).

In the historical-critical line of questioning, it becomes of utmost importance to decide whether Romans was indeed a real letter or perhaps something else. In historical-critical terminology (indicated with italics in the following quotation), Donfried (1977b:xi) states the importance of this issue as follows: '. . . the implications and challenge of New Testament scholarship for the twentieth century can *only* be made clear when one knows the *setting* of each New Testament book in its *original context*. In other words, if one does not know the *original intention* of a document one can hardly interpret its contemporary meaning with *accuracy* and *precision*' (my italics). On the basis of this assumption, Donfried (1977b:xvii) concludes: 'Obviously, Romans will have a very different meaning if it was conceived by Paul as an eternally valid summary of his theological position, or, if he conceived it as a response to an actual, acute problem of the first century . . . .' In recognition of the importance which is ascribed to this problem, the so-called 'Romans debate' has evolved, where a whole range of solutions were offered to solve the basic question: Why did Paul write Romans? (see the essays in Donfried 1977). As yet, there is no agreement what this 'actual, acute problem of the first century' might have been.

Commentators like A. Nygren and T. W. Manson continued in the line of Melanchton by interpreting Romans as a doctrinal treatise, so also G. Bornkamm with his characterization of Romans as Paul's 'last will and testament.' A purely dogmatic understanding of Romans, however, is not seriously considered today. G. Klein maintains that Paul wrote Romans to establish the apostolic foundation that was still lacking in the Christian communities in Rome. Both J. Jervell and R. J. Karris argue that the reason for Romans was *Paul's own existential situation*, and not that of the community in Rome: Paul wrote the letter because he sought the support of the Roman Christians when he would have to face the Christians in Jerusalem in due course (Klein), and Romans was not written to address a conflict between Jewish Christians and Gentile Christians (identified by P. Minear as respectively 'the weak' and 'the strong') (Karris). Others like W. Weifel and K. Donfried (1977a) look to *the actual situation in Rome* for an explanation as to why Paul wrote the letter. Wedderburn (142) surveys the arguments for each of these differing positions and opts for a compromise, a 'cluster of interlocking factors' why Romans was written: '. . . the presence of both Judaizing and Law-free Christians in the church there, the present situation of the church in Rome and the present situation of Paul, the visit to Jerusalem now being undertaken and the prospect of a future visit to Rome.'

Interpreters have made a number of proposals for the specific historical occasion of Romans 13:1-7.

Käsemann (1969:196-216) argues that there were 'enthusiasts' in Rome who propagated that obedience to earthly societal structures had become irrelevant for them since they had become Christians, citizens of a heavenly *polis*. Against this background Paul warns in 12:3 against pompousness (a possible allusion to the enthusiasts) and urges his readers in 12:6 to humbleness. In 13:1-7 he explicitly warns them that they still have to live and function within earthly structures.

Friedrich, Pöhlmann and Stuhlmacher (153-159) argue from a remark of Tacitus (*Annales*, XIII, 50) that Nero had made major tax reforms in 58 C.E., that there had been problems and tensions in the application of the indirect taxes (τὸ τέλος) during the immediately preceding years — that is, the time when Paul wrote his letter to the Romans. These problems were caused by the abuses of the revenue collectors. Some of the people of the Christian communities were of the commercial class and would have been exactly those most affected by the revenue abuses of the middle fifties. Friedrich *et al.* argue that Paul was urging his readers in Rome to pay all the taxes for which they were obligated, the direct taxes (ὁ φόρος) as well as the controversial indirect taxes (τὸ τέλος), in order that they may not suffer (again) an expulsion from Rome as had happened to the Jews a few years earlier (49 C.E.) under the edict of Claudius. He did this because he was eager to get to Rome — the capital of the world of the first century — and to be received by the Christians there, because of his recognition of the importance such a visit would have for his own mission (see also Furnish 1985:133-134).

Borg (205-218) explains Romans 13:1-7 against the background of Jewish nationalism. When Romans was written (55-56 C.E.) conflict had been simmering for decades and in 66-70 it finally exploded in the Roman-Jewish war. The edict of Claudius in 49 C.E., ordering all Jews to leave Rome, gives evidence that the Jews in Rome were also causing trouble. It is possible that Jewish messianic expectations (according to which the Jews would be liberated from Roman oppression) were promulgated by Jewish nationalists in Rome. Since Judaism and Christianity were at this stage still closely interwoven (for which there is much evidence in the Letter to the Romans), it was hardly possible for Christians to escape the Roman-Jewish conflict — although they did not any longer share the political and violent messianic expectations of the militant Jewish groups. If the Roman authorities acted again against the Jews, as they did in 49, that would also seriously harm the Jewish and Gentile Christians in Rome. Therefore, for their own good as well as for his own missionary ideals which involved the Roman Christians, Paul warned them in Romans 13:1-7 to conform with rather than to confront the Roman authorities.

Wedderburn's proposal (for the historical occasion of Romans) and a combination of Friedrich *et al.* and Borg's proposals (for the historical occasion of specifically Romans 13:1-7) are perhaps as far as one can get with such a historical line of questioning. The limits of this approach have been demonstrated convincingly by Petersen (1978:24-48), W. S. Vorster (1984a) and J. N. Vorster (1991:3-16). Leaving the historical question aside, we again turn our attention to the epistolary situation of the letter.

6.3.2 *Analysis of the epistolary situation in terms of ancient epistolary categories*

According to Koskenniemi three literary elements constitute the epistolary situation of the ancient letter, namely, φιλοφρόνησις, παρουσία and ὁμιλία (see §4.4). Consideration of how these elements function in the case of Romans will provide us with a framework from which implications for the interpretation of Romans 13:1-7 can be drawn.

6.3.2.1 Epistolary φιλοφρόνησις in the Letter to the Romans

The degree and type of 'friendship' shared by the correspondents are usually expressed in the opening and closing conventions of the letter (Koskenniemi 128, 148; White 1986:219). The maintenance of contact (φιλοφρόνησις) in Romans is somewhat peculiar since it is indicated that the addresser has not previously met the communities to whom he wrote (see 1:13 and 15:22-23). Therefore, an important feature of this letter's epistolary situation is that it has as its aim to *establish* contact and not to maintain existing contact. This situation is perhaps one of the reasons for the exceptionally long self-introduction of the addresser in the letter-opening (1:1-6), the thanksgiving (1:8-12) and the self-recommendation (1:13-15). Paul wants to make it clear to the recipients exactly who he is and what his credentials are: he introduces himself as a servant of Jesus Christ and an apostle for the gospel of God (with an elaboration on the nature of this gospel as he sees it, 1:2-5). He has not appointed himself as an apostle, but his apostleship is a gift (χάρις) which he has received (ἐλάβομεν) (1:5). The recipients are included among those to whom he must, in obedience to the One who appointed him, serve as an apostle: 'you also are among them' (ἐν οἷς ἐστε καὶ ὑμεῖς, 1:6). He wants them to know that he always prays for them (1:9-10). Among the credentials he mentions in his self-recommendation is the fact that he has often intended to visit them (1:13), that it is not of his own doing that he has not yet been able to do so (1:13) and that he is eager (τὸ κατ᾽ ἐμὲ πρόθυμον) to preach the gospel to them (1:15).

The recipients are localized as 'all who are in Rome' (πᾶσιν τοῖς οὖσιν ἐν 'Ρώμῃ, 1:7), further characterized as κλητοὶ 'Ιησοῦ Χριστοῦ (1:6), as ἀγαπητοῖς θεοῦ (1:7) and as κλητοῖς ἁγίοις (1:7). The religious nature of the epistolary setting is indicated both by the important religious terms with which the addresser and addressees are characterized (δοῦλος Χριστοῦ 'Ιησοῦ, κλητοί, ἀγαπήτοι, ἅγιοι et cetera), but more particularly by the thanksgiving. The relationship between the correspondents is in the first place (πρῶτον, 1:8) characterized by a situation in which God is thanked by the addresser for certain qualities of the addressees. The thanksgiving is a peculiar Pauline deviation from the *proskunema*-formula and statements of remembrance (see Doty). As such it represents some of the most typical philophronetic phrases of ancient letters (see Koskenniemi 139ff). These philophronetic characterizations of addresser and addressee in the letter-opening are important indicators of the epistolary situation of Romans.

Typical of ancient letter-conventions (see Koskenniemi 148ff; White 1986:219), more indications of the 'friendship' relation are given at the closing of the letter (15:13 - 16:24). A good example of philophronetic elements in the letter-closing is the confidence-formula in 15:14: Paul emphasizes that he himself (αὐτὸς ἐγώ) has confidence (πέπεισμαι) in his recipients. The basis of his confidence is three characteristics that he ascribes to them, namely, that they are full of goodness (μεστοί ἐστε ἀγαθωσύνης), filled with knowledge (πεπληρωμένοι πάσης {τῆς} γνώσεως) and able to instruct one another (δυνάμενοι καὶ ἀλλήλους νουθετεῖν). This is another clear indication of Paul's goodwill and positive attitude towards the recipients.

The exceptionally long list of people to whom greetings are conveyed at the end of the letter (16:3-16a) is perhaps also due to the specific epistolary situation of not having been personally acquainted with the Roman communities previously: Paul wants to overcome this complicating factor of the epistolary situation by indicating that he, in fact, does know a whole number of people who were, according to his knowledge at the time of the writing of the letter, at that stage among the recipients of the letter. These people are greeted with a very positive attitude and by means of the most explicit philophronetic terminology (for more examples of this terminology in ancient Greek letters, see Koskenniemi 128-130): Epaenetus, Ampliatus, Stachus and Persis are characterized as ἀγαπητοί of Paul; Andronicus, Junias and Herodion as συγγενεῖς and συναιχμαλώτους; Urbanus as συνεργόν; Apelles as δόκιμον ἐν Χριστῷ; Rufus as τὸν ἐκλεκτὸν ἐν κυρίῳ; others as ἀδελφοί and ἅγιοι. From this it is clear that he wants to maintain and promote good relations with those in the community whom he already knows. This factor, however, does not change the more fundamental characteristic feature of the epistolary situation, namely, that he was not previously acquainted with the recipients and that the letter serves to establish and promote such an acquaintance.

By introducing himself as an 'apostle' in the letter-opening as well as through the elaborate implementation of the 'apostolic *parousia*' (see the analysis of 15:15-32 in §5.2), Paul indicates that he sees himself in a *position of authority* in relation to his recipients. Although he does not know them, this authoritative position enables him 'to dare to write rather boldly to them' (τολμηρότερον δὲ ἔγραψα ὑμῖν, 15:15). The implications of this feature of the epistolary situation for the interpretation of Romans 13:1-7 will be discussed in §6.3.3.2

6.3.2.2 *Epistolary παρουσία in the Letter to the Romans*

According to White (1986:219) the sense of presence (the παρουσία) is most often communicated in the body of the letter, usually towards the end. In

Romans this aspect of epistolary presence is found in the section which White (1972:59) calls the 'body-closing' (15:15-33). Specific conventions in this regard in Romans which are in accord with the general practice of ancient Greco-Roman letter-writing are the following: Paul states his disposition and purpose (15:15-16); he states the basis of his apostolic relation to the recipients (15b-21), his desire and eagerness to see/come to them (15:23b) and his hope (ἐλπίζω) to see/to come to them (15:24b). Perhaps the most explicit and most characteristic feature (in terms of general ancient epistolary conventions) of the apostolic παρουσία in Romans is the announcement or promise of a visit (15:28b): ἀπελεύσομαι δι' ὑμῶν εἰς Σπανίαν. Paul invokes divine approval and support for this apostolic παρουσία: he appeals to them to pray for his presence (15:30-31) and uses the convention "if God will" (15:32): διὰ θελήματος θεοῦ. Finally, he indicates the benefit from the apostolic παρουσία accruing to himself (15:32b) — he will be refreshed in the company of the recipients.

Funk (258-261) observes that Paul made use of three methods to enforce his apostolic authority to persuade recipients into adopting his prescribed course of action, namely, an apostolic letter, an apostolic messenger or an apostolic visit. The theory that Phoebe, 'commended' (συνίστημι) in 16:1, was to serve as apostolic messenger to the recipients of the letter to the Romans is widely held (see Schnider & Stenger 101-102). Therefore, in the situation envisioned by the letter and in his desire to make a personal visit to them, she had to represent him. The commendation of Phoebe is therefore another example of the epistolary παρουσία in the letter to the Romans.

6.3.2.3 Epistolary ὁμιλία in the letter to the Romans

In addition to the maintenance (or establishment) of contact, two other basic characteristics of the ancient letter are the desire to communicate information and to state a request or a command (White 1986:218) — both are aspects of the ὁμιλία which characterize the epistolary situation. In Romans Paul is concerned to convey information. He uses the epistolary formula οὐ θέλω δὲ ὑμᾶς ἀγνοεῖν more than once (1:13; 11:25). He also makes requests; he appeals (παρακαλῶ) to the recipients to 'strive together with me in your prayers . . . that I may be delivered from the unbelievers in Judea' (15:30); he requests that they should 'receive' (προσδέξησθε) Phoebe and 'help' (παραστῆτε) her in whatever she may require from them (16:1-2); he appeals (παρακαλῶ) to them to 'take note' (σκοπεῖν) of those who create dissensions and difficulties and to 'avoid' (ἐκκλίνετε) them (16:17).

These are all examples of the communication of information and the making of requests at points where Paul is directly addressing his recipients, and where such a direct interaction is specifically indicated in the text (inter alia by the use of the personal pronouns 'I' and 'you'). The body of the letter, however, consists mainly of ὁμιλία where the relation between the addresser and addressee is more indirect. So for example, if he writes in 2:1 'therefore *you* have no excuse, O man,' there is a greater distance between this 'you' and the 'I' of the addressee than between the 'you' in 15:30, 16:1–2 and 16:17 and the 'I' of the addressee. This does not mean, however, that the recipients are excluded from the 'you' in 2:1 (and almost right through the body of the letter where this more general 'you' is used). The text-immanent literary reading of Romans (in §6.3.3) will contain a more detailed analysis of these deictic elements. At this stage it is enough to note that in general the body of Romans consists of the exchange of information and the conveying of requests, as specific characteristics of the ὁμιλία of the epistolary situation.

To summarize: the letter supposes a situation where an addresser, 'Paul,' writes a letter to addressees, identified as communities 'in Rome.' The relationship between them is based on (shared?) religious convictions. Although it seems as if the addresser knows some of the addressees with whom he seeks to maintain and promote cordial relations, the basic characteristic of the epistolary situation is that he wants to establish a relationship with his addressees, most of whom he has never met and does not know personally. One of the specific aims of this to-be-established relationship is to enlist their assistance for his personal plans to preach the gospel in new places, more particularly, Spain. To accomplish this aim, the addresser deems it necessary to give an elaborate exposition of how he understood this gospel. He is in a position of authority over his addressees, and that enables him to share information with them and to convey requests to them 'rather boldly' (15:15), although he writes primarily to obtain their cooperation for his own future plans.

From this a number of implications for the interpretation of Romans 13:1–7 can be drawn. The commands in Romans 13:1–7 ('every person should subject to the governing authorities,' 13:1; 'you must pay taxes,' 13:6; 'you must pay all your dues,' 13:7) should be seen against the background of a relationship that exhibits a certain duality. The one who gives the commands is in a rather delicate situation. On the one hand he is the disadvantaged one in the relationship: he does not know them personally, and he is the one who wants their cooperation for his personal plans. This is usually not the best position for someone who wants to give commands to others. Therefore, the influence of this particular situation in which the commands were given must be taken into account in the interpretation of the tone of the commands given in Romans 13:1–7 (see chapter 3, §7, for an analysis of these rhetorical aspects). On the other hand, because of the way in which Paul envisioned the religious nature of their relationship and because of the status which he ascribed to himself in terms of these religious convictions, Paul is in a position of authority over them. Therefore, he is in a position to give commands. To reflect this dual situation and its influence on the nature and tone of the 'commands,' the term 'exhortation' is more appropriate.

Another implication of our construction of the epistolary situation for the interpretation of Romans 13:1–7 is the decidedly *religious* nature of the basis of the to-be-established relationship between addresser and addressees. The exhortations to submit to the authorities and to pay taxes are not given by a (secular) governmental institution who would directly benefit from such a submission and the payment of taxes. These exhortations have a 'friendly' and 'advisory' character rather than being clinical, official and enforceable commands given by someone/somebody in a formal position of authority. The exhortations in Romans 13:1–7 are, in fact, part of a whole series of exhortations given in the latter part of the letter (12:1 – 15:13). These should therefore be understood against the background of this construction of the epistolary situation. More implications of these observations will become clear when the rhetorical dimensions of this text are analyzed (in chapter 3, §7).

6.3.3 Analysis of the epistolary situation in terms of modern epistolary categories

The point of departure for this section is well expressed by the following general observation of Classen (7):

> Wer Briefe interpretieren will, muß sich zunächst das Wesen und die Eigenart des Phänomens > Brief < als Mittel menschlicher Kommunikation verdeutlichen und bei der Interpretation die Vielfalt der möglichen Faktoren vergegenwärtigen, die Struktur und Ton des einzelnen Briefes bestimmen oder bestimmen können.

Classen's (7–9) subsequent exposition of 'was ein Brief eigentlich ist,' however, is simplistic since he seems to have a blind eye for the particularities of the *textuality* of letters. He equates the 'Empfängers' with the real addressees and the 'Schreiber' with the real author. He does not distinguish between the historical situation of the letter and its epistolary and rhetorical situations (see chapter 3, §5). Furthermore, for him the letter serves primarily to transfer *information*, disregarding the rhetorical and social *interaction* performed by letters.

A combination of the theoretical frameworks proposed by Violi and Altman is more suitable for our purposes. According to Violi (149) the determinative characteristic of the letter is its *communicative function*. The way in which this function is inscribed in the text identifies the letter as a specific genre. Although letters differ in structure, the basic frame of the letter as genre accounts for the inscribed communicative axis present in every letter.

The way in which *deixis* functions in the letter is of particular importance for the description of the meaning created and communicated by means of the letter genre (Violi 150). Levinson (54) defines 'deixis' as follows:

> Essentially, deixis concerns the ways in which languages encode or grammaticalize features of the *context of utterance* or *speech event*, and thus also concerns ways in which the interpretation of utterances depends on the analysis of that context of utterance.

Usually an interpreter distinguishes five types of deixis: *personal deixis* (that is, the identity of the interlocutors in a communication situation); *place deixis* (that is, the place in which these individuals are located); two types of *time deixis* (*encoding* time is the time at which the message is sent and *decoding* time is the time at which the message is received); *discourse deixis* (that is, the matrix of linguistic material within which the utterance has a role, namely the preceding and following parts of the discourse); and *social deixis* (that is, the social relationships of the participants in the conversation which determine, for example, the choice of honorific or polite or intimate or insulting speech levels) (see Fillmore 40 and Levinson 61–96). These different types of deixis can be identified and described in any discourse. Violi's point is, however, that the specific way in which the first three (personal, place and time deixis) function in a letter characterizes the letter as letter and provides the most appropriate means to describe and interpret a letter. Therefore, the following discussion considers aspects of the function of these three types of deixis in the letter to the Romans.

6.3.3.1 General characteristics of epistolary language

In order to provide a theoretical framework for the analysis of different types of deixis in letters, Violi (150) utilizes the fundamental distinction between *énonciation* (the 'utterance') and *énoncé* (the 'sentence' in the text). The situation in which the text is produced concretely and in which the categories of space and time and participating people are contained is called the *Situation of the Utterance*. This situation, however, is defined by the elements inscribed within the text itself, that is, by the *Situation of the Sentence*. The 'traces' that the 'real' addresser and addressee leave in the text refer to the 'utterance' and not to the 'sentence.' On this basis it is possible to distinguish between *discourse* as 'those linguistic productions whose description entails reference to the Situation of Utterance' and *story* as 'those linguistic productions whose description does not.'

Violi (151) argues that two fundamental characteristics of letters can be defined by using these categories: (i) letters are linguistic productions that belong to discourse rather than to historical narrative, and (ii) letters constitute a genre in which traces of the utterance (which separate discourse from story) are constitutive of the genre. For example, the subject of an utterance as it reveals itself in a letter must express itself in the first person — assuming the role of narrator (this is not the case with forms of discourse other than the letter, except perhaps for poetry written in the first person).

In the analysis of any literary text it is of fundamental importance to distinguish between the addresser as a real person (the empirical author of the text) and the narrator as a figure of discourse (a textual abstraction inscribed in the linguistic production). The same distinction holds true for empirical reader and narratee. As Violi (158) puts it:

> The communicative structure inscribed in the letter turns the figure of the narratee into simultaneously both a more concrete and a more ambiguous figure in that although on the one hand it can be defined in its textual configuration, it seems at the same time to be continually referring to an extratextual presence *which can not be reduced to a mere sum of the inscriptions in the text*' [my italics].

Violi (151) emphasizes that these distinctions are crucial in the analysis of letters for two reasons: (i) to prevent the real subjects (addresser and addressee) from being identified with the inscribed subjects (narrator and narratee) and (ii) to enable us to describe how both these processes of identification and their accompanying 'reality effects' are constituted in discourse.

Petersen (1978; 1985) is to be credited for bringing about in New Testament studies this awareness that the 'world' created by the text and the so-called 'real' world cannot be simplistically equated (see §4.6). Specific awareness of the *textuality* of letters has led to new levels of sophistication in the analysis of letters. In our analysis of deixis in Romans, these fundamental distinctions will therefore always be borne in mind. To reflect this distinction, I will from now on use the terms 'narrator' and 'narratee' (proposed by Violi 151), instead of the terms 'addresser' and 'addressee' used so far.

As general background for the analysis of deictic elements Altman's (186) observation that the letter is unique because it defines itself in terms of *polarities* is very illuminating. She (186–187) lists a number of the polar dimensions that characterize epistolary language:

* bridge/barrier — the letter is both a distance maker and a distance breaker. It is an instrument that both connects and interferes;
* confidence/non-confidence — a letter has a dual potential for transparency

(portrait of the soul,[12] confession, vehicle of narrative) and opacity (mask, weapon);

* writer/reader — the epistolary situation evokes simultaneously the acts of writing and reading, as correspondents alternate, even within the same letter, between the roles of narrator/narratee or encoder/decoder. The letter connotes privacy and intimacy; yet as a document addressed to another, the letter reflects the need for an audience. The audience may suddenly expand when the document is confiscated, shared, or published. Therefore *reader consciousness* explicitly informs the act of writing itself;
* I/you, here/there, now/then — (that is, personal, place and time deixis) in letters reflects a polarity characteristic of the letter genre. The letter writer is engaged in the impossible task of making present both events and narratee. To do so, he or she attempts to close the gap between his or her locus and the narratee's (here/there) and creates the illusion of the present (*now*) by oscillation between the *then* of past and future;
* discontinuation/continuation of writing — the potential for finality of the letter's signature and the open-endedness of the letter as a segment within a chain of dialogue.

Against the background of these general characteristics of the letter genre, I will now analyze three types of deixis as represented in the letter to the Romans. In each case the analysis will point out implications for Romans 13:1-7.

6.3.3.2 Personal deixis

Since each letter is written by someone whose appearance in the text is unavoidable, it is structurally impossible to eliminate the presence of the narrator in the letter. The narrator is marked by the signature — the most concrete trace of the subject's utterance. The presence of a specific narrator as an abstract moment of utterance is always announced in the text. Since the signature represents an 'anchorage' in the text which functions as a marker of the genre, the narrator's presence in a letter is more concrete than other forms of text narrated in the first person. In a letter the narrator is always in reality presented as complementary and co-present with the narratee (Violi 151). Although ancient conventions for signing letters differ from modern conventions, these differences do not influence the validity of this theoretical observation of the presence and function of the narrator in letters. The very first word in the Letter to the Romans serves as the 'signature' and 'anchorage' of the letter: Παῦλος.[13]

---

[12]This notion was widely held among ancient epistolographers: the letter reflects the personality of its writer (Cicero *Epistulae familiares* 16, 16, 2; Seneca *Epistulae Morales* 40, 1; Demosthenes *De Elocutione* 227; Philostratus *De Epistulis* II 257ff. See Malherbe [1988] for texts and translations).

[13]Another way in which ancient letters were 'signed' was the convention that authors themselves (instead of the amenuensis) sometimes wrote a few words at the end of letters,

The presence of the narratee in a letter is generally marked by an explicit form, either in the letter's opening ('Dear X') or in the pronominal structure ('I am writing to tell *you*') (Violi 1985:152). In the letter to the Romans, the narratee is marked (according to ancient convention), in the letter opening, πᾶσιν τοῖς οὖσιν ἐν Ῥώμῃ ἀγαπητοῖς θεοῦ (1:7), the repeated direct invocation of the narratees with the philophronetic term ἀδελφοί (1:13; 7:1, 4; 8:12; 10:1; 12:1; 15:14, 30; 16:17), as well as by the use of the second person plural throughout the letter (for example, χάρις ὑμῖν . . . 1:7; εὐχαριστῶ . . . περὶ πάντων ὑμῶν 1:8; μνείαν ὑμῶν ποιοῦμαι 1:9; παρακαλῶ οὖν ὑμᾶς 12:1; φόρους τελεῖτε 13:6; παρακαλῶ δὲ ὑμᾶς 16:17; etc.). In letters such an explicitly marked narrator/narratee alliance is a necessary condition for the identification of the genre (Violi 152).

Although Altman (117–141) does not use the term 'personal deixis,' she nevertheless provides a valuable theoretical description of exactly these elements in her description of the peculiarities of epistolary language. She maintains that epistolary discourse is distinguishable from other types of discourse 'by certain basic pronominal and predicative traits' (117). She calls the first such trait 'the particularity of the I-you in epistolary discourse.' The *I* of epistolary discourse always has as its (implicit or explicit) partner a specific *you* who stands in a unique relationship to the *I*. Epistolary language is a coded language (although it is not necessarily obscure), whose code is determined by the specific relationship of the *I-you*. The interpersonal bond is basic to the very language of the letter and necessarily structures meaning in letters (Altman 118).

The implications of this observation for the interpretation of New Testament letters are rather sobering: pushed to its logical extreme, epistolary language can be so relative to its *I-you* that it would be unintelligible to an outside reader (Altman 120). Or as Violi (159) puts it, 'the letter personalizes its relationship with its own addressee to a maximum: the *shared knowledge* of addresser and addressee can be *highly idiosyncratic.*' Depending on the degree of the shared information between the *I* and the *you* that is not explicitly indicated in the letter itself, letters may be more or less intelligible to an outsider. In addition to the cultural and linguistic distance between us and the New Testament, this specific feature of letters should make us humble in our claims on the meaning New Testament letters might have had for their original recipients. Lars Hartman has written an informative essay on

---

for example Philemon 19, ἐγὼ Παῦλος ἔγραψα τῇ ἐμῇ χειρί (see also Galatians 6:11). On the originals of ancient letters, different handwritings can be clearly noticed in cases like these. Although Romans was written by an amenuensis (16:22, ἀσπάζομαι ὑμᾶς ἐγὼ Τέρτιος ὁ γράψας τὴν ἐπιστολὴν ἐν κυρίῳ), there is no evidence, however, of this practice in the letter to the Romans.

the implications on this problem, aptly titled 'On reading others' letters' (Hartman). In the context of this study's plea for an ethics of reading, this sobering thought is very important: it should urge us to be even more cautious when we want to infer any ethical implications for our own situation from New Testament letters.

In the letter to the Romans, a specific relationship between the epistolary *I* (identified as Paul) and *you* (identified as Christian communities in the city of Rome) is clearly marked and maintained throughout the letter. The *I-you* structure is, in accordance with ancient epistolary conventions, most explicitly present in the letter-opening and the letter-closing. Although the greater part of the body of the letter consists of theological reflection, a sense of 'presence' for the *I-you* is maintained by the repeated direct invocation, ἀδελφοί (1:13; 7:1, 4; 8:12; 10:1; 12:1; 15:14, 30; 16:17).

The pronominal structure upholds the basic communicative axis of the letter. For example, the first explicit pronominal reference to the epistolary *I* is in the first person *plural* 'we' (1:5).[14] In the rest of the letter-opening (particularly the thanksgiving and self-recommendation, 1:8–15), as well as in the letter-closing (15:13 – 16:23), the narrator uses the first person singular ('I' or 'me') repeatedly. The second person plural (ὑμεῖς and its derivatives) consistently indicates the epistolary *you*. The distance between the epistolary *I* and *you* is bridged by, among others things, the use of the first person plural to *include* both the epistolary *I* and the *you*, for example, the προεχόμεθα and προῃτιασάμεθα in 3:9, the εἰρήνην ἔχομεν in 5:1, and the 'we' in the hymnic language in 8:31–38.

A particularly interesting phenomenon in Romans is the difference in distance between the interlocutors created by the personal deixis in the letter. In the letter-opening and letter-closing, the personal deixis refers more or less consistently to the narrator and narratees themselves. In different sections of the letter-body an 'internal' communicative axis is created by means of the so-called imaginary interlocutor, typical of the diatribe-style.[15] Within the conversation represented by the epistolary frame, another conversation takes place. So, for example, the 'you' in 2:1, 2:17 and particularly the well-known 'I' of Romans 7:14ff do not refer to the epistolary narratees or narrator.

---

[14]The rhetorical implications of this plural instead of the singular are analyzed in detail by J. N. Vorster (1991).

[15]For our argument here we need not enter the debate on the diatribe in Romans, which after Bultmann's (1910) study was recently revived with two doctoral theses on the subject (Stowers 1981 and Schmeller 1987). In this context we only note the literary phenomenon of a 'conversation within a conversation' as represented by the diatribe in Romans.

In Romans 13:1–7 the personal deixis follows a particular pattern that has implications for a literary interpretation of this passage. The paraenetic section (12:1 – 15:13) which frames 13:1–7 is introduced with explicit personal deictic markers, παρακαλῶ οὖν ὑμᾶς, ἀδελφοί (12:1). This 'I' and the 'you, brothers' refer to the epistolary *I* and *you*, or narrator and narratees. Within this framework, the first section of Romans 13:1–3 uses only non-deictics[16] in the *third person*: 'let *every person* be subject' (ὑποτασσέσθω — present imperative third person singular), '*he* who resists' (ὁ ἀντιτασσόμενος — present participle nominative singular masculine), '*those* who resist will incur' (λήμψονται — future indicative active third person plural). This is an indication of the general, gnomic, nature of these statements. Not only the narratees of the letter are involved here, but a broader, general audience.

In the next section, Romans 13:3b–4, a conversation takes place *within* the discourse of the epistolary narrator/narratee communicative axis. The 'addressees' of this conversation are indicated with non-deictic elements in the *second person singular*: 'would *you* have no fear?' (θέλεις δὲ μὴ φοβεῖσθαι — present indicative second person singular), 'do good' (τὸ ἀγαθὸν ποίει — present imperative second person singular), '*you* shall receive praise' (ἕξεις — future indicative second person singular), the authority is God's servant 'for *your* good' (σοὶ εἰς τὸ ἀγαθόν), 'if *you* do wrong' (ἐὰν δὲ κακὸν ποιῇς — present subjunctive active second person singular), 'fear!' (φοβοῦ — present imperative medium second person singular). Note that the second person *singular* is used consistently. Although the narratees are therefore not directly addressed, the use of the second person and, specifically, the use of the singular, serves rhetorically to create a sense of intimacy and closeness (for more on these rhetorical implications, see chapter 3). Yet it is important to remember that this singular 'you' may not be identified directly with the epistolary *you*, the narratees of the letter.

In the summary statement (13:5) an impersonal third person is implied, 'therefore it is obligatory to be subject' (διὸ ἀνάγκη ὑποτάσσεσθαι). The third person is only implied here and not marked with explicit morphological markers. This may be taken again as an indication of the gnomic character of the statement, but this time perhaps even more 'general' in nature as was the

---

[16]Levinson (66) explains the difference between deictic and non-deictic usages of the same word or morphemes by means of the following examples:

(a) *You*, *you*, but not *you*, are dismissed.
(b) What did *you* say?
(c) *You* can never tell what sex they are nowadays.

The first two sentences are examples of the deictic and the last one the non-deictic use of the pronoun *you*. The use of the pronomina in Romans 13:1–5 is similar with the third sentence, and they are therefore labelled 'non-deictics.'

case in 1:1–3a where explicit third person non-deictics were present. This change in the pronominal structure also serves as a marker of closure for the end of the theoretical reflection of which the first sections of the passage consist. The absence of any explicit deictics in 13:1–5 marks this section as gnomic in nature.

It is only in the final section of the passage (13:6–7) that explicit personal deictics return. The second person plural is used consistently, 'you (must?) pay taxes' (τελεῖτε — present indicative [or imperative?] active second person plural), and, 'you must pay all your dues' (ἀπόδοτε — present imperative second person plural). This ἀπόδοτε governs the rest of verse 7, where four possible dues to be paid are specified. In this last section, therefore, the personal deictics refer to the narratees of the letter on the level of the relationship specified in the letter-opening and letter-closing, as it was re-emphasized by the personal deictics in Romans 12:1.

With its structure of personal deixis, therefore, Romans 13:1–7 presents a picture of diminishing distance between the interlocutors. From general gnomic statements (presented initially in the third person and then explained in a sort of 'impersonal second person'), the narrator zooms in on his narratees by invoking them directly in the last section of the passage.

One final observation about personal deixis: Altman (121) stresses the crucial importance of reciprocity in the epistolary *I-you*. She observes that the moment of reception of letters is as important and as self-consciously portrayed as the act of writing: 'In no other form of dialogue does the speaker await a reply so breathlessly; in no other type of verbal exchange does the mere fact of receiving or not receiving a response carry such meaning.' This was perhaps even more true of ancient letters, considering the effort it must have been to produce and deliver a letter (see White 1986:213–214). The ancient epistolary convention identified by White (1972:60) as the 'confidence formula' bears witness to this characteristic of letters. The narrator expresses his or her confidence and conviction that the letter will invoke the appropriate response. In our formal analysis (§5.2), Romans 15:14 was identified as a confidence formula (πέπεισμαι δέ, ἀδελφοί μου, καὶ αὐτὸς ἐγὼ περὶ ὑμῶν, ὅτι καὶ αὐτοὶ μεστοί ἐστε ἀγαθωσύνης, πεπληρωμένοι πάσης {τῆς} γνώσεως, δυνάμενοι καὶ ἀλλήλους νουθετεῖν). Depending on how the letter-type and social action are explained (protreptic or epideictic) (see §5.3), the relationship of this formula to the paraenetic section of the letter can be explained in two ways. If the letter is seen as protreptic, the confidence formula expresses confidence for reciprocity on the part of the narratees with a life-style corresponding to the exhortations given in the paraenesis. An actual pattern of behavior with the regard to the authorities, namely that of obedience/submission (Romans 13:1–7), is the reciprocity expected/hoped for by the narrator. If the letter is seen as epideictic, however, these exhortations focus on the narrator and not the narratees. The reciprocity longed for/hoped for in this case is another level, namely the support of the narratees for the narrator's personal plans. For this the credibility of the narrator needs to be established. The kind of attitude towards authorities promoted by Romans 13:1-7 serves as 'credential' for the narrator: in his perception the narratees would find it acceptable to identify themselves with such an attitude towards governing authorities. Because they can identify with him on these (and all the other issues he has raised, specifically in the paraenetic section of the letter), they will respond favorably and cooperate with him in his future plans. By doing this the longed-for reciprocity of the letter will be fulfilled.

6.3.3.3 Time and place deixis

Place deixis encodes spatial locations on coordinates anchored to the place of utterance, and time deixis encodes times on coordinates anchored in the time of utterance (Levinson 62). The possible implications of these deictic phenomena for our interpretation of Romans 13:1-7 may best be introduced with a few observations on the processes of space-time referentiality in letters as described by Violi (152-157) and Altman (122-141). A specific feature which separates letters from other forms of discourse (for example, the diary) is the setting up of a distance within the text, separating both the narrator from the narratee, and the time and place of the narrator from the time and place of the narratee. The letter's system of time and place localization refers to the 'here' and 'now' of narration, and consequently, we find explicit references to it. But *also* inscribed in a letter are *the time and locus of the narratee*, that is, reference to the 'here' and 'now' of the reading of the letter. The future time and place of the reading are anticipated within the text. In this case the focalization moves on to the narratee. Altman (127) speaks of the 'Janus-like' character of epistolary language: it is grounded in a present that looks out toward past and future. 'Now' defines itself relative to a retrospective or anticipated 'then.' This modality which describes the *distance* between time and place of narration and time and place of reading is more specifically inscribed in the letter than in any other text. This distance is a constitutive element in that it is often the main reason the letter exists in the first place (Violi 156).

The addressee has to activate the addresser's structure of utterance by interpreting it and subsequently reconstructing the 'presence' of the Situation of Utterance. This effect is very characteristic of the letter: it produces an *effect* of *immediacy* (or, as the ancients called it, παρουσία, see §6.3.2.2) derived from particular textual strategies. This effect runs parallel to another effect, the effect of *distance*. Two situations are inscribed in the text (narration and reception-reading) — this characteristic determines a simultaneous presence in the text of a *double reference to the time and locus* of both narrator and narratee. Thus, letters create two effects: the 'effect of presence' or 'reality effect,' and the communicative axis between addresser and addressee which produces a parallel complementary effect of distance (see Altman 187).

Now, to turn to our passage. There are no explicit time or space deictics in Romans 13:1-7 itself. However, the passage is embedded within a letter, and a whole network of discourse deictics (such as the γάρ in 12:1) links it with the rest of the letter. A few remarks with regard to the space and time deictics in the letter as a whole are therefore needed to provide a framework for the interpretation of space and time categories presupposed and implied in Romans 13:1-7.

Typical of epistolary language, there is a distance both in space and time between the narrator and narratees in the letter to the Romans. The narratees were not present at the time of utterance, that is, when the letter was written. The narrator, Paul, wants to visit the narratees in a time future to his writing (encoding time) of the letter as well as future to their receiving of it (decoding time). Consideration of a number of explicit space deictics in Romans will be helpful to get a picture of the space-time processes presupposed by the letter. Other than modern conventions (with the addresser's address and date of the letter at the top), no indication of the time and place of utterance is given in Romans. The location of the narratees, however, is indicated with an explicit space deictic, 'Rome.' This provides a fixed point in terms of which the other detail of the narrators past movements and future ideals can be explained. Perhaps a rather superficial[17] construction of the 'story' (i.e. the actions represented in 'chronological' time sequence) behind this letter will be helpful to point out the relations between the different places and actions (see Petersen 1985:43-88 on the theory and practice of this move 'from letter to story').

---

[17]It is superficial since only the space and time deictics that are of direct relevance in terms of the epistolary situation are taken into account for the construction of the 'story.' More implicit deictics, such as the references to the past (for example, Abraham in Romans 4 and Adam in Romans 5), to the future (for example, 'the day that is at hand,' Romans 13:12), the narrator's and narratees' places within this broader framework, and the way in which they are plotted in the poetic sequence of the letter are not taken into account.

Story time	*Plotted time*
1 Paul works 'from Jerusalem and as far as around Illyricum' (15:19)	2
2 During this period and in this region (specifically in Macedonia and Achaia), he collects offerings for the Christians in Jerusalem (15:26)	6
3 He writes a letter to the Christian communities in Rome (15:15)	1
4 He goes to Jerusalem to give the collected offering to the people there (15:28)	3
5 The letter is received in Rome	
6 The Romans respond favorably to the letter	
7 Paul visits Rome and stays there for a while (15:24)	4
8 Paul's anticipated visit to Spain (with the help of the Roman Christians) (15:24, 28) takes place	5

Actions 4 and 5 may happen the other way around or simultaneously. Action 3 represents the time and place of utterance. Actions 1 and 2 precede it and actions 4–8 are subsequent to it.

In terms of this framework, the implicit time deictics in Romans 13:1-7 may be explained. Both instances of direct appeals to the narratees (13:6, 7) are given in the *present tense*: τελεῖτε and ἀπόδοτε. The time of these 'payments' relative to the time of the situation of utterance (action 3) or the situation of reception (action 5) is not specified. This is very important, because the vagueness in time deixis indicates that it is not a new action which the narrator expects from his narratees in reaction to his letter. Nor is it explicitly marked as an action in which the narratees had been engaged prior to the situations of utterance and reception, or, whether or not they were still doing so at the time of reception. The fact that the time for the fulfillment of these exhortations in relation to the time of utterance is not specified (as the visits to Jerusalem, Rome and Spain are) confirms their gnomic nature. The payment of taxes and dues is a natural consequence of submission to the authorities, which in its turn is argued in even more gnomic terms in 13:1-5. None of the explicit space deictics identified above (Rome, Jerusalem, Spain) has any particular relevance for the interpretation of Romans 13:1-7, except that it provides a general locus for the world created by the text. An analysis of that 'world' will take us beyond the *literary* perspective of this chapter.

7. Summary and conclusions

The aim of this chapter was to provide a reading of Romans 13:1-7 from a literary perspective. Since 'literary' is such a wide-ranging term, a number of concepts were clarified, and the focus for this particular literary reading was set (§2). This was followed by a brief overview of the impact of modern literary theory on New Testament studies (§3) and a more elaborate overview of the current study of New Testament letters as literary documents (§4).

On the basis of this background material and historical overviews, a literary reading of Romans 13:1-7 was subsequently undertaken. Romans was analyzed as a literary letter from a formalistic perspective in order to identify the place of Romans 13:1-7 within the letter as a whole (§5.2). The formal characteristics of Romans 13:1-7 as Paraenetic Literature was subsequently analyzed (§5.3). After the formal analysis was completed, I indicated the need for and limits of such a formal literary analysis within the context of my particular position on the ethics of reading. Since I have indicated that an ethics of reading necessitates a reading that moves beyond formal analysis, Romans 13:1-7 was subsequently read in terms of a communicative approach, although still within a literary perspective. This reading consisted of a description of the letter-type and the possible social action performed by the letter to the Romans (§6.2) as well as an analysis and description of the epistolary situation created and presupposed by the letter (§6.3).

Proposals to identify Romans as protreptic or epideictic were considered and preference was given to view it as epideictic with, however, an important qualification: the letter does not merely intend to strengthen the existing values of the recipients, it does so with the more particular aim that, by being strengthened in these values, the cooperation of the recipients for Paul's personal future plans will be ensured. For this identification of the possible social action performed by the letter, a clear and consistent distinction between a pure textual approach and a mixture of textual and historical considerations was not possible.

In line with developments in the literary study of New Testament material, the final phase of the analysis consistently followed a textual approach in order to describe the intra-textual communication in the letter. The difference between such an approach and a historical approach was illustrated and the concept of the 'epistolary situation' as textual construct was explained (§6.3.1). Following this the epistolary situation was analyzed both in terms of ancient (§6.3.2) and modern (§6.3.3) epistolary categories. From this analysis the following conclusions have been drawn:

* The commands given to the recipients in Romans 13:1-7 should be seen against the background of a relationship that exhibits a duality. The one who gives the commands (the narrator, Paul) is in a delicate situation. On the one hand he is disadvantaged in the relationship: he does not know the narratees personally, and he is the one who wants their cooperation for his personal plans. Therefore the influence of this particular situation in which the commands were given must be taken into account in the interpretation of the tone of the commands given in Romans 13:1-7. On the other hand, because of the way in which Paul envi-

sioned the religious nature of their relationship and because of the status which he ascribed to himself in terms of these religious convictions, Paul is in a position of authority over them. Therefore, he is in a position to give commands. To reflect this dual situation and its influence on the nature and tone of the 'commands,' it is better to use the term 'exhortation' rather than 'command' for the utterances in Romans 13:1-7.

* Romans 13:1-7 should be read against the decidedly *religious* nature of the basis of the to-be-established relationship between narrator and narratees. The exhortations to submit to the authorities and to pay taxes are not given by some or other secular governmental institution who could benefit from such a submission and the payment of taxes. Therefore these exhortations have a 'friendly' and 'advisory' character rather than being clinical, official and enforceable commands given by someone/somebody in a formal, secular position of authority.

* The personal deixis in Romans 13:1-7 presents a picture of diminishing distance between the interlocutors. From general gnomic statements, the narrator narrows the focus on his narratees by invoking them directly in the last section of the passage.

* The attitude towards authorities advocated by Romans 13:1-7 serves as 'credential' for the narrator: in his perception the narratees would find it acceptable to identify themselves with such an attitude towards governing authorities. Because they can identify with him on these issues (and all the other issues he raised, specifically in the paraenetic section of the letter), they will respond favorably and cooperate with him in his future plans. Therefore, the longed-for reciprocity of the letter is fulfilled.

* The vagueness in time deixis in Romans 13:1-7 can be understood as an indication that it is not a new action that the narrator expects from his narratees in reaction to his letter. Nor is it explicitly marked as an action in which the narratees were engaged prior to the situations of utterance and reception, or whether or not they were still doing so at the time of reception. This provides additional motivation for the observation that the letter to the Romans, and thus also Romans 13:1-7, is primarily concerned with enlisting the cooperation of the narratees for the personal plans of the narrator.

* None of the explicit space deictics in other places in the letter (Rome, Jerusalem, Spain), have any particular relevance for the interpretation of Romans 13:1-7 from a literary perspective, except that they provide a general locus for the 'world' created by the text.

These conclusions give an indication of the type of results to be gained from reading a text from a literary perspective. When the ethics of reading in such a mode is considered, it is necessary to reflect on the view of literature and the view of the text presupposed by such a reading. Of particular importance is the distinction between the 'world created by the text' and the 'historical world.' One of the implications of this distinction, is the subsequent distinction between 'real historical addressee' and 'narrator,' and 'real historical readers' and the 'implied readers' as a textual construction. I submit that a study of the 'textual world' (with all its consequences and complications) has to precede any inferences or conclusions about either the first century historical world or the historical world of the modern interpreter which are made on the basis of this text. Careful consideration of the literary features of the text is an essential aspect of the respect due to the text and for the constraints in its interpretation.   Although this distinction should be heeded consistently, the interpreter also has the responsibility to go further. Talking *only* about fictive literary or textual worlds without drawing any implications for the 'real world' or the context in which interpreters live is a specific reflection of the interpreter's ideology and stance regarding contextual matters.   It may therefore also be a specific manifestation of an irresponsible act of reading.   Although this is a necessary characteristic of an ethics of *reading*, an ethics of *historical* reading and in particular an ethics of *public accountability* in interpretation compels the interpreter not to end the act of interpretation prematurely.   While I want to underscore all this as important and essential aspects of the ethics of New Testament interpretation, the point that I want to make in this study is that none of this can or should happen before or worse, without, a careful literary reading of the text in all its complexity.   In this chapter I have illustrated what I mean by saying that an ethics of reading compels the interpreter to take the 'literariness' of the text seriously.   Yet, an ethically responsible reading must also take the rhetoricity of the text seriously. That will be the concern in the next chapter.

CHAPTER 3

READING ROMANS 13:1-7 FROM A RHETORICAL PERSPECTIVE

1. Introduction

The aim of this chapter is to propose a reading of Romans 13:1-7 from a rhetorical perspective against the background of the preceding linguistic and literary readings. I have argued (see the Introduction) that an ethics of responsible interpretation of the New Testament compels us to take the rhetoricity of the text seriously. To illustrate what I mean by that is one of the concerns of this chapter.

Although somewhat more specific than a linguistic perspective (chapter 1) or a literary perspective (chapter 2), the concept 'reading from a rhetorical perspective' also needs to be qualified and specified. This is done in §2. Following this, an overview of the impact of rhetorical criticism on the modern study of the New Testament is given (§3). In the next two sections, the relationship between rhetoric and epistolography (§4) and the similarities and differences between the notions of 'historical situation,' 'epistolary situation' and 'rhetorical situation' (§5) are discussed. These sections serve as a theoretical orientation for the actual reading of Romans 13:1-7 from a rhetorical perspective in the latter part of the chapter. In §6 some of the conclusions of modern rhetorical critical studies of the letter to the Romans as a whole are summarized to provide the broader framework in terms of which Romans 13:1-7 is then analyzed from a rhetorical-critical perspective (§7).

2. A 'rhetorical perspective': definitions and foci

Rhetoric is an ancient and wide-ranging discipline — a highly developed intellectual activity already established in antiquity (see Kennedy 1963:13). From its history it is clear that no single and simple definition, covering the whole field of reference of this phenomenon, is possible. Part of the reason for this is the fact that a uniform or unified system of classical rhetoric never existed (Thurén 50, 51; Wuellner 1991:171) despite efforts of modern studies of classical rhetoric to present such a system (for example, Lausberg; Corbett; Leeman & Braet). After a survey of rhetorical theory in Plato, Isocrates, Aristotle and Quintilian, Kraftchick (1985:69-94) concludes: 'It became clear that rhetoric was a *flexible discipline* concerned more with the persuasion of its listeners (function) than the production of set forms of speech (text),' and: '. . . rhetoric remained *multifaceted*. We find no set formulae or understandings of the discipline which absolutely governed the production and form of a speech' (1985:95) [my italics]. To this he adds in a later study: 'The existence of the rhetorical handbooks notwithstanding, it is well to remember that ancient rhetoric, in its rules as well as the manifestation of those rules, was *extremely fluid*' (Kraftchick 1990:61) [my italics]. The twentieth century has witnessed a renewed interest in rhetoric (see Sloane 807), widening the field of reference of the term 'rhetoric' even further. To define modern, and more recently, post-modern rhetoric (see Wuellner 1991:177–178) has become a very complex matter.

Yet, since not everything that can possibly be done under the rubric of a rhetorical critical reading of Romans 13:1–7 can in fact be undertaken in this chapter, we need to establish a definition of the nature and focus of the rhetorical reading to be undertaken here.

2.1 Classical definitions of rhetoric

Four definitions can be regarded as representative of classical views on the nature of rhetoric (Quintilian, *Institutio oratoria* 2.15.21):

*   πείθους δημιουργός (creator of persuasion) — a definition attributed to Corax and Tisias, Gorgias and Plato (Kennedy 1963:52–67).

*   ἡ δὲ ῥητορικὴ περὶ τοῦ δοθέντος ὡς εἰπεῖν δοκεῖ δύνασθαι θεωρεῖν τὸ πιθανόν (rhetoric appears to be able to discover the means of persuasion in reference to any given subject) — Aristotle's definition (*Rhetorica* I.1.2).

*   δύναμις τοῦ εὖ λέγειν τὰ πολίτικα ζητήματα (the faculty to speak well regarding public affairs) — one of the definitions ascribed to Hermagoras.

*   *scientia bene dicendi* (the science of speaking well or adequately) — Quintilian's definition (*Institutio oratoria* 2.15.21), following Stoic rhetoricians.

The differences between these definitions are obvious. It is also important to note that these are only four of the many definitions of rhetoric in antiquity. Leeman and Braet (52–57) interpret these definitions with regard to the following four elements of meta-theoretical reflection on the nature of rhetoric: (i) the methodological status, (ii) the purpose, (iii) the object and (iv) the value-free character of rhetoric. Some highlights from their discussion will help us to get an insight into the nature of rhetoric as it was seen in antiquity (see also the thorough discussion of ancient understandings of rhetoric by Kraftchick 1985:62–96).

2.1.1 The methodological status of rhetoric

Regarding the methodological status of rhetoric, the famous problem of classical discussions was: *an rhetorice ars sit*, whether or not rhetoric was an 'art' (*ars*, τέχνη). Related to this was the didactic problem of how one can be best trained in eloquence: with or without the rules of rhetorical theory? According to the teachers of rhetoric, rhetoric was indeed a τέχνη, or even a science (ἐπιστήμη, *scientia*). Knowledge of rhetorical theory was deemed absolutely necessary, in addition to the natural ability (φύσις, *natura*) and practice (μελήτη, *exercitatio*) of making speeches. Philosophers, on the other hand, did not see rhetoric as a science or a τέχνη. They recognized only the rhetorical experience (ἐμπείρια, *usus*), and this experience had didactic value only for natural ability and practice.

The discussion of what a τέχνη is presents a confusing picture. All four definitions have in common that τέχνη is defined as a corpus of knowledge which is organized into a system or method in order to accomplish a practical purpose. The concept is used on three levels: (a) τέχναι refers to the rhetorical handbooks, (b) the term can also refer to the content of such handbooks and, confusingly, it can also (c) refer to the skill of a person to practice what is taught by the handbooks. The third sense overlaps with the term δύναμις (*vis*, *facultas*) (ability or skill). The basic difference between Aristotle and Plato is that Aristotle maintains that τέχνη was value-free, while Plato wants to use the term only when an ethically acceptable purpose is pursued. And here lies the basis of the conflict between rhetoric and philosophy: can rhetoric be a 'neutral' act in itself, employed in each situation to achieve the envisioned persuasion ('anything goes,' as long as the argument/case is won), or should any argument in the first place be based on truth, which can only be given by philosophy? Later classical rhetoricians such as Cicero and Quintilian maintain that rhetoric is in itself ethically good and thus, it can be seen as a science (according to the Platonic criteria).

2.1.2 The purpose of rhetoric

In classical reflections on the purpose of rhetoric, the theoretical level of rhetoric and the practical level of eloquence are not clearly distinguished. When classical authors speak about the purpose of rhetoric, they mean the purpose of *rhetores* (the public speakers). This is clear in the definition of rhetoric as πείθους δημιουργός. But the teacher of rhetoric *teaches*, he does not persuade. Thus he is only indirectly involved with the purpose of rhetoric, that is, if we accept that persuasion is the purpose of rhetoric. And here the question has to be asked whether the rules of rhetoric are only applicable to persuasive texts, or whether any text can be produced by means of these rules. With Quintilian's definition of rhetoric as *scientia bene dicendi*, it seems as if he regards rhetoric as the science of all forms of purposeful speaking. The purpose of speaking is not only persuasion, but speaking adequately (*bene*). Thus, already Quintilian (and before him also Cicero) sees rhetoric as a general science of the production of speeches and texts. However, the limitation of rhetoric to the persuasive function was more familiar, as can be seen in the first two definitions.

2.1.3 The object of rhetoric

When discussing the object of rhetoric, classical authors again have in mind the object of eloquence as such (and not the theory of eloquence). A minimalist and a maximalist view on the object of rhetoric can be distinguished. In the minimalist view the object of rhetoric is limited to discourse about public affairs (πολίτικα ζητήματα, *quaestiones civiles*). In terms of the theory of rhetoric this means that only the three well-known types of public discourse (forensic, deliberative and epideictic) fall within the rhetorician's purview (see the definition of Hermagoras).

The proponents of the maximalist view were not willing to accept this restriction. Aristotle represents the formalistic variant of the maximalist view: rhetoric is not a subject bound discipline. For him the rules of rhetoric are applicable to any subject, regardless of whether special knowledge of the subject is required. Cicero (and before him also Gorgias and Isocrates) represents the materialist variant of the maximalist view: the ideal orator must be able to speak adequately (that is, with expertise) about any subject. For them rhetoric became a super-science having the total reality as object.

2.1.4 The value-free character of rhetoric

Another major point of difference discernible in writers of antiquity was whether rhetoric should be ethically neutral or ethically committed. Plato champions the view that rhetoric should be ethically committed and responsible, while Aristotle is of the opinion that it should be a neutral ordering of the means of persuasion that was the most effective. For Aristotle the responsible (or irresponsible) use of persuasion is vested not in the rhetorical system itself, but in an orator (just as methods of interpretation as such can not be ethically evaluated, but how *people* use these methods is a matter for consideration in the ethics of interpretation). The orator is the one who has to decide whether he or she will use the rhetorical principles for good or bad purposes. The definition of Quintilian (to speak *bene*) represents the normative view. *Bene* means purposeful as well as ethically acceptable. For Quintilian eloquence is a virtue (*virtus*) and the orator is a *vir bonus* who is able to speak well (*dicendi peritus*).

Classic conceptions of the nature of rhetoric thus comprise a whole spectrum of views. In one respect, however, there is general agreement: rhetoric and the study of rhetoric are oriented towards the *creation* of speeches (or texts) and on the instruction of those wishing to initiate communication. Another shared view among classical rhetoricians is the implicit belief that the truth can be detached from the forms of discourse and can be divided into the demonstrable and the probable.

2.2 Modern conceptions of rhetoric

Cox and Willard (xii-xlvii) provide a valuable overview of the development of rhetoric since the beginning of the twentieth century. With the renewed interest in rhetoric in American universities at the beginning of this century, the emphasis has been on the creation of discourse, and rhetoric was viewed in a formal and positivistic way. For instance, the conviction-persuasion duality dominated. Strict distinctions were made between reason and passion, between logic and emotion. Conviction was thought to issue from logical processes while persuasion resulted from appeals to the passions (Cox & Willard xv). The formal relationships expressed by syllogistic logic were believed to replicate the essential realities of the world. The majority of textbooks on argumentation distinguished their subject matter from that of formal logic essentially in terms of *probability* versus the *certainty* of knowing in practical affairs. This monistic logical model dominated the study of argumentation for the whole first half of our century. The switch to a postpositivistic, audience-centered conception of rhetoric came in the middle of the century with the work of Toulmin and Perelman and Olbrechts-Tyteca (Cox & Willard xxii).

Modern rhetoric is therefore marked by its shift of focus to the auditor or reader (Sloane 803, 807). Modern rhetoric is as involved with the process of interpretation, or analysis, as it is with the process of creation, or genesis. Yet, it distinguishes itself from literary criticism (which is also oriented towards interpretation) by viewing a message through situations. That 'a text must reveal its context' (Sloane 804) is for Wuellner (1987a:450) the most important difference between rhetorical criticism and literary criticism. By 'context' is meant more than historical situation or genre or the generic *Sitz im Leben*. For modern rhetoric 'context' means the 'attitudinizing conventions, precepts that condition (both the writer's *and* the reader's) stance toward experience, knowledge, tradition, language, and other people' (Wuellner 1987a:450). In modern linguistics the study of language-in-use, or how utterances have meaning in context, has come to be known as pragmatics (see Leech x). That is why Thurén (52) can maintain that 'in a sense, the text-linguistic term for rhetoric is pragmatics.' Of particular importance for the modern rhetorical critic's understanding of context are the interests, values or emotions of the audience and the strategies through which a speaker or writer is engaged with that through his or her discourse (Sloane 804).

Most notable among those who have devoted themselves to the theory of rhetoric in modern times, is Ch. Perelman (1969; 1982). Perelman and Olbrechts-Tyteca (4) define the object of their theory of argumentation (which they term 'the new rhetoric') as 'the study of the discursive techniques allowing us *to induce or to increase the mind's adherence to the theses presented for its assent.*' Three observations may serve to highlight the significance of Perelman's treatise (see Mack 15).

> a) Whereas ancient rhetoricians were primarily concerned with the art of public speaking in a persuasive way, Perelman and Olbrechts-Tyteca (6) want to go far beyond that: they do not limit their study to the presentation of an argument by means of the spoken word or restrict the kind of audience addressed to a crowd gathered in a square. In the new rhetoric argumentation is placed within a rhetorical framework — the soundness of an argument is equated with its effectiveness on the audience for whom it is intended. By emphasizing argumentation, Perelman and Olbrechts-Tyteca revived the ancient classical definition of rhetoric as 'the act of persuasion,' described a logic of communication that could be applied to widely ranging modes of human discourse, and immersed the study of speech events in social situations.

> b) Perelman and Olbrechts-Tyteca thus have succeeded in demonstrating the importance of the situation or speech context when calculating the persuasive force of an argumentation. They offered a way of talking about the persuasive power of various modes of discourse, thereby offering the apparatus to bridge the gap between literary criticism and social history.

> c) Perelman and Olbrechts-Tyteca have demonstrated the rhetorical coefficient that belongs to every human exchange involving speech (aural or written), including common conversation and the daily discourse of a working society. By doing this, they have taken rhetoric out of the sphere of mere ornamentation and stylistics (see §2.3.1), and the extravagance of public oratory, and placed it at the center of a social theory of language. Their contribution to the factors that impinge on the speaker-audience relationship has been a special and important contribution.

In their influential *Handbook of Argumentation Theory*, Van Eemeren, Grootendorst and Kruiger (55–77) consider rhetoric as a predecessor to, or as part of, modern theories of argumentation and they define argumentation as 'a social, intellectual, verbal activity serving to justify or refute an opinion, consisting of a constellation of statements and directed towards obtaining the approbation of an argument' (7).

For Thurén (52) modern rhetoric is 'a method of practical criticism' and is as such linked with the literary study of ancient rhetoric as well as with modern pragmatic research. Modern rhetoric, like pragmatics, focuses not only on the communicative, but also, and especially, on the *interactive* dimension of a text: 'a discourse is regarded not only as the sender's message to the recipients, but also as a bi-directional, interactive relationship between author and reader' (Thurén 53). In a similar vein, Vorster (1990) has worked out a model combining insights from rhetoric, conversational analysis and reader response criticism for the analysis of letters as *interaction*.

Many other modern conceptions of rhetoric can be considered (which will take us well beyond our immediate purposes). From what has been presented here, it is clear that, although a great variety can be discerned in the definitions and applications of modern rhetoric, certain basic tenets can nevertheless be identified. Two interrelated aspects of (ancient and modern) rhetoric are (i) the study of discursive techniques and (ii) the functioning of these techniques to persuade. Most important in modern rhetoric, however, is the shift of focus to the audience/reader. This shift entails consideration of the values, beliefs and emotions of the audience (as seen by the speaker/writer) and the various strategies used to influence this by means of discourse, a development concomitant with the shift away from a positivistic monism that discarded the role of persons and passions in favor of logic alone.

Wuellner (1991:176) aptly summarizes what has been said about modern conceptions of rhetoric in this section, by pointing out that four features can be distinguished as the characteristics of modern rhetoric: (i) the turn toward argumentation and the designation of arguments as text-type distinct from narrative and description (that is why modern rhetoric came to be seen as theories of argumentation, see Cox & Willard), (ii) the focus on a text's intentionality or exigency, (iii) the social, cultural, ideological values embedded in the argument's premises, *topoi* and hierarchies, and (iv) to see rhetorical or stylistic techniques as means to an argumentative end and not as merely formal and decorative features. In order to set this conception of rhetoric (which serves to make clear what we will do in our rhetorical reading of Romans 13:1–7) more specifically in focus, it is necessary to consider briefly a number of limitations and distortions of rhetoric.

2.3 Misconceptions regarding rhetoric

Rhetoric and rhetorical criticism have been and are still frequently hampered by a number of misconceptions that represent a distortion of what rhetoric is all about. Four such misconceptions can be discerned.

2.3.1 Rhetoric reduced to style

The most general and most persistent distortion is the conception that rhetoric is only concerned with stylistics, or, what Kennedy calls *Litteraturizzazione* (1984:3). Wuellner (1987a:451) speaks of this distortion as

> "rhetoric restrained," i.e., victims of the fateful reduction of rhetorics to stylistics, and of stylistics in turn to the rhetorical tropes or figures. Reduced to concerns of style, with the artistry of textual disposition and textual structure, rhetorical criticism has become indistinguishable from literary criticism . . . .

A good example of this reduced conception of rhetoric can be found in Cranfield's commentary on Romans. He writes (1975:26):

> For the most part the real grandeur of Romans as a piece of literature derives from its content and from the sincerity, directness and personal involvement of the author. At the same time, it would be quite incorrect to assume that the epistle is totally devoid of literary elegance; for it affords clear evidence that Paul knew *the various figures of speech of the rhetoricians* and that it came naturally to him to make use of them from time to time. [Cranfield then gives examples of stylistic figures used by Paul in Romans: assonance, climax, paranomasia and parallelism, and then he continues:] . . . *But* these things are used by Paul unselfconsciously, not as ends in themselves but *as natural means to the forceful and compelling expression* of what he has to say. *It is the content that is all-important.* And it is to this content of what has to be expressed and *subordination of outward form* to it that at any rate some of his anacolutha should be attributed [my italics].

It is clear that Cranfield subordinates form to content, that the stylistic features are for him part of the less important form of Paul's letter, and that the purpose or function of these stylistic figures is 'a means to forceful and compelling expression,' but it is not integral to 'what he has to say' (= the 'content'). The reference to the Greek rhetoricians is made in the context of the presence of stylistic figures in Paul's letters.

For the classical rhetoricians, however, rhetoric was primarily a system or collection of advice on how to find and arrange the content of a speech (Kennedy 1963:88). In the two oldest rhetorical handbooks, the *Rhetorica ad Alexandrum* and the *Rhetorica* of Aristotle, almost three quarters of each are devoted to the finding and arrangement of the content of the material, and not much attention is given to style, while recitation is treated only in passing. In the later Roman rhetoric style indeed became more important, but it always remained less important than the finding and arrangement of the material for the purpose of effective argumentation (Leeman & Braet 58).

After a development of several centuries rhetoric was, by the time of Cicero considered to be a discipline that encompassed five *officia*: *inventio* (analyzing the speech topic and collecting the materials for it), *dispositio* (arrangement of the material into an oration), *elocutio* (fitting words to the topic, the speaker, the audience and occasion), *memoria* (lodging ideas within the mind's storehouse) and *actio* (or pronunciation: delivering the speech orally) (see Lausberg 146-149, 241, 248, 525-527). Stylistic figures are treated under *elocutio*. Although *inventio* and *elocutio* are treated separately, Cicero is emphatic that it is not possible in principle to separate 'content' and 'form' because neither can exist without the other (Cicero, *De oratore*, 3.55).

Because of the dominance of *inventio* in classical rhetoric, it is justified to conclude that stylistic features were not as prominent then as generally understood today. In a careful and well-documented study, Wuellner (1989) traced the development of rhetoric (and its relation to biblical hermeneutics) since late antiquity, through medieval times, the Renaissance, the sixteenth-century religious reforms, Ramus's sixteenth-century educational reforms, to the hostility to and the death of rhetoric in the eighteenth and nineteenth centuries, right through to its revival in the twentieth century. It is particularly due to the influence of Ramus, who considered style (*elocutio*) and delivery (*actio*) as the only proper parts of rhetoric, leaving aside the other parts traditionally associated with rhetoric (*inventio*, *disposition* and *memoria*), to which Wuellner (1989:10) ascribes the preoccupation of rhetoric with style — up to the revival of stylistics-oriented rhetoric with the Muilenberg school in twentieth century biblical scholarship (Wuellner 1989:33; on the reduction of rhetoric to stylistics, see also Snyman 1988a:94-99; Thurén 47-52; Wuellner 1991:171-172.)

Against this fateful limitation of rhetoric to stylistics, Wuellner (1987a:462) claims that:

> [r]hetorical criticism . . . promises to take biblical exegetes at last out of the ghetto of an aestheticizing preoccupation with biblical stylistics which has remained for centuries formalized, and functionless, and contextless.

With the emphasis of modern rhetoric and theories of argumentation on audience, interaction within situations, social values and strategies to bring about changes in beliefs, values and attitudes (see §2.2), it is clear that rhetorical criticism is much more than merely a study of the stylistic figures and tropes as optional extras added to decorate language.

2.3.2 Rhetoric as an inferior form of argumentation

A conception of rhetoric as consisting of irrational, emotional techniques used to promote an uncritical acceptance of a message (Thurén 48) or rhetoric being involved in the willful manipulation of facts for dubious ends (Kraftchick 1985:68) is also widespread. According to Kraftchick (1985:68) this has been the perception because the visible part of rhetoric was the manipulation of words and sentences and not the reasoned construction of proof and argument. The charges made against rhetoric were therefore actually protestations against its textual side.

This issue has already been touched on in the consideration of the value-free character of rhetoric and how ancient opinions on this matter differed (see §2.1.4). Although such abuses of rhetoric cannot be denied, I have argued that it is not an inherent characteristic of rhetoric which is responsible for this. Especially with the modern shift toward audience-oriented, and more specifically, toward rhetorical criticism as practical criticism and as *analysis*, this perception need not discredit the ethical standards of rhetorical criticism as such.

2.3.3 Rhetoric bound to Greco-Roman school rhetoric

From our consideration of modern conceptions of rhetoric (see §2.2), it has become clear that, although indebted to classical rhetoric, modern rhetoric has moved beyond the classical traditions in important ways. Emphasizing this, Kraftchick (1990:78) calls for 'a movement away from the formal categories of ancient classical rhetoric to the functionally-oriented categories of modern rhetoric . . . ,' because:

1) it does justice to the rhetorical aspects and strategies in a discourse allowing us to recognize and appreciate more facets of an argument.
2) the recognition of these strategies helps us to refrain from stressing various parts of the discourse at the expense of others.
3) given the nature of the rhetorical situation we may better assess the 'authoritative function' of the discourse in present rhetorical situations.
4) investigating techniques or argument based on shared premises, and especially, shared values, we may be able to utilize these arguments to discover what those initial premises were for the speaker/writer.

This is not to say that the 'long and illustrious tradition of rhetoric at the heart of Western education and culture' (Mack 9) is to be discarded altogether. Building on certain ancient classical categories, but also moving beyond them in the light of these four considerations, a method of rhetorical criticism will be developed that can provide insightful results when applied to a New Testament text. In this rhetorical reading of Romans 13:1-7, I take up Wuellner's (1987a:455) suggestion to use the framework proposed by Kennedy (1984:33-38), which is based on the legacies of Hellenistic-Roman textbooks on rhetoric, but build on it and adapt it to incorporate the essential insights of modern rhetoric and theories of argumentation.

When rhetoric is understood in this way, the problem of whether Paul in fact received formal rhetorical training or not (see Forbes 1-30; Du Toit 1989:194-195; see also Weiss; Betz 1987; Hughes 19-30) can be seen in a new perspective. Paul need not to have studied rhetoric formally to be influenced and to act/write in terms of rhetorical categories (Kraftchick 1985:94–95; Thurén 49). As Kennedy puts it, 'it is not a necessary premise . . . that . . . Paul had formally studied Greek rhetoric . . . . [T]he rhetorical theory of the schools found its immediate application in almost every form of oral and written communication' (1984:9–10), and, 'rhetoric is a universal phenomenon which is conditioned by basic workings of the human mind and heart and by the nature of all human society' (1984:10). Classen (2–3) concurs:

> Die Frage, ob die Kategorien der Antiken Rhetorik sinnvoll zur Erklärung der Paulus-Briefe herangezogen werden können, gibt Anlaß zu einer grundlegenden Feststellung: Das Instrumentarium der griechisch-römischen Rhetorik kann mit Gewinn zur Analyse jedes geschrieben oder gesprochenen Textes verwendet werden.

Wuellner (1979) has illustrated how digressions in Paul's letters are illustrative of his rhetorical sophistication and how they serve to support his argumentation. Betz (1987) analyzed a number of passages in Paul's letters and illustrated how Paul dealt with the challenges of the rhetoric of his time. After a consideration of the technical rhetorical terminology λόγος καὶ γνῶσις in 1 Corinthians, Betz (1987:32) concludes that '. . . when Paul in 1 Cor 1,5 uses with approval the formula "eloquence and knowledge," he must have known its nature and origin.'

Many more such influences of classical rhetoric on Paul's letters can be detected — as, for example, Melanchton indicated in his commentary on Romans (see Classen). This does not imply that rhetorical criticism may be applied profitably to the study of Paul's letters *only* if classical rhetorical categories are used. Classen (6) holds a balanced view:

> Es besteht kein besonderer Grund dafür, bei der Interpretation der Paulus-Briefe nur antike Kategorien zu verwenden, obwohl Paulus dank seiner Kenntnis der griechischen Sprache Zugang zu von der Rhetorik geprägten literarischen Werke hatte.

In terms of modern conceptions of rhetoric as argumentation the issue of whether or not Paul had formal rhetorical training becomes even less important. It is evident that in his letters Paul is involved in an act of argumentation. This argumentation takes place within certain situations, which presupposes a form of interaction in which social values and strategies are at stake. In my analysis these considerations will be in focus.

2.3.4 A new captivity: fixation on genre

Kraftchick (1990:64–66) issues a timely warning against a fixation on the question of genre in recent New Testament scholarship from a rhetorical critical perspective (as can be seen in the Betz-Kennedy dispute on the rhetorical genre of Galatians — see §7.2.3 for more detail), which has detracted from the analysis of the letters themselves. He appropriately calls this fixation on genre '. . . a new form of parallelomania' (1990:64). Kraftchick (1990:78) emphasizes that analysis of social values and strategies of argumentation is a better way to use insights of rhetorical criticism than the debate on rhetorical genre. Kraftchick's warning needs to be taken seriously. In our rhetorical reading of Romans 13:1-7, genre-considerations will not be ignored but will also not dictate the results. This procedure will be explained in more detail in §5 and §7.2.

2.4 Rhetorical criticism and literary criticism

The close relationship between rhetoric and pragmatics, reader response criticism and conversational analysis has already been mentioned, as well as some of the differences between rhetorical criticism and literary criticism (see §2.2). In order to distinguish the aim of this chapter more clearly from what has been done in chapter 2, some remarks on the relationship between rhetoric and literary criticism are necessary.

With the shift toward the auditor or reader in modern rhetoric, it is obvious that rhetorical criticism and audience or reader-oriented criticism are very closely related. Suleiman (7) indicates that a rhetorical approach and the literary approaches (particularly structuralism and semiotics) are similar in one respect: they share a model of the text as a form of communication. According to this model (which was explained and applied in chapter 2), the author and the reader of a text are related to each other as the sender and the receiver of a message. The transmission and reception of the message depend on the presence of a shared code of communication between sender and receiver. Although both are interested in the process of communication, literary criticism and rhetorical criticism differ in the more specific interest of the modern rhetorical critic. The rhetorical critic 'seeks not only to formulate the set of verbal meanings embedded in the text, but above all to discover the values and beliefs that make those meanings possible — or that those meanings imply' (Suleiman 8). The values and beliefs that underlie and ultimately determine the meaning which a work may have are attributed by the rhetorical critic to the implied or encoded author, the second self of the actual author. Suleiman (8) defines the encoded author as 'the shadowy but overriding presence who is responsible for every aspect of the work and whose image must be constructed (or rather, reconstructed) in the act of reading.' In the same sense, the audience towards which the encoded author aims his argumentation, or rather, with whom he is in interaction, is a textual construct — a creation of the encoded author — not to be identified with the real recipients of the letter. Thus the interaction which the rhetorical critic of written texts seeks to describe is a text-internal phenomenon, taking place between an encoded author and the implied readers.

For Mack '[r]hetorical criticism may in fact be the most promising form of literary criticism for the task of reconstructing Christian origins with social issues in view' (17) and 'rhetoric, therefore, has the capacity of joining forces with other theoretical disciplines that seek to describe the dynamics of social intercourse and formation' (93). Wuellner (1991:180) warns that the implications of rhetorical criticism for the analysis of social factors should not be overemphasized (as Mack tends to do). Although social factors are indeed very important for rhetorical criticism, the larger complex of the rhetoric of basic communication (namely the rhetoric of 'what goes without saying' or the ideological aspect of communication, Wuellner 1991:180) is unavoidable and inescapable for rhetorical criticism. Rhetoric cannot be reduced to a social science, nor to linguistics, speech act theories, or a communication science, although it does overlap with these disciplines. The realm of rhetoric has its own integrity and its own constraints (Wuellner 1991:180).

The rhetorical critic is primarily interested in the ethical and ideological 'content' of a message (whether transmitted in oral or written form), how such 'content' comes into existence in the process of interaction between the sender and receiver (encoded author and implied reader in the case of a written text), and finally, how the discourse functions as a power that influences the values and actions of people. Rhetorical criticism, therefore, has a more specific aim than literary criticism: discourse is studied as argumentation, as interaction, and not only as communication, or the transmission of information. Aesthetic codes as such, which are such an important aspect of the 'literariness' of a text, do not play such an important role here, although aesthetically attractive language may sometimes prove to be more effective in persuasion than 'un-aesthetic' language.

2.5 Summary, focus and method

It it is possible to summarize the most important choices I have discussed so far and thereby set the focus of what will be done in this chapter.

* In contrast to classical rhetoric, modern rhetoric is not only concerned with the production of oral speech. All discourse (oral and written, therefore also letters) falls within the purview of the rhetorician.

* A fundamental presupposition for this chapter is that Romans 13:1–7 forms part of an argumentative text and can therefore be interpreted in terms of a rhetorical critical approach.

* The aim of this rhetorical critical reading of Romans 13:1–7 is to investigate and describe the discursive techniques in the text and their persuasive effect.

In this process special attention to the beliefs and values that serve as basis for the argumentation is necessary.

* The rhetorical critical approach to be used here is not restricted to an investigation of the style of the passage as such, nor is it restricted to classical school-rhetoric.

* In this approach the text is understood as a form of interaction between the intra-textual phenomena of an encoded author and an implied reader.

* The audience, which is the determining factor in the composition of rhetorical discourse, is never the real audience, but always the image that the author has of the audience, and it is consequently always a construct of the author.

* An adaptation of Kennedy's model (1984) based on classical rhetoric is used as general framework and expanded to incorporate some of the advances and new perspectives of modern developments in rhetoric.

3. Rhetorical criticism and New Testament interpretation

The surveys of Mack (9-24) and Hughes (19-30) of the renewed interest in rhetoric in recent New Testament scholarship provide a broader context for our intended reading and are briefly summarized here. For many centuries it was taken for granted that the writings produced by early Christians were to be read as rhetorical compositions, as can be seen in the work of Origen, Augustine, Cassiodoris and other Patristic exegetes of the New Testament (see Wuellner 1979; Betz 1987:17-21; Classen 15-16). Through the centuries, up to the *Aufklärung*, scholars of the New Testament have learned rhetoric in the normal course of their education in the humanities.[1] The commentary of Melanchton on Romans, in which he made extensive use of classical rhetorical categories, indicates how deeply he was influenced by this tradition (Classen 16-24). This is also true of the interpretive work of Lorenzo Villa, Jacques Lefèvre d'Etaples, Desiderius Erasmus, Luther, Zwingli, Bucer, Brenz, Bullinger and Calvin, although to a lesser extent than Melanchton's commentary on Romans (Classen 25).

With the rise of the critical study of the New Testament in the seventeenth and eighteenth centuries, knowledge of classical rhetoric was deemed essential for those areas on which scholarly interest was then focused, namely the establishment of texts, apparatus, translations and philological interpretations. Rhetorical observations abound in the major lexica, grammars and

---

[1]Rhetoric was one of the three fields of study in the *trivium* (grammar, dialectic, rhetoric) which formed the foundation for the seven liberal arts (the *trivium* and the *quadrivium* — geometry, arithmetic, astronomy and music) (see Kennedy 1980:35, 163-169, 175-177, 188-196 for more detail).

commentaries (including the Liddell & Scott *Greek-English Lexicon* and the Blass-DeBrunner-Funk grammar of the New Testament — both stemming from the nineteenth century), although they are mainly concerned with figures, stylistic traits, and ways of putting words together. Nevertheless, their observations are an indication of the legacy of the Western rhetorical tradition. During this early period a number of studies that specially addressed the question of the rhetoric of the New Testament also appeared, a tradition that eventually developed through the works of Johannes Weiss, Hans Wendland and in the commentaries of Hans-Dieter Betz on Galatians (1974) and 2 Corinthians 8 and 9 (1985) (see Hughes 22–23 for more detail).

In 1975 Betz published a seminal article in which he argued that Paul wrote Galatians with the standard parts of a rhetorical speech in mind. Late in 1979 his commentary on Galatians appeared in which he put his ideas in practice. He structured his commentary around his rhetorical analysis of Galatians as an 'apologetic letter.' Although in a tradition of German rhetorical commentaries, Betz's work has nevertheless been hailed as a precursor[2] of the current rediscovery of rhetoric in biblical criticism (see Hester 1986:388; Wuellner 1987a:452; Schüssler Fiorenza 1987:386; Furnish 1989: 324; Kennedy 1984:4). The reason for this is the fact that interest in rhetoric waned around the turn of the century and was actually lost for a great part of twentieth century New Testament scholarship. The dominant trends in the twentieth century, namely the theological exegesis in the tradition of Barth and the existentialist interpretation in the wake of Bultmann were in fact openly hostile toward rhetorical criticism (Mack 12). Betz's Galatians commentary was therefore indeed a surprising development.

Since the mid-seventies a wealth of rhetorical studies of New Testament texts have made their appearance, yet there has been no programmatic essay to announce its presence, no school or acknowledged master or canon of methods at its center. Three significant influences or (groups of) figures can nevertheless be discerned, although their concerns differ rather significantly (see Hughes 23ff).

Firstly, the 1968 SBL presidential address by James Muilenberg, 'After Form Criticism What?' (Muilenberg) has often been heralded as the beginning of rhetorical criticism in modern biblical studies (Watson 1988:465; Patrick & Scult 11–13). As an answer to the shortfalls of form criticism, he suggested a return to rhetorical criticism, by which he meant the analysis of the formal features of a composition that could take account of authorial accomplishment and creativity — against the form-critical tendency to bracket

---

[2]The Galatians commentary of Betz also sparked off a debate on rhetorical criticism and New Testament interpretation which still continues (for a summary of the debate, see Classen 21 note 9).

all historical considerations. However, Muilenberg, as well as the school that subsequently followed his suggestion (for a recent example, see Patrick & Scult), practiced a 'rhetoric restrained,' that is, a rhetoric reduced to stylistic features and composition. That is why Wuellner (1987a:451; 1989:33) has repeatedly emphasized the difference between what he conceptualizes and practices and what the Muilenberg school understands and practices under the rubric of rhetorical criticism.

A second major influence has been the book *Early Christian Rhetoric: The Language of the Gospel* of Amos Wilder. Wilder's work, however, was more attuned to poetics and the aesthetic effect of style on the imagination, and less to the sociology of literature. Following Wilder's lead, many scholars became interested in the work of Kenneth Burke and Wayne Booth (1961) on rhetoric and literary studies. This development has eventually led to literary studies of the parables and studies on the Christian imagination (see chapter 2, §3.2).

The questions about the role of literature within a given culture and about the effective difference a text might make within a given social history, enhanced with the social and cultural upheavals of the late sixties, brought to the fore the likes of Betz and Wuellner as a third, and perhaps most significant, contributing force to the rise of rhetorical criticism in modern New Testament interpretation. Mention has already been made of Betz's indebtedness to classical rhetoric and the tradition from which his work on rhetorical criticism emerged. Wuellner's 1976 essay on Paul's rhetoric of argumentation in Romans stands as a landmark in this regard (Jewett 1982:6–8; Furnish 1989:324; Vorster 1991:2, 73). Although Wuellner consistently expresses his indebtedness to classical rhetoric (1976:333; 1979:179–181; 1987a:454; 1991:172–173), he is also a strong advocate for working out the definition of rhetoric in the larger context of modern scholarship, namely as a rhetoric of argumentation taking full cognizance of modern developments, especially the work of Perelman (see §2.2). Without detracting from the pioneering work of either one of them, the clear differences between Betz's and Wuellner's rhetorical criticism should not be overlooked.

Since the work of Betz and Wuellner in the seventies, studies of the New Testament with 'rhetoric' in its title have reached tidal wave proportions (see Watson 1988, 1990, 1991). It is hardly possible to review this development exhaustively. This overview of the impact of rhetorical criticism on New Testament interpretation in recent times therefore concludes with a summary of four characteristics of modern rhetorical criticism in New Testament interpretation as they were identified by Mack (19–24) (Modern rhetorical studies dealing specifically with the letter to the Romans will be considered in §6).

* The single most important feature of the new rhetorical criticism is the move toward rhetoric as argumentation.

* The discovery of rhetorical units: a large number of modern studies have identified textual units of argumentation in the New Testament, many of them coming close to, and complementing, the more traditional interests of literary criticism in questions of form and genre.

* The question of authority: the stature and credibility of the speaker and audiences in the process of interaction is a natural concern for rhetorical criticism.

* Engaging social histories: although not (yet) a dominant feature of modern rhetorical studies, particular attention to the social implications of the investigations of rhetorical situations will undoubtedly form an important part of this attempt.

All four of these characteristics of rhetorical criticism will be dealt with in the rhetorical reading of Romans 13:1-7 in the latter half of this chapter. Two theoretical concerns will first have to be discussed to provide additional conceptual clarity on the nature of the rhetorical reading to be undertaken, namely the relation between rhetoric and epistolography (a discussion which also serves to highlight the difference between what was done in chapter 2 and what will be done further on in this chapter), and the relation between a historical situation, epistolary situation and a rhetorical situation.

4. Rhetoric and epistolography

The problem of the relationship between rhetoric and epistolography, between speech and letter, between oral discourse and written text continues to provoke different opinions among scholars (see, for example, Betz 1974; Aune 1981; Hübner 242-249; Berger 1984b; Thurén 57-65; Vorster 1991:73-77). Since this problem is at issue in this chapter (a part of a *letter*, namely Romans 13:1-7, is read in terms of *rhetorical* critical categories), the issue needs further clarification.

Schlier's (17, 33) characterization of Romans 1:1-7 as *Präskript* (epistolographical terminology) and Romans 1:8-17 as *Proömium* (rhetorical terminology) is typical of the traditional way in which this relationship is perceived: an epistolary framework frames the 'content' of the letter, which may be analyzed in rhetorical categories (for a similar approach, see Snyman's [1989] analysis of Philemon). Wuellner (1976:337-338) criticizes this perception, maintaining that epistolographical conventions (such as the prescript and closing) form part of the act of persuasion intended by the letter as a whole. Therefore the rhetoricity of the letter does not begin only after the epistolary prescript and stop short of the epistolary closing. On the other hand, Petersen (1987:9–12) objects to this handling of the material, maintaining that to 'map the rhetorical structure onto the epistolary structure obscures the latter.' In response, Wuellner (1988:5) insists that 'it is in and through every one of the epistolary conventions that Paul makes his argument.'

The problem is aggravated because both ancient rhetorical handbooks and treatises on epistolography treat this issue rather superficially or not at all (see the survey of Cornelius 18–30). Both Kraftchick (1990:56) and Vorster (1991:74) ascribe the problem to an absolutization of ancient rhetorical genres. Many ancient letters are hortatory or paraenetic in nature, and this is a category not included in the classification of rhetorical genres (see Stowers 1986:51–57). Yet it appears from a comparison of Pseudo-Demetrius's typification of letters with the rhetorical genres that at least some of the technical rhetorical terminology became part of the terminology of the relatively little we know about ancient systematic teaching about letters (Hughes 27). Kraftchick (1990:56) warns that '. . . in the desire to find rhetorical forms among Paul's letters, the letters themselves are forgotten. Instead of allowing the texts their rightful shape, the letters are often fitted to the canons of rhetoric.'

This problem is assessed in a number of ways by modern scholars: (i) those who emphasize that New Testament letters are real letters and that rhetorical considerations can only play a secondary role (White 1972, 1986; Doty 1973; Hübner), (ii) those who consider the New Testament letters as speeches in written form, embedded within an epistolary frame (Berger 1984a:216–217 — New Testament letters are 'schriftliche fixierte apostolische Rede'), and (iii) those who analyze the whole text using both epistolographical and rhetorical categories, some by creating a higher level of epistolography (Schnider & Stenger and Johanson) and some by incorporating epistolography within a broader conception of rhetoric (Wuellner 1976, 1988; Thurén 58; Vorster 1991). For the purpose of this study, the suggestion of Vorster (1991:75–76) provides a satisfactory perspective: when both epistolography and rhetoric are redefined in terms of human social behavior, letter writing can be seen properly as a *species* of the *genus* rhetoric, and rhetoric therefore encompasses epistolography. Both epistolography and rhetoric seek to address a need in a particular situation; thus they are both goal-oriented. In rhetoric this goal-oriented social behavior includes both verbal and non-verbal behavior, while a letter is always restricted to written language. As written language, an essential condition for a letter is its own communicativeness (see chapter 2, §6.3.3.1). Against this background Vorster (1991:75–76) arrives at the following conclusion:

Both [epistolography and rhetoric] use language to perform a certain action, namely to remove or modify the need of the exigence of the situation. In the case of the letter, distance always forms an essential part of the exigence of the situation and the sending of the letter becomes the first step in the removal or modification of the exigence of the situation. If a letter is as such an attempt to remove the exigence of the situation, the letter should be seen as part of the rhetorical act. Accordingly, all elements of a letter are rhetorical. All rhetorical elements are not, however, epistolographical. As a matter of fact, all epistolographical elements are specific rhetorical entities.

In a certain sense, what was done in the previous chapter can be characterized as an epistolographical study of Romans 13:1-7, although elements of literary communication also played an important role (see for example, chapter 2, §2 and §6.3.3). As was argued earlier in this chapter (§2.4), however, rhetorical criticism has a more specific aim than literary criticism (or an epistolographical approach): discourse is studied as argumentation, as interaction, and not only as communication, or the transmission of information. In a sense, therefore, a literary (or epistolographical) study has a broader perspective than a rhetorical study, and in another sense, epistolography is included within rhetoric, since all elements of a letter are rhetorical. In the final instance, therefore, it is a matter of perspective, and considerable overlapping cannot — and need not — be excluded. The important thing is to define the focus of the perspective from which one is working at a given point and to work consistently within those parameters.

To conclude this section on the relationship of rhetoric and epistolography, a short word about rhetoric and paraenetic literature would be helpful. Since Romans 13:1-7 has been identified as paraenetic literature (see chapter 2, §5.3), this issue is also at stake here. Controversy on this matter was initiated by Betz's (1979:14-25) classification of Galatians as forensic apology (although the typical forensic speech did not contain a paraenetic section, such as can be found in Galatians) and his remark (1979:253-254) that paraenesis belongs to the realm of epistolography and not rhetoric. In his review of Betz's commentary, Aune (1981:323-324) criticized this typification and wrote that in general '. . . the relationship between the setting of the paraenesis, epistolary paraenesis and the paraenetical sections of the Pauline letter remains a subject for investigation.'

Betz' typification of the genre of Galatians led to the now well-known Kennedy-Betz controversy. Kennedy (1984:145) described Galatians as deliberative rhetoric and accused Betz of overemphasizing the presence of narrative in Galatians and underestimating the presence of exhortation (1984:146). On the basis of this genre which he ascribes to Galatians, Kennedy (1984:146-147) arrived at a totally different analysis of the rhetorical disposition of the letter. Entering the debate, Lyons (1985:175) and Kraftchick (1990) sharply criticized what they regarded as a fixation on genre and form at the expense of the proper and satisfactory description of the role of paraenesis in the argumentation of the letter as a whole. Emphasizing the particular focus of rhetorical criticism to deal with the premises (and thus, the values) of argumentation, Kraftchick (1990:73) maintains that Paul's use of maxims, proverbs and metaphors in his paraenetic materials reflects the common value system that underpins his argumentation. Discovering and describing that value system is the proper goal of rhetorical criticism of paraenetic material. This is also the direction I will follow in the rhetorical reading of Romans 13:1-7 later in this chapter. Once rhetoric has been freed from the fixation on genre and form (see §7.2.3) and focuses on argumentation as social interaction (see §2.2), all discourse, including paraenetic literature, can be approached from a rhetorical critical perspective. It does not matter any longer whether and how paraenetic literature as such was treated in classical rhetoric. From a modern rhetorical perspective, the paraenetic sections of letters form part of the argumentation of the letters, that is, the process of social interaction performed by letters, and can be studied as such.

From this discussion of the relationship between rhetoric and epistolography, and between rhetoric and paraenetic literature, it has become clear how important it is not to confine one's conception of rhetoric to classical rhetoric alone (see §2.3.3), but to work with the broader perspective proposed by modern rhetoric. This broader perspective, however, necessitates the consideration of yet another theoretical issue before we can get to the rhetorical criticism of Romans 13:1-7 itself.

5. *Historical situation, epistolary situation and rhetorical situation*

As a document dating from the first century C.E., the letter to the Romans is the product of a certain historical situation. As a letter it presupposes a certain epistolary situation. As a manifestation of a goal-specific social interaction, it presupposes a certain rhetorical situation. What are the differences and similarities between the concepts 'historical situation,' 'epistolary situation,' and 'rhetorical situation?' Is there any interdependence among them? Where is the categorical difference? Can these concepts be equated to the concept *Sitz im Leben* (as Kennedy 1984:34 and Hughes 30 seem to do)? In this section these questions will be addressed, because these concepts play an important role in more than one section of this study. It is a rather complicated matter, as can be seen, for instance, in the accusation of Thurén (54–56) that Schüssler Fiorenza (1987:387–388) mixes the historical and the rhetorical situations in her attempt to reconstruct the historical situation of Corinthians *by means of* the identification and description of its rhetorical situation and rhetorical genre.

Firstly, a definition and description of the concept 'historical situation' will be given. By way of illustration a number of reconstructions for the rhetorical situation of Romans 13:1–7 will be dealt with in a short excursus. Secondly, some of the important developments in the modern debate on the concept 'rhetorical situation' will be traced. Against this background, the difference between these concepts will be formulated. The rhetorical situation of Romans 13:1–7 as such will be dealt with in the rhetorical reading of the passage (§7.2). Thirdly, the relation between rhetorical situation and epistolary situation will be addressed briefly.

5.1 Definition and description of the concept 'historical situation'

As a preliminary working definition we may say that *'historical' situation* is a concept with a very broad field of reference, encompassing the events, objects, persons, abstractions and relations (social, political, personal, cultural, ideological, ecological, or whatever) that constituted a situation which existed in the past in time and space, and which could have been or was in actual fact experienced by human beings. Understood in such a comprehensive way, a historical situation consists of a 'complex chaos,' a 'complex, bewildering world,' or, as Vatz (156) has formulated it: 'The world is not a plot of discrete events. The world is a scene of inexhaustible events which all compete to impinge on what Kenneth Burke calls our "sliver of reality."' In similar vein Petersen (1985:10–14) speaks of the impossibility of representing the enormous mass of 'events' which we perceive, even in a single day, exhaustively. Narration of history is therefore always a construction of the one who tells the story, and not simply a *re*construction of 'historical facts.' In the description of this 'complex chaos,' therefore, those who undertake such a description make a construction — or *re*description — (Lategan 1985a:75–85) of reality. The constructions of different people may, and often do indeed, differ. This is the basic factor (in addition to the availability of sources et cetera) which is responsible for a 'vast uncertainty of judgment' regarding the historical situations in which New Testament texts originated.

Excursus:

This is evident in the case of Romans 13:1–7. Many different descriptions of its historical situation have been given: (a) Romans 13:1–7 was written from an apocalyptic point of view with the expectation of the immediate return of the Lord to establish the kingdom of God. The parallel with anti-enthusiastic admonitions of Paul in 1 Cor 11:2ff (Käsemann 1969) should be noted and the text should be understood against this background; (b) Romans 13:1–7 was written against revolutionaries who wished to overthrow Roman rule (Borg); (c) The text was written to Jewish-Christians who had lost their property when they had to leave Rome under Claudius and who returned to Rome after his death in 54 and then had to be kept under the thumb, (d) the tax-issue in Rome in the 50's C.E. is the most important issue that forms the historical background against which Romans 13:1-7 should be understood (Friedrich *et al.*; Furnish 1985). It might be possible to come up with even more possibilities, but the problem seems to be 'insoluble.' This line of enquiry ends in the same gridlock as the Donfried-Karris debate about the historical situation of the letter to the Romans as a whole against which Wuellner (1976) protested (see Donfried 1977). Because external information from contemporary writings and other sources is limited, it is almost impossible even to reconstruct a probable historical setting for Romans 13:1-7 (Vorster 1984a:109).

Despite the ambiguity of historical data and the creation of more ambiguities in the process of describing these data, everything is not so vague that the text can be cut loose totally from the ideal of providing and clarifying historical information. To do so is to retrograde to advocating a 'spiritual exegesis' which, for example, 'wrests the parables of Jesus or the letters of Paul from their first century environment without further ado' (Nations 66).

The methods used to describe a historical situation fall under the rubric 'historical method(s),' or in the case of written texts, 'historical criticism.' Nations (63) warns against the fallacy of speaking about '*the* historical-critical method,' when in fact there is a plurality of historical methods. 'Historical paradigm' is therefore a broad and general term for the presuppositions, values, beliefs, techniques and historical methods used to provide perspectives on the data of events, people and phenomena of the past (Vorster 1984a:104). When the description of the historical situation of a text is the purpose of an investigation, 'historical critical method(s)' are usually used. The general perception of the nature of such methods is formulated by Nations (63) in the following way:

> What is ordinarily meant [by a historical-critical method] is not a uniform method but rather a set of assumptions thought to be operative in doing historical research; i.e. criticism must be freed from dogmatic presuppositions, maintain a high degree of objectivity, eschew ecclesiastical controls, and accept secular historians' notions of historical homogeneity, of cause and effect relationships and of the criticism of sources.

The dominance of the historical paradigm in critical New Testament scholarship since the *Aufklärung* is well known, and it is not necessary for our immediate purposes to describe or evaluate it here (see Krentz).[3]   The

---

[3]The arguments of Nations (61-63) regarding the limitations of historical criticism can be summarized in the following points: (1) its distancing effect — Scripture becomes a strange object to be dissected and examined instead of acknowledging it to be a Word that must be heard and obeyed in the present moment; (2) its positivistic underpinnings, (3) oversimplification of the complexities of the ancient period due to the limitation of sources, (4) vast uncertainty of judgment and open skepticism often prevail, and there is no such a thing as a critical consensus; (5) it is doubtful or even impossible to discover the

possibilities and limitations, and the goals and perspectives of an historical approach can be debated in many directions (see, for example, the Vorster-Van Aarde debate in W. S. Vorster 1988 and Van Aarde 1988), yet, in some way or another, historical considerations remain inevitable within the purview of New Testament scholarship. Historical interpretation of the New Testament is necessitated by the very nature of these writings as historical documents. I concur with the following assessment of Vorster (1984a:113):

> One of the basic flaws in the underlying theory of traditional historical-critical interpretation is the assumption that texts are windows through which reality behind the text can be seen . . . . The next flaw is the assumption that historical interpretation is understanding and leads to appropriation and application. One should be very clear about this. The problem of 'what the text says' and 'what the text means' . . . cannot be addressed by historical explanation.

On the basis of this I conclude that, although they cannot be totally isolated from their historical situations, there are facets of New Testament texts which need to be approached from other perspectives (such as linguistics, literary criticism and rhetorical criticism). To address the problems of 'what the text says' and 'what the text meant' satisfactorily, the historical situation of the text needs to be bracketed, and a more specific focus, allowing for the peculiarities of the textuality (for example its literariness and rhetoricity) of the material under investigation deserves priority. But it will be impossible to come up with convincing answers to the questions of the meanings and intentions of these texts if historical considerations are totally disregarded. At a later stage, *after* the textuality and rhetoricity have been taken fully into account, historical considerations again come into play — although then in a quite different manner. To link this point directly with the overall problem with which this volume deals, I submit that an ethics of *reading* thus has preference over an 'ethics of *historical* reading' (see the Introduction, pp. 4–8). On the other hand, an ethically responsible reading of an ancient text inevitably has to deal with historical matters somewhere in the act of interpretation — a matter that will not be taken up in this study.

---

original meaning and intention of a biblical text, (6) it is atomistic and disintegrative, (7) the results of historical critical research cannot be effectively communicated to non-specialists; (8) criteria in terms of which historical methods function (for example the principle of analogy) are inadequate to deal with historic novelty since in biblical narratives there are numerous events without analogy; (9) historical criticism is responsible for a sterility in the academic study of the Bible; (10) historical critical perceptions of myth are reductionist and anti-historical and ignore the power of myth for modern society; (11) the study of the direct, genetic or casual relationships of units with each other is inadequate for a full understanding. I disagree with some of these arguments, but since historical criticism as such is not at issue here, I shall not argue this matter any further.

5.2 Definition and description of the concept 'rhetorical situation'

The academic reflection on the nature of the concept 'rhetorical situation' already has a history of its own. It was first introduced by Bitzer in 1968. The same journal contained responses from Larson, Vatz, Consigny and Brinton. Bitzer himself elaborated on his original proposal in an article in 1980. In New Testament studies Kennedy (1984:34) reintroduced the concept of the rhetorical situation as the first issue to be investigated in rhetorical criticism after the rhetorical unit has been determined. Wuellner (1976) uses the concept in his discussion of Paul's rhetoric of argumentation and later (1987a:450) makes reference to the concept again, underscoring its importance. The concept is also used very prominently by Plank (11–33) in his book on the language of affliction in 1 Corinthians. The identification and the description of the rhetorical situation of Romans are the focus of the thesis by Vorster (1991). In order eventually to define my own perception of the rhetorical situation and distinguish it from the historical situation and the epistolary situation, I will now introduce the basic points in Bitzer's original article and two significant responses to it.

5.2.1 Bitzer's definition

Bitzer (1968:8) maintains that the situation controls the response of the rhetor and proposes the following definition:

> Rhetorical situation may be defined as a complex of persons, events, objects, and relations presenting an actual or potential exigence which can be completely or partially removed if discourse, introduced into the situation, can so constrain human decision or action as to bring about the significant modification of the exigence.

Larson (165) summarized the main elements of Bitzer's definition:

> . . . there are in the world sets of circumstances ("situations") such that they exhibit imperfections ("exigencies") that are (1) urgently in need of correction, and (2) capable of being partly or completely remedied by acts to which a hearer or hearers (an "audience") can be led or moved ("constrained") by some piece of discourse (large or small).

Prior to the creation and presentation of discourse there are three constituents of any rhetorical situation: the first is the exigence; the second and third are elements of the complex, namely the audience to be influenced in decision and action, and the constraints which influence the rhetor and can be brought to bear upon the audience (Bitzer 1968:6).

These three constituents are more specifically described in the following way:

*   Exigence: Exigence is defined as 'an imperfection marked by urgency; it is a defect, an obstacle, something waiting to be done, a thing which is other than it should be . . . . An exigence which cannot be modified is not rhetorical' (Bitzer 1968:6).

*   Audience: Since rhetorical discourse produces change by influencing the decision and action of persons who function as mediators of change, it follows that rhetoric always requires an audience — even in those cases when a person engages himself or an ideal mind as audience. A rhetorical audience consists only of those persons who are capable of being influenced by discourse and of being mediators of change (Bitzer 1968:7, 8).

*   Constraints: Every rhetorical situation contains a set of constraints made up of persons, events, objects and relations that are part of the situation because they have the power to constrain decision and action needed to modify the exigence (Bitzer 1968:8).

Six general characteristics or features of the rhetorical situation and its constituents can be identified:

1)   The situation invites rhetorical discourse. The situation is not a function of the speaker's intention. Discourse remains un-rhetorical as long as it does not fit a situation of real events (Bitzer 1968:9).

2)   The rhetorical situation does not invite any response; it invites a response that fits the situation (Bitzer 1968:10).

3)   If it makes sense to say that situation invites a 'fitting' response, then the situation must somehow prescribe the response that fits. A rhetorical response fits a situation when it meets the requirements established by the situation (Bitzer 1968:10).

4)   The exigence of persons, objects, events and relations that generate rhetorical discourse is located in reality, are objective and publicly observable historic phenomena in the world we experience, and are therefore available for scrutiny by an observer of critic who attends to them (Bitzer 1968:11).

5)   Rhetorical situations exhibit structures that are simple or complex, and more or less organized (Bitzer 1968:11).

6)   Rhetorical situations come into existence, then either mature or decay, or mature and persist — conceivably some persist indefinitely (Bitzer 1968:12).

Rhetorical and non-rhetorical discourse can be distinguished in the following way: if the situation is not real, not grounded in history, neither the fictive situation nor the discourse generated by it is rhetorical (Bitzer 1968:11). Thus, the designation 'rhetorical' should be reserved exclusively for discourse generated in circumstances that have these characteristics.

5.3 Responses to Bitzer's definition

5.3.1 Vatz: rhetoric is the cause, not an effect of meaning

Vatz's (154) main point is that the rhetor is free to create a situation at will. Statements of speakers do not tell us about qualities within a historical situation — they only inform us of the phenomenological perspective of the speaker. A statement can hardly do more than convey the attitude of the person making the reference: 'No situation can have a nature independent of the perception of its interpreter or independent of the rhetoric with which he chooses to characterize it' (Vatz 154).

Vatz (154) maintains that Bitzer works with a 'realist' philosophy of meaning. For this philosophy meaning resides in events, thus, 'meaning is regarded as intrinsic to the thing that has it, being a natural part of the objective makeup of the thing.' This presupposition is responsible for Bitzer's view of the relationship between 'situations' and rhetoric, namely that there is an intrinsic nature in events from which rhetoric inexorably follows or should follow. For Vatz Bitzer's views are consistent given Bitzer's Platonistic *Weltanschauung*. Bitzer sees a world in which

> the exigence and the complex of persons, objects, events and relations which generate rhetorical discourse are located in reality, are objective and publicly observable historic facts in the world we experience, and are therefore available for scrutiny by an observer or critic who attends to them.

Such a perception is labelled by Vatz as 'The myth of the rhetorical situation' (Vatz). His critique is that '[f]ortunately or unfortunately meaning is not intrinsic in events, facts, people, or "situations" nor are facts publicly observable.' Except for those situations which directly confront our own empirical reality, we learn of facts and events through someone's communicating them to us. This involves a two-part process, namely, (i) a choice of events to communicate and (ii) the 'translation' of the chosen information into meaning.

* Choice: The 'facts' or 'events' communicated to us are choices by our sources of information. Which facts or events are relevant is a matter of pure arbitration (Vatz 157).

* 'Translation': The translation of chosen information into meaning is an act of creativity — it is an interpretive act and is a rhetorical act of transcendence. To the audience, events become meaningful only through their linguistic deception. Therefore, meaning is not discovered in situations, but *created* by rhetors (Vatz 157).

Vatz's (157) valid conclusion is that '[n]o theory of the relationship between situations and rhetoric can neglect to take account of the initial linguistic depiction of the situation.'

The ethical implications of such a view of rhetoric can be formulated in the following way: If you follow Bitzer (subscribing to a 'realistic' philosophy), you ascribe little responsibility to the rhetor with respect to what he or she has chosen to give salience. If you follow Vatz (by holding that the communication of an event is a choice, interpretation, and translation) the rhetor's responsibility is of supreme concern:

> To view rhetoric as a creation of reality or salience rather than a reflector of reality clearly increases the rhetor's moral responsibility . . . . He must assume responsibility for the salience he has created (Vatz 158).

On the issue of the relationship between rhetoric and situation, Vatz (159) therefore takes converse positions on each of Bitzer's major statements:

> I would not say "rhetoric is situational," but situations are rhetorical; not ". . . exigence strongly invites utterance," but utterance strongly invites exigence; not "the situation controls the rhetorical response . . ." but rhetoric controls the situational response; not ". . . rhetorical discourse . . . does obtain its character-as-rhetorical from the situation which generates it," but situations obtain their character from the rhetoric that surrounds them or creates them.

Vatz (160) underscores his position by quoting Edelman:

> Language does not mirror an objective "reality" but rather creates it by organizing meaningful perceptions abstracted from a complex, bewildering world.

Thus rhetoric is a cause, not an effect of meaning. It is antecedent, not subsequent, to a situation's impact. The *sine qua non* of rhetoric is that it is *the art of linguistically or symbolically creating salience.* After salience has been created, the situation must be translated into meaning. It is only then — when the meaning is seen as the result of a creative act and not a discovery — that rhetoric will be perceived as the supreme discipline it deserves to be (Vatz 161).

5.3.2 *Consigny: rhetoric as an 'art' as mediating factor*

Consigny (176) maintains that Bitzer and Vatz together pose an antinomy for a coherent theory of rhetoric: for Bitzer the situation controls the response of the rhetor; for Vatz the rhetor is free to create a situation at will. Consigny argues that 'this apparent antinomy arises from particular views which fail to account for actual rhetorical practice, and that this antinomy disappears with a complete view of the rhetorical act' (Consigny 176). Consigny argues that Bitzer correctly construes the rhetorical situation as characterized by 'particularities,' but misconstrues the situation as being thereby determinate and determining. Vatz, on the other hand, correctly treats the rhetor as creative, but he fails to account for the real constraints on the rhetor's activity.

The rhetor cannot create exigencies arbitrarily, but must take into account the particularities of each situation in which he actively becomes engaged (Consigny 176).

To resolve the apparent antinomy of rhetor and situation, Consigny (179-181) proposes a mediating third factor which he calls 'rhetoric as an art.' The two conditions that 'art' must meet to allow the rhetor to become creatively engaged in particular situations are integrity and receptivity.

* Integrity demands that rhetoric as an 'art' provides the rhetor with a 'universal' capacity such that the rhetor can function in all kinds of indeterminate and particular situations as they arise (Consigny 180). The rhetor's universality is restricted to the particular and indeterminate situations which Consigny characterizes as 'rhetorical.' The rhetor must be constrained in that he can function in novel but real situations, being true to the particularities of each.

* The 'art' of rhetoric must meet the condition of receptivity allowing the rhetor to become engaged in individual situations without simply inventing and thereby predetermining which problems he is going to find in them (Consigny 181).

5.3.3 Brinton: exigence and interest

Brinton (242-245) also, and to my mind, justifiedly, objects to Bitzer's (somewhat naive) notion of the 'objectivity' of the exigence which Bitzer identifies as one of the three constituent elements of the rhetorical situation. Instead of thinking about 'objective' facts in the world we experience as necessary constituents of the exigence as Bitzer proposes, Brinton (246) argues that the rhetorical situation only comes into existence when the exigence of the situation comes into relation with the interest of the rhetor. The exigence is a constituent of the situation, but it is exigent only in relation to an external term. Exigence becomes exigent only when *interest* is imposed on the situation (Vorster (1991:30).

By introducing a relational view on the rhetorical situation and the rhetor, Brinton offers a helpful way to cope with the subject-object dualism that has dominated the Bitzer-Vatz debate, without allowing total relativism. Vorster's (1991:30) presentation of this relational perspective is satisfactory, and with that we conclude our discussion of the rhetorical situation:

> If the 'interest' of the rhetoric then acts upon a basic set of facts to constitute a (*sic*) exigency the creative role of the rhetor in regard to the rhetorical situation must be conceded. If the interest of the rhetor plays the role of catalyst in the constitution of the exigency of the rhetorical situation 'objectivity' has been minimized to the existence of a basic set of facts . . . that there are objective matters of fact cannot be denied, but how they constitute the exigency of the rhetorical situation is determined by the 'interest' of the rhetor . . . that these facts can be combined in an exigency is due to the interest of the rhetor.

5.4 The relation between the historical situation and the rhetorical situation

Historical situation can be understood in quite a comprehensive manner, encompassing all the events, objects, persons, abstractions and relations (social, political, personal, cultural, ideological, ecological, or whatever) that constituted a situation which existed in the past in time and space and which could have been or was in actual fact experienced by human beings (see §5.1). Within this 'complex and bewildering chaos,' human discourse and social interaction take place. Rhetoric has been identified as one (among other) possible types or modes of discourse (§2.2). Therefore, any rhetorical situation is of necessity embedded within an historical situation. Yet, historical situation and rhetorical situation are not identical. Rhetorical situation is more specific in many respects. It is always an element in/of a human communication situation, in which language usually plays the dominant (though not exclusive) role (depending on how broadly one defines 'language'). Rhetorical situation is always an element in/of a specific type of human communication, namely goal-oriented social interaction, or persuasion. Historical objects or events, or 'facts,' or 'givens,' obviously do not vanish from this situation. The important thing, however, is that the exigency of a rhetorical situation is constitutive for the rhetorical situation only if the interests of the rhetor are brought into relationship with the existence of such a set of 'facts.' Related to the historical situation, therefore, this basic set of 'facts' comes into existence *as a creation of the rhetor*. In a rhetorical approach the aim is not to describe historical information about the text or its possible referents. Rhetorical criticism is interested in the historical situation of the text for the sake of argumentation. Its objective is not to reconstruct the original historical readers or the real author. It focuses on the text as 'a more or less independent argumentative unity' (Thurén 55). Rhetorical criticism, therefore, does not ignore the historical aspect of a text, neither does it solely depend on it. In a rhetorical approach, the notion of the rhetorical situation is of fundamental importance.

5.5 The relation between epistolary situation and rhetorical situation

Since the notion of the epistolary situation and its relation to historical situation were defined and described in some detail in chapter 2 (§6.3.1), we can be brief at this point. The epistolary situation must not be confused with the actual historical situation or occasion which caused the letter to be written. The epistolary situation is primarily a text-internal, literary, phenomenon. It is the situation created by the structural framework that identifies the writing as a letter.

When the rhetorical situation is understood as an element in/of a specific mode of human discourse, namely goal-oriented human interaction (or persuasion), the epistolary situation is one possible specific manifestation of a rhetorical situation, coming into existence when this interaction takes place by means of a letter. Furthermore Wuellner (1987a:456) writes:

> The rhetorical situation differs both from the historical situation of a given author and reader and from the generic situation or conventions of the *Sitz im Leben* of forms or genres in one point: the rhetorical critic looks foremost for the premises of a text as appeal or argument.

The implication of these conceptions of the epistolary situation and the rhetorical situation is that the 'actors' in this goal-oriented interaction by means of the letter to the Romans (Paul and the Roman communities to whom the letter was addressed) should not be simplistically equated with the real historical people to whom these names referred (see Du Toit 1989:196, who calls such an equation a 'referential fallacy'). Both need to be understood in the first place as abstractions and constructions created in the processes of the textuality and the rhetoricity of the letter. This does not imply that they cease to refer to historical people. Although modern rhetoric has realized that the situation and the audience are in a real manner a construct of the rhetor (or in case of a letter, the author), this construction cannot be completely at odds with the historical situation if the argument is to be effective (Kraftchick 1990:57). The letter to the Romans came into existence as a rhetorical act and as such as an historical artifact embedded in the culture of the first century. Consideration of the codes, conventions, general knowledge and value systems of this culture must form part of any plausible interpretation of this letter. Part of the purpose of the rhetorical reading of Romans 13:1–7 is to 'discover' or lay bare some of the elements of this code and to determine how they functioned in the argumentative strategy of this passage. But it must be clear by now that this process, is an intermediary step, preceding and differing from any conclusions or claims about the real historical first century situation in which the passage came into existence. In the next chapter, 'Reading Romans 13:1–7 from a Social-scientific Perspective,' these considerations will be closer to the focus of our attention.

On the basis of the theoretical aspects discussed up to this point, we are now in a position to focus specifically on the text of the letter to the Romans, reading it from a rhetorical critical perspective. This reading consists of two stages. First (in §6) the rhetorical situation of the letter as a whole is considered in order to provide a framework and broader context for the reading of specifically Romans 13:1–7 in more detail (in §7).

6. The rhetorical situation of the Letter to the Romans

6.1 Part and whole in a rhetorical critical reading

In the practical method that Kennedy proposes for rhetorical criticism, he indicates that the determination of the rhetorical unit is the first thing to be done (1984:33). It will be argued in §7.1 that Romans 13:1–7 satisfies all the requirements to be identified as a rhetorical unit. Kennedy (1984:33) maintains that the rhetoric of large units (such as the letter to the Romans as a whole) often has to be built up from an understanding of the rhetoric of smaller units. If a rhetorical analysis of the whole of Romans is the purpose, it might be necessary to begin with analyses of smaller units within the letter and to build up towards the whole. A more practical approach for the present study, however, is to take over some of the conclusions of scholars who worked with Romans as a whole as the object of their rhetorical analyses and to use those analyses as a framework and context for a more detailed and more specific analysis of Romans 13:1–7.

A rhetorical analysis of a part of Romans in isolation from the larger context or rhetorical situation of the letter as such (for example Snyman 1988b) forfeits its plausibility. This position is well argued by Plank (11):

> Literary and rhetorical criticism seek to illumine the interaction of textual part and whole. Over against the legacy of piecemeal reading — habits of interpretation that sever given bits of text from their relationship with other portions of a common text — the literary or the rhetorical critic emphasizes the vital role of textual context in discerning the meaning of any given passage. No portion of text bears meaning in general, but only in terms of some context which locates it in a specific sphere of discourse. In context, the meaning of a text becomes perceptible and particular. Yet not just any context will suffice. For the literary or rhetorical critic, a portion of a text is first of all a textual reality, shaped and enriched by its place within a larger textual whole. The interaction between that whole and part reveals the underlying values of the world which the text creates. It maps the textual foreground and obligates the critical reader to take seriously the full dimensions of literary context.

Jüngel went a long way towards this ideal in his study of Romans 13:1–7 (Jüngel). In his reading of Romans 13:1–7 within the context of the letter as a whole, however, he does not work with rhetorical critical categories but within a semantic (or content-oriented) paradigm. For my purpose here, I need to consider the rhetorical situation of the letter as a whole to fill in the context for our subsequent rhetorical critical reading of Romans 13:1–7.

6.2   Approaches to a rhetorical critical reading of the Letter to the Romans and a description of its rhetorical situation

Four approaches to the rhetorical critical study of the letter to the Romans can be distinguished, namely, (i) a form-critical approach, (ii) a structural or dispositional approach, (iii) an argumentative approach, and (iv) an interactional approach.

6.2.1   A form-critical approach

A general characteristic of form-critical rhetorical analysis is that formal features of the letter to the Romans are identified on the basis of genealogical and analogical relationships with Greco-Roman oratorical genres, and probable sociological contexts are then constructed (Vorster 1991:17–20; Robbins 1990:262–263).   Exponents of this approach are Scroggs (1976), Stowers (1981) and Schmeller.

Scroggs (1976:271–298) identifies two homilies in Romans, namely an exegetical homily (Romans 1–4 and 9–11) and a diatribal homily (Romans 5–8).   For the former he visualizes a sociological context of the Jews and for the latter a Hellenistic-synagogal milieu. Both are concerned with preaching.

Stowers and Schmeller concentrate on the diatribe in Romans. Comparing Romans with works of Stoic-Cynic popular philosophers, they describe the typical formal features of the diatribe and its composition.   Stowers (1981:175–184) concludes that the form of the diatribe in Romans and the way it functions presuppose a student-teacher relationship. Thus, for him the use of the diatribe indicates that Paul's intentions to visit the Roman Christians (ἵνα τινὰ καρπὸν σχῶ καὶ ἐν ὑμῖν καθὼς καὶ ἐν τοῖς λοιποῖς ἔθνεσιν, 1:13) should not be subordinated to the allusion to his hoped-for support for a trip to Spain (15:24) (Stowers 1981:182).   The rhetorical situation of Romans, thus, is that of a teacher, written to address the Romans' pedagogical needs.   The dialogical style of Romans is evidence for Paul's 'school.'   In the letter to the Romans, two activities of this 'school' can be found, namely the exegesis and interpretation of the Scriptures and ethical-religious instruction in the style of indictment and protreptic (Stowers 1981:183).

It is clear, then, that in these studies the form that is identified in the letter is used to identify the actual reality of its origin, social context, and purpose.   However, I concur with Vorster (1991:19) that, in doing this, they confuse the generic context of the homily or diatribe with the specific context of the letter.

6.2.2 A structural or dispositional approach

In the structural or dispositional approach, meaning is largely seen as some-thing that is constituted by the relationship between linguistic entities on dif-ferent levels. Therefore, the classical rhetorical phase of the *dispositio* plays an important role. One of the most important determinants for the *dispositio* is the rhetorical genre (Leeman & Braet 94–95). Accordingly, in this approach, the structural analysis of the letter serves to determine its rhetorical genre. Genre forms one component of the rhetorical situation; therefore it helps to determine the meaning of the discourse, and by doing this, the ques-tion of the purpose of the discourse comes into view (see Vorster 1991:21–27). Exponents of the structural or dispositional approach are Wuellner (1976), Kennedy (1984), and Jewett (1986).

There seems to be general agreement that the rhetorical genre of Romans should be seen as epideictic (Wuellner 1976:337; Kennedy 1984: 152; Fraiken 92; Jewett 1986:383; Aune 1987:219; Snyman 1988b:228). Because the genre is epideictic, it follows that the purpose of Romans is to affirm communal values shared by Paul and the Romans (Wuellner 1976:337; see Burgess and Perelman & Olbrechts-Tyteca 47–51 on the purpose of epi-deictic discourse). More specifically, but still based on its identification as epideictic, Jewett (1986:383) sees the purpose of the letter as the unification of the various house churches in Rome and the suspension between the 'weak' Jewish Christians and the 'strong' Gentile Christians to avoid the jeopardizing of Paul's intended mission to Spain. In his turn, Fraiken (98, 103) infers from the identification of the genre of Romans as epideictic that the purpose of the letter is the restoration of Paul's credibility among a Gentile Christian audience. Still on the basis of rhetorical genres, Aune (1987:219) argues for two levels on which the purpose of Romans should be understood: the presentation of Paul's gospel in Romans 1–11 is epideictic within the epistolary situation of the letter, but in the prior situation of his ministry it was protreptic, that is, its function was to demonstrate the truth of the Christian gospel and to convince the hearers to commit themselves to it by becoming Christian converts.

It is clear that rhetorical genre consistently forms an important element in dispositional or structurally oriented rhetorical analyses and is used to dis-cover and describe the letter's purpose and rhetorical situation. Vorster (1991:24–27) convincingly demonstrates the limitations of reading Romans (solely) from the perspective of Greco-Roman rhetorical genres (see also §2.3.4 and §7.2.3). For instance, he demonstrates that good arguments can be presented to identify the genre of Romans as either deliberative[4] or

---

[4]The letter functions as a preparation for Paul's visit. Preparing for his visit implies

forensic[5] (Vorster 1991:26–27). This is not to say, however, that the results of genre-oriented rhetorical analyses of Romans are without value. The important point, though, is that genre-considerations are but one aspect to be taken into account in the determination of the rhetorical situation of the letter. It is not the sole determinative factor.

6.2.3 An argumentative approach

A unifying factor in the argumentative approach is a focus on the argumentative or persuasive strategies used by Paul. Exponents of this approach are Siegert, Fraiken, Du Toit (1989), N. Elliott (1990) and Hester (1991). In general the objective of these studies is to analyze and describe Paul's persuasive or argumentative strategies, for example, in the letter-opening and letter-closing (Elliott), in Romans 9–11 (Siegert), or the use of maxims as argumentative strategy (Hester). The results of the dispositional approach are used, but the analyses are not restricted to disposition and genre. Argumentation is seen as a social event (Siegert 91).

6.2.4 An interactional approach

In the interactional approach the argumentative approach is developed further, in particular its interdisciplinary leanings. A major exponent of this approach is J. N. Vorster (1990; 1991). Prompted in part by the direction taken by Siegert towards rhetoric as a social event, Vorster has worked out an interdisciplinary model for an interactional reading of the letter, utilizing elements from speech act analysis, reception criticism and conversational analysis (1990) and has put it to practice in his study of the rhetorical situation of Romans (1991).

Vorster works with a very sophisticated model, providing as far as possible for the particularities of the epistolarity of Romans, language as social

---

that the audience has to be persuaded to accept him, has to be persuaded to assist him financially, and has to be persuaded to assist him in establishing a base in Rome from where further missionary enterprises can be undertaken (15:23). Therefore he indicates that his visit to them would be to their advantage also (1:11, 13; 15:16, 29). References to hope and fear, two of the important elements of the deliberative genre, abound in the letter.

[5]Paul must defend his past absence. He does this by emphasizing that he was hindered from doing so (1:13; 15:20, 22, 23). The case for the forensic genre is strengthened by the presence of the *conquestio* (in which sympathy for his own party is sought) when Paul refers to the possible threat awaiting him in Jerusalem (15:30–31). The main theme is formed by the various passages in which controversy with the Jews appears, and these seem to confirm that this is a *Leitaffekt* in the letter.

interaction, and the role of interactional (or rhetorical) strategies in the letter. He has analyzed the frame of the letter, that is, the letter-opening (which he takes as 1:1–17) and the letter-closing (which he takes as 15:7 – 16:23) in detail (1991:94–233). On the basis of this analysis he arrives at a rather elaborate description of the elements of the rhetorical situation of the letter to the Romans, namely, the concretization of the exigence (or *causa*) of the letter and the parties who have an interest in the rhetorical situation (namely the encoded author and the implied readers) (1991:234–258). The rhetorical situation described could be inferred from Paul's perspective on the situation, expressed in written language. This perspectivistic element of the rhetorical situation was used by Vorster to formulate the question or need as well as the persons who have an interest in the rhetorical act. Since the conception of the rhetorical situation as worked out by Vorster (1991:234–258) will be used as the larger context for our own rhetorical analysis of Romans 13:1–7, the basic elements of that conception are presented here.

6.2.4.1 The causa of the Letter to the Romans

That Paul wants something from his readers is more probable than that he is merely providing them with information. Paul wants cooperation from his readers on five different levels. Their future cooperation is the *factum* of the rhetorical situation. The *dubium* is whether Paul has the right to demand this cooperation. As such the rhetorical situation can be qualified as *status qualitatis* (see §7.2). Although the *status* seems to remain the same, the genre oscillates between epideictic and deliberative, with the emphasis on the latter. The reciprocal action expected from the readers is to decide whether they will give Paul their cooperation or not. Characteristic of the deliberative genre, a decision in the future is expected from the audience.

Paul seeks cooperation on five levels:

* He asks his readers' cooperation in accepting him as their apostle too. His being apostle-to-the-Gentiles includes them. He wants to persuade them that he is also their apostle and therefore has the right to request their cooperation.
* The cooperation of the readers is necessary for the establishment of a base in Rome. Despite the salient fact that he describes his proposed visit as 'passing through' (15:23, 24, 28), he sees Rome not merely as a temporary station. His repeated references to his past intentions to visit the Romans (1:10, 13; 15:23) and the frequently mentioned movement which has Rome as its goal (1:10, 11, 13, 15; 15:22, 23, 24, 28, 29, 32), as well as the activities that he foresees for himself when he is in Rome, suggest that he intends a longer stay there. Playing down the length of his stay in the letter is an understandable politeness strategy, considering the delicate rhetorical situation.
* He needs cooperation for further enterprises beyond Rome, particularly his envisioned mission to Spain. He hopes that the believers in Rome will play an

important role in his future missions by providing him with comprehensive assistance (15:24c).

* He also requests the cooperation of the readers for the period between their reception of the letter and his arrival in Rome: he requests the cooperation of the readers for his visit to Jerusalem. He asks them to join him in prayer that his ministry will be acceptable to the believers in Jerusalem (15:30–31).

* The final level on which Paul seeks cooperation from his readers is in their attitude towards the Jews. The Jews' rejection of the gospel is perceived by Paul as a threat to the incipient Christian movement, and this threat is another reason for the letter. The role and position of the (non-Christian) Jews in the salvation plan of God seem to have been, in Paul's perception, very delicate. Paul sees his relationship with his readers, namely the Gentile-Christians in Rome, as part of the broader picture of the Jew-Gentile relationship (yet the Jew-Gentile problematic in the letter does not necessarily reflect a particular historical situation in Rome). For him the Gentiles' relationship with the Jews has salvation-historical significance (11:11–24). A general conflict looms between the mother (Jewish) and daughter (Christian) movements — according to Paul the mother-movement seems to deny the daughter-movement her rightful status. In this delicate situation, the letter aims to restore the credibility of Paul's gospel and those who adhere to it. The position of the implied readers, the Gentile Christians, must therefore be clarified. He does so by making the values of the Jewish theological system his point of departure, and in the process redefines Israel: adhering to Paul's gospel is actually a continuation of God's universal design which originated in Israel. Defining the Gentile believers in terms of a redefinition of the Jewish value-system, specifically the covenant (which must, according to Paul, not be understood in an exclusivist sense), the roles of the Gentiles and Jews are reversed. The Gentiles become instrumental in conveying the gospel to the Jews. Paul wants to persuade his readers that the rejection of the Jews should not be reciprocated with rejection, but a strategy of compromise instead of confrontation should be followed. He wants to integrate rather than segregate the Jews and the Christians.

In sum, we may say that Paul wants to persuade his readers that he can and must request their cooperation and that they can and should provide it.

6.2.4.2 The encoded author in the Letter to the Romans

The encoded author corresponds to the rhetorical notion of 'person-construction' or the establishment of ethos. The construction of Paul's person serves to remove any doubt and establish his right to ask their cooperation. His authority, therefore, is the question to which the construction of his person is the response.

A number of uncertainties concerning his person could, from Paul's perspective, have prevailed among his audience:

* He was relatively unknown to them.
* They may have doubted whether his apostleship included them too (his apostleship as such seems not to be at issue — Romans is therefore not an apologetic letter).

    *   He has not visited them yet.

    *   His visit to them is yet again postponed because of a visit to Jerusalem.

As a response to these perceived uncertainties, the encoded author is constructed so as to indicate the appropriateness of his response for the situation.

Regarding his relationship with the Gentiles, Paul consistently portrays himself as apostle to the Gentiles, including the Romans. All his statements about his Gentile ministry in general are followed or preceded by a specific statement concerning his ministry to the implied readers (1:5 with 1:6; 1:13d with 1:13e; 1:14 with 1:15; 15:15 with 15:16; 15:18-21 with 15:23). The encoded author always functions in the role of benefactor. Sharing a spiritual χάρισμα could produce τινα καρπόν (1:11, 13) and a εὐπρόσδεκτος ἡ προσφορά (a more acceptable offering) (15:16). The role of benefactor provides the encoded author with a pragmatic component — to cooperate with him will be to the advantage of the implied readers. His apostleship to the Gentiles also provides the encoded author with an authoritarian component — although this authority is rather disguised in the letter. Although the implied readers belong to Paul's sphere of ministry and are as such, in his perception, under his authority, his need of their cooperation puts them in a position of power. He cannot expose his authority too bluntly, because then he runs the risk of offending the implied readers whom he has not yet met and who could doubt whether his authority is applicable to them. In this situation, he disguises his authority by making it relative to external powers, namely God (1:2) or Christ (15:18-19a).

Regarding his relationship with the Jews, he defines himself in terms of Jewish values shared by him and the implied readers. The Gentile Christian audience of the letter, although Gentile, hold to (redefined) Jewish values since they have become Christians. His apostleship is firmly rooted in Jewish tradition, as redefined by him. By emphasizing their shared common values, he also confirms these values. This is a powerful means of association with his readers. Paul and his readers belong to the same 'in-group,' sharing the same values, and, by virtue of these values he has been, as apostle to the Gentiles, assigned to them too.

6.2.4.3 The implied readers in the Letter to the Romans

The audience, as it is described here, is an intratextual construct, and should therefore not be identified with the actual historical readers of the letter. It is Paul's image of his audience. The implied readers are situated in Rome.

They consisted of a homogenous group of non-Jews who have become Christians, or Gentile Christians. There may (historically) have been Jewish-Christians in Rome, but they are not included in Paul's image of his intended readers.[6]

The Gentiles are contrasted with the Jews in many respects: they are not circumcised (2:25-27; 4:11-12), they are not under the law (3:19), their past does not characterize them as 'people of God' and thus they have not been given the privileges of the Jewish nation (2:19-20; 9:4-5; 11:17ff). They are by nature a wild olive tree and grafted, contrary to nature, onto a cultivated olive tree (11:24). They do not have the same priority as the Jewish nation. Because of their inferior past and uncircumcised state they are rejected by the Jews. Yet Paul defines the Gentile Christian in terms of a redefinition of the Jewish religion. He becomes the 'true Jew,' with the law written in his heart, and being circumcised in his heart (2:15-16, 25-29). The designations exclusive to Jews (for example, Abraham as forefather 4:11-12) are reinterpreted to include the Gentiles in God's overall design for the world. All the privileges of the Jews are transferred to the Gentiles, they are called $\kappa\lambda\eta\tauo i$ (1:6), $\upsilon io i$ $\theta\varepsilon o\hat{\upsilon}$ (8:14) and $\kappa\lambda\eta\rho o\nu\acute{o}\mu o\iota$ (8:17); they receive a $\pi\nu\varepsilon\hat{\upsilon}\mu\alpha$ $\upsilon io\theta\varepsilon\sigma i\alpha\varsigma$ (8:15). All this, of course, has been valid of Jewish believers also. But, with regard to Jewish non-believers, the Gentile implied readers get the role to function as co-workers of Paul's ministry in that their election is an act of mercy (11:17-24) with a purpose beyond themselves, namely to the Jews also (11:25-32). They have an obligation towards Israel, a situation that distinguishes them from the Jewish Christians.

Paul identifies with the implied readers: both he and they (although they are Gentiles) have been made part of God's salvation plan with God's people, the Jews. Consequently, they stand in continuation with Israel. They are clothed with Jewish honorific titles (such as $\kappa\lambda\eta\tauo i$ 1:5; $\dot{\alpha}\gamma\alpha\pi\eta\tauo\hat{\iota}\varsigma$ $\theta\varepsilon o\hat{\upsilon}$ 1:6; $\kappa\lambda\eta\tauo\hat{\iota}\varsigma$ $\dot{\alpha}\gamma i o\iota\varsigma$ 1:6). They are pictured as well-acquainted with the Jewish value-system, and they adhere to these values. As people of God they and Paul belong to the same 'in-group.' They are held in high esteem. They are expected to appreciate the honors bestowed on them (namely, the honorific titles and Paul's identification with them). Paul's apostolate and his interest

---

[6]That the intended audience of the letter to the Romans consists of Gentile Christians, *excluding* Jewish Christians, is convincingly argued by Vorster (1991:101-103, 105-106). The implied readers are identified with $\pi\acute{\alpha}\nu\tau\alpha$ $\check{\varepsilon}\theta\nu\eta$ in 1:5: $\dot{\varepsilon}\nu$ $o\hat{\iota}\varsigma$ $\dot{\varepsilon}\sigma\tau\varepsilon$ $\kappa\alpha\grave{\iota}$ $\dot{\upsilon}\mu\varepsilon\hat{\iota}\varsigma$. The $\check{\varepsilon}\theta\nu\eta$ do not include the Jewish nation. In fact, it functions rhetorically as an opposite to the Jews. As ethnographical designation $\check{\varepsilon}\theta\nu\eta$ does not refer to all nations *per se*, but to all *non-Jewish* nations (Vorster 1991:102, with reference to Käsemann 1980:15; Cranfield 1975:67; Ridderbos 27; Schlier 29-30; Wilckens 1978:67). Vorster (1991:103) asserts emphatically: 'To include the Jewish nation within the designation $\check{\varepsilon}\theta\nu\eta$ is to do exactly what Paul does not want to do in the *prescript*!'

in them are described from the perspective of Israel's history. By affirming and strengthening their mutual Jewish value-system, Paul hopes to move them to a positive response towards his request for cooperation.

The implied readers are portrayed as a group that has power (δυνατοί, 1:5). They are cautioned not to overestimate themselves (11:18–24) or to judge others (14:13). They know the law (7:1) and share the Judaic tradition, and they can read the signs of the times (13:11). As such (since they are powerful) they can be Paul's co-workers and share in his ministry. That is exactly what he requests from them. But at the same time, they are depicted as belonging to Paul's sphere of authority, and he can act as benefactor towards them. They can be of benefit to him; that is why he asks their cooperation. But he can also be to their benefit (1:11). They are portrayed as people in power, but they can also derive their power from Paul. A certain tension can thus be detected in Paul's relationship with the implied readers.

In summary: The purpose of writing the letter to Gentile Christians is to request their future cooperation. In order to persuade them to do this, the letter functions to identify the encoded author with the implied readers by confirming their mutual value-system. In the general tension between Jews and Gentiles, the letter serves to enhance and confirm the status of the Gentile Christian implied readers. To determine how Romans 13:1–7 fits within this picture will now be our concern. This will be done by means of a rhetorical critical reading of Romans 13:1–7.

7. A rhetorical critical reading of Romans 13:1–7

Based on classical rhetorical theory, Kennedy (1984:33–38) proposes five stages for a rhetorical critical reading of New Testament texts: (i) the identification of the rhetorical unit, (ii) the identification of the rhetorical situation, (iii) the identification of the rhetorical disposition or arrangement, (iv) the identification of the rhetorical techniques or style, and (v) the identification of rhetorical criticism as a synchronic whole. Within this framework our own rhetorical critical reading of Romans 13:1–7 will now be undertaken, although we will not limit ourselves to classical school rhetoric but elaborate on the framework to include elements of modern rhetorical theory.

7.1 The identification of the rhetorical unit

Kennedy (1984:34) defines a rhetorical unit as a textual unit having '. . . some magnitude. It has to have within itself a discernible beginning and ending, connected by some action or argument.' For Wuellner (1987a:455) a rhetorical unit is in all respects similar to a literary unit, except in one point namely that it '. . . defines a text unit as an argumentative unit affecting the reader's reasoning or the reader's imagination. A rhetorical unit is either a convincing or persuasive unit.' Romans 13:1-7 satisfies both these definitions and can therefore be taken as a rhetorical unit.

The semantic and structural arguments put forward above to identify Romans 13:1-7 as a distinctive unit (see chapter 1, §9) are all relevant here. I have indicated a number of them, for example: introduced with an exhortation, a new one in a series of exhortations stretching from 12:9, Romans 13:1 has a discernible beginning. In contradistinction to the previous exhortations (12:9-21), the exhortation in 13:1 is followed by demonstrative argumentation, with the repeated use of argumentative indices such as γάρ (13:1, 3, 4, 6), ὥστε (13:2), διό (13:5), and διὰ τοῦτο (13:6). The end of Romans 13:1-7 as a rhetorical unit is marked by formal stylistic devices (see §7.4), wrapping up the argumentation on the issue of conduct towards governing authorities.

With regard to its argumentative nature, specifically its inner logic and persuasive strategy, more arguments can be raised in favor of treating Romans 13:1-7 as a distinct rhetorical unit. McDonald (342-343) identifies three roles in Romans 13:1-7, namely:

* that of the authorities, indicated with ὑπέρ (ὑπερεχούσαις)
* that assigned to the 'everyone' (πᾶσα ψυχή), indicated with ὑπό (ὑποτασ-σέσθω) — a role with which the implied readers are identified in 13:6-7
* the illegitimate response to the basic command, denoted by ἀντί (ἀντιτασ-σόμενος, ἀνθέστηκεν).

McDonald argues that the interplay of these parties constitutes the interactive structure of the text and reveals the persuasive strategy of the encoded author. Integral to the persuasive strategy is an appeal to 'conscience' (διὰ τὴν συνείδησιν, 13:5). The interaction of these three roles (analyzed in more detail in §7.3) and the specific persuasive strategy operative in this interaction are peculiar to Romans 13:1-7 — these roles are not present in its co-text. On the basis of this inner logic the passage is completely self-contained and in some respects an isolated unity. However, McDonald (342) overstates his case by maintaining that '. . . the primary base of authentic interpretation is to be located in the inner logic of the passage *rather* than in its literary context' (my italics; on the part-whole issue, see §6.1.). Since it has a discernible beginning and end, and since it can function as an argumentative unit affecting the reader's reasoning, Romans 13:1-7 can be identified as a rhetorical unit.

7.2 The identification of the rhetorical situation

The rhetorical situation of Romans 13:1–7 will be described in terms of the four constitutive elements of a rhetorical situation: (i) its *status*, (ii) the creation of persons and their roles, (iii) the rhetorical genre and, (iv) the identification of *topoi* and persuasive strategies.

7.2.1 The status of the rhetorical situation of Romans 13:1–7

The 'need' or the exigence of a situation becomes concrete in the *quaestio* or the question of the situation. The question dominates the rhetorical situation and therefore determines its *status* (Vorster 1991:54). Since Hermagoras (thus, after Aristotle but before the first century of the Common Era), the classical doctrine of *status* has been the cornerstone of classical rhetorical theory of argumentation, in particular the Greek and Roman doctrines of *inventio* and hence the entire rhetorical system (Braet 79). Braet (79–93) illustrates that a rhetorical theory of argumentation with a doctrine of status at its core presupposes a critically reacting audience (contrary to a popular misconception that a rhetorical approach pays all its attention to effecting a passive response in an audience by means of a monologue). The doctrine of *status* developed in the situation of ancient legal proceedings. Argumentation is seen as a critical discussion: it is an interaction between a protagonist and an antagonist of a particular standpoint in respect of an expressed opinion. Seen in a broader perspective (namely as any type of interaction between rhetor and audience, not only that of legal proceedings), the concept is applicable as a heuristic device in the analysis of any argumentation.

From ancient rhetoric we know that the concept of *status* (Greek: στάσις) was linked to the so-called κρινόμενον-scheme. The purpose of this scheme is to steer the *inventio* of the prosecutor and the defendant in legal proceedings. Both parties imagine the courtroom during their preparations. They anticipate their opponent's arguments and decide on their reaction to them. In this way they deduce the κρινόμενον, that is, the crucial question that the judge must answer. Then, with the aid of *topoi*, they look specifically for arguments to back up their position with regard to the κρινόμενον (Braet 81). The notion of *status* can be rendered in English in a number of ways (Braet 89–90):

* starting point (of the *inventio*: the seeking of argumentation for the standpoint)
* main issue (of the argumentation)
* point of questioning, judgment, or decision (for the judge) (Braet 81).

Four types of *status* were identified in classical rhetoric, depending on the type of question the rhetor would put to himself (Quintilian *Institutio Oratoria* 7; see also Lausberg 85–108; Corbett 35–38; Leeman & Braet):

* *An sit?* (εἰ ἐστι;) (whether a thing is). When focused on legal proceedings, the question is phrased *an fecerit?* Did he or she in fact do it? For example, did Brutus, as has been alleged, kill Caesar? The type of *status* created by this question is called the *status coniecturae* (στοχάσμος). The emphasis is on the subject of the deed.

* *Quid sit?* (τί ἐστι;) (what is it?). When focused on legal proceedings, the question is phrased as *quid fecerit?* What has the accused done? How can the deed be described or defined? For example, if it is granted that Brutus *did* kill Caesar, was the act murder or self-defense? The type of *status* created by this question is called the *status definitivus* (ὅρος). The emphasis is on the deed and the appropriateness of the linguistic qualification of the deed. Uncertainty exists as to the precise definition or naming of the deed.

* *Quale sit?* (ποῖον τί ἐστι;) (what kind is it? How should it be judged?). When focused on legal proceedings, the question is phrased *an iure fecerit?* Did the accused act justifiedly? For example, if it is established that Brutus did kill Caesar and that it was indeed murder, was Brutus justified in murdering Caesar? The type of *status* created by this question is called the *status qualitatis* (ποιήτης). Uncertainty exists as to whether the deed was justified, or the need exists to indicate that a certain line of action would be the correct one to follow. The emphasis is on the quality of the deed.

* *Ad aliquid?* (πρός τί ἐστιν;) (to what does it relate?). In legal proceedings the question is phrased *an iudici in iudicium debeat?* Should the case be brought to court? The type of *status* created by this question is called the *status translatio* (μεταλήψις). The whole process is questioned.

Usually the *status* of a rhetorical situation is not given in the text. It has to be inferred.

If one phrases the question to which Romans 13:1–7 is the response as *Should the implied readers obey the Roman authorities or not?*, a case for *status coniecturae* could be made: a decision concerning a specific (future) action must be made. Formulated in this manner, it presupposes a specific situation, namely, whether something was done or should be done by a *specific person* at a *specific time* — a prerequisite for *status coniecturae* (Kennedy 1984:18). In Romans 13:1–7, however, the textual evidence points to a more general situation. It is a general exhortation to πᾶσα ψυχή, and explicit space, time and personal deictics are totally absent (see chapter 2, §6.3.3.2 – §6.3.3.3). Therefore *status coniecturae* must be ruled out for Romans 13:1–7. Romans 13:1–7 is also not the result of a rhetorical situation that has *status definitivus* as its starting point. To *define* obedience (or to define authorities) as such is not at issue.

The question to which Romans 13:1–7 is the response should rather be phrased as *What is the right conduct with regard to the governing authorities?* Submission or resistance? The need exists to indicate that a certain line of action would be the correct one to follow. The emphasis is on the quality of the deed (and not on whether a specific deed should be done or on a definition of the nature of the deed). The *status* of the rhetorical situation of Romans 13:1-7 is therefore identified as *status qualitatis*.

This identification fits well within the broader framework of the rhetorical situation of the letter. Paul wants to enlist the future cooperation of the implied readers, including the establishment of an operational base for his future missionary activities (see §6.2.4.1). If his implied readers were to live in constant conflict with the authorities in Rome, it would seriously hamper their ability to provide him with such an operational base. He himself and his mission could be put in danger. Therefore he argues that the right conduct toward the authorities in this particular situation is that of submission. Compromise rather than confrontation will be to the mutual benefit of the encoded author and the implied readers.

> *Digression:* If historical considerations are taken into account, it could be argued that two of the most plausible constructions of the historical situation of Romans 13:1-7 also confirm this conclusion. The expulsion of the Jews from Rome by Claudius in 49 C.E. because of Jewish nationalist zealots stirring unrest in the city (see Borg), or the problems with regard to the paying of taxes in the mid-first century to which Tacitus *(Annales*, XIII, 50) refers (see Friedrich *et al.* 153-159) give credence to the idea that a situation of conflict between the authorities in Rome and those social groups to whom the implied readers belonged may have existed. Paul might have known about this situation of conflict existing before and during the time when the letter was written. This might have been the exigence which prompted him to address the topic of conduct towards the authorities in his letter. However, no specific and explicit *textual evidence* (that is, from the Letter to the Romans itself) for either of these constructions can be forwarded. That is why it is not taken into consideration in this rhetorical critical reading. This does not imply, however, that this historical information is necessarily false or that it is of no value at all. However, when this information is taken into consideration here, I would not be working consistently within a rhetorical paradigm. Therefore it is bracketed for the moment (see §5.4).

7.2.2 The creation of 'persons' and their roles

Those persons active in the rhetorical process who are able to modify the exigence are fulfilling the rhetorical roles. Interested parties who cannot modify the exigence (for example Onesimus in the letter to Philemon) do not act as 'persons' in the rhetorical process, although they have a definite interest in the outcome of the argumentation. In Romans 13:1-7 the authorities do not act as a 'person' in a rhetorical process, although they have a definite interest: they want peace and harmony among their citizens, and, of course, they want their taxes!

In the rhetorical theory of Perelman and Olbrechts-Tyteca (10) the notion of audience (that is, those whom the speaker wishes to influence by his argumentation) has become of paramount importance (see Snyman 1986). They distinguish between different types of audiences, which we need not consider here.[7] The important thing to note is that the audience created in the letter to the Romans is located as a functional entity in the epistolary situation. It serves as an 'inventional tool,' namely as a construct of the speaker, and, as the most important constituent of argumentation, it is sociologically and psychologically embedded in the social codes of the first century. An intimate relationship exists between the encoded author and the audience, or as it is called in this chapter, the implied readers.

The argumentative interaction in Romans 13:1–7 takes place between the encoded author and the implied readers. The creation of three roles in the argumentation, identified above as (i) the authorities, (ii) the $\pi \hat{\alpha} \sigma \alpha \ \psi v \chi \acute{\eta}$, and (iii) those who resist, is one of the *strategies* by means of which the encoded author aims to move his audience, the implied readers. None of these three roles as such constitutes the audience of the argumentation, although in the final section (13:6–7) the implied readers are included under the $\pi \hat{\alpha} \sigma \alpha \ \psi v \chi \acute{\eta}$.

A number of characteristics of the implied readers of the letter to the Romans — as pictured by Paul, of course — were identified above (see §6.2.4.3). As Gentile Christians, although different in many respects to the Jews, they embrace a Jewish value system (which holds positive views regarding conduct towards the authorities; see §7.2.3). Furthermore, they are pictured as people in a position of power with regard to the encoded author. They are in a position to offer (or to refuse) the cooperation that Paul is seeking. This picture of the implied readers, compiled only from the letter-opening and letter-closing, is specified in Romans 13:1–7. In a certain sense their 'power' is confirmed and simultaneously limited. If they were in no position to resist the authorities, why then the exhortation to submit? It is granted, therefore, that they do have the power to cause serious trouble if they should decide to resist the authorities. On the other hand, although they have power, their power is limited and subjugated to that of the authorities. They do not have absolute power. The right conduct in their situation is to submit to the authorities.

The role created for the encoded author in the letter-frame is also maintained in Romans 13:1–7. The nature of the argumentation in Romans 13:1–7, or in fact, in the whole paraenetic section (12:1 – 15:13), necessitates careful explanation to fit this role. The dual position of the encoded author has been pointed out: as an apostle he exercises authority, which, so he argues, includes also those in Rome to whom the letter is addressed. Yet,

---

[7]Perelman and Olbrechts-Tyteca (19) distinguish between a particular and a universal audience, a composite audience or a single person (the deliberating self) and an elite audience.

while not yet known to them and particularly because he writes to ask something from them, the exhortations in the paraenetic section may appear strange. Is he in a position to 'command' them to do something, or, put more softly, to 'advise' or 'exhort' them to follow a certain way of life? Is it strategically wise to do so? On the basis of the nature of paraenetic material (being usually well-known traditional material, see chapter 21, §5.3.1), I would argue that these exhortations do not function as exhortations as such in this specific rhetorical situation. Their function should rather be understood as one of the strategies employed by the encoded author to enhance his credibility. Their presence serves as one more way of identification with the implied readers: I, Paul, share your (Jewish) values because I also hold that the right conduct towards the authorities (in the normal course of things) is to submit to them and to pay your taxes.[8] The roles of both the encoded author and the implied readers in Romans 13:1–7 are therefore consistent with the manner in which these roles are created in the letter-frame. Furthermore, it enables us to interpret the tone and argumentative function of the paraenetic material in Romans, including Romans 13:1–7.

7.2.3 The rhetorical genre

It has been argued above (see §2.3.4 and §6.2.2) that the value of the identification of rhetorical genre should not be overestimated. I have indicated that Kraftchick (1990:60, 61, 66) gives a fair assessment of the value of genre-analysis in rhetorical criticism. He reminds us that the primary focus of ancient rhetoric was to make the argument effective. It is for this reason that forms of argument were so fluid and that the rhetorical genres were not precisely delimited. Therefore judicial, deliberative and epideictic speeches could each incorporate elements of the others, depending on the rhetorical situation being faced. Fixation on genre often has the result that it imposes upon Paul a structure that is neither demonstrable in terms of his habit of constructing arguments nor in terms of classical rhetoric. Therefore it seems to be a more fruitful method of appropriating rhetoric to consider how arguments and techniques function in Paul's letters (this is done in §7.2.4). This does not imply, however, that genre-considerations should play no role at all. This is considered here as *one* element in the rhetorical situation and not as an over-riding determinative factor.

Following Aristotle (*Ars Rhetorica* 1.2.22.3), ancient rhetoricians divided oratory into three types according to the intended effect on the

---

[8]In the literary critical reading of Romans 13:1–7 a similar conclusion was reached (see chapter 2, §7).

hearer: the δικανικόν (or judicial), the συμβουλευτικόν (or deliberative) and the ἐπιδεικτικόν (or demonstrative/epideictic). Judicial oratory (with its two basic types, accusation and defense) attempted to convince judges about *past* events. Deliberative oratory focused on persuading the assembly about a *future* course of action. It also has two basic types, persuasion (*protreptic*) and dissuasion (*apotreptic*). Epideictic oratory in classical rhetoric was ceremonial oratory. It does not ask the audience to make judgments, but it tries to provide pleasure in the *present* by celebrating common values (see Burgess for classical conceptions of epideictic oratory). In modern rhetoric Perelman and Olbrechts-Tyteca (47–51) have incorporated the epideictic genre as an important element of their 'new rhetoric.' They maintain that epideictic oratory forms a central part of persuasion (49) 'because it strengthens the disposition toward action by increasing adherence to the values it lauds' (50). By employing the epideictic genre the speaker sets out to increase the intensity of adherence to certain values . . . and tries to establish a sense of communion centered around particular values recognized by the audience . . .' (51). Directly relevant in the case of Romans 13:1–7 is the following statement of Perelman and Olbrechts-Tyteca (51):

> Epideictic speeches are most prone to appeal to a universal order, to a nature, or a god that would vouch for the unquestioned, and supposedly unquestionable values.

From the analysis of the enthymemes in Romans 13:1–7 (see §7.2.4) it becomes clear just how universal in nature the values are which serve as premises for the argumentation. Appeals to God in order to substantiate the claims made with regard to the authorities are consistently made by means of a transitive argumentation strategy (for more detail see §7.2.4).

Kennedy (1984:19) indicates that there is sometimes a utilization of more than one genre in a single discourse, and that the definition of the genre as a whole can become very difficult. Usually, however, a discourse has one dominant genre which reflects the author's major purpose in speaking or writing. Vorster (1991:237) concluded that the rhetorical genre in the letter to the Romans does indeed oscillate between the deliberative and the epideictic, with the emphasis on the former.

I want to argue that Romans 13:1–7 is an example of the epideictic genre (*contra* Wuellner 1987b who regards the whole paraenetic section of Romans 13 as deliberative), since the aim of the argumentation in this passage 'is not, like demonstration, to prove the truth of the conclusion from the premises, but to transfer to the conclusion the adherence accorded to the premises' (Perelman 21). In the next section (§7.2.4) the values on which the argumentation is built are identified and described in detail. If we consider those values it becomes clear that Paul *confirms* the existing values of his audience.

In fact, all of these values are not only well-known Jewish values, but in the wider context of the Hellenistic world, they also were held as more or less self-evident truths (see Michel 299–400; Käsemann 1980:353–354; Wilckens 1982:33). That the argumentation aims to confirm values is also supported by both the rhetorical role of the encoded author and the *status* of Romans 13:1–7 as a rhetorical unit: by confirming shared values, the *ethos* of the encoded author is established and enhanced and this, consequently, serves to move implied readers to react positively to the request for cooperation.

7.2.4 The identification of topoi

Once the student of ancient rhetoric has converted the subject into a sharply defined thesis, that is, once the *status* has been defined, one is faced with the task of developing the theme. In the case of persuasive discourse, one must find 'arguments' to develop the topic. Ancient rhetoricians compiled lists of 'arguments' or *topoi*.[9] *Topoi* are the underlying premises (literally the 'places' where appropriate arguments are found), the basis for the meeting of minds in the process of argumentation. With the aid of *topoi* the rhetors look specifically for arguments to back up their position with regard to the *krinomenon* (Braet 81). The finding of the 'places' (or, as Corbett 96 puts it, the 'suggesters,' or 'prompters' or 'initiaters' or 'checklist' of ideas on some subject) forms a very important element in the *inventio*, the first task of the rhetorician in the process of the rhetorical *creation* of discourse (Lausberg 146). When engaged in the process of a rhetorical *analysis* of discourse (see Sloane), as we are here, the process is reversed: we need not invent our own *topoi* to argue a specific point. We need to analyze the argumentation in Romans 13:1–7 in order to lay bare the *topoi* that are used to substantiate the existing argumentation in the passage under consideration. That can be done by way of an analysis of the syllogisms and enthymemes in Romans 13:1–7. Through this analysis the premises of the argumentation that are usually not explicitly present in the text can be discovered. These premises usually reflect the social values that are, in the perception of the encoded author, shared by his audience and on the basis of which a meeting of minds can take place, resulting in effective and successful argumentation.

The syllogism is a schematic device that Aristotle invented to analyze and test deductive reasoning (Van Eemeren *et al.* 60–70; Corbett 45–61). A

---

[9]A distinction should be made between *topos* in its association with argumentation as we are using it here and the understanding of the *topoi* to describe the main 'themes' appropriate for certain types of oratory for which Aristotle (*Ars Rhetorica* 1.4–15) used the term ἴδιοι τόποι (see also Quintilian *De institutione oratoria* 5.10.20; 10.5.12 and Wuellner 1978:466–470; Vorster 1991:65).

syllogism consists of two premises and a conclusion. A model syllogism runs like this:

Major premise:
1. All <u>humans</u> are **mortal**   <u>middle term</u>   **major term**

Minor premise:
2. All **Australians** are <u>humans</u>   **minor term**   <u>middle term</u>

Conclusion:
3. All **Australians** are **mortal**   **minor term**   **major term**

In this example the middle term in the major premise is thus in the position of the subject, and in the minor premise it is in the position of the predicate. However, there are in all four different possible combinations for the position of the middle term in the major and minor premises. These four combinations correspond to the four figures for syllogisms that Aristotle has described (see Van Eemeren *et al.* 62). Two rules govern the validity of a syllogism, namely, (i) there must be three terms and only three terms, and (ii) the middle term must be distributed at least once. The middle term is the term that occurred in both premises but not in the conclusion.

The rhetorical equivalent of the logical syllogism is called the *enthymeme* (Corbett 62). There is a formal difference between the syllogism and the enthymeme because one of the formally mandatory premises, ordinarily the major premise, is usually not explicitly articulated in actual argumentation or discourse. The enthymeme takes the form of a statement with a supporting reason, with a syllogism standing behind it. Leeman and Braet (70) describe the enthymeme as follows:

> Vormlijk onderscheidt een enthymeem zich van een syllogisme doordat van de twee formeel noodzakelijke premissen met name de majorpremisse vaak onuitgesproken blijft. De reden hiervoor is dat deze bekend verondersteld mag worden en daarom door het publiek aangevuld kan worden.[10]

An enthymeme is therefore a shortened syllogism with the mandatory major premise usually omitted. However, this does not exclude the possibility that an enthymeme may sometimes appear in the form of a full syllogism with both premises explicitly stated.

In Romans 13:1–7 the following enthymemes and syllogisms can be identified (the major premise not stated explicitly in the text is printed in **bold** letters):

---

[10]My translation: "The enthymeme differs from the syllogism because one of the mandatory premises, usually the the major premise, is often left out. This occurs because the major premise is supposed to be known and could therefore be provided by the audience."

Enthymeme 1:

Major premise:[11]
(1) [πᾶσα ψυχὴ   τῷ θεῷ   ὑποτασσέσθω]
     every soul   to God   should submit
     (major term)   (middle term)

Minor premise:
(2a) οὐ γὰρ ἔστιν   ἐξουσία   εἰ μὴ ὑπὸ θεοῦ
      there is no   authority   except by God
                      (minor term)   (middle term)

(2b) αἱ δὲ οὖσαι   ὑπὸ θεοῦ   τεταγμέναι εἰσίν
      those who   by God   are ordained
      (minor term)   (middle term)

Conclusion:
(3) πᾶσα ψυχὴ   ἐξουσίαις ὑπερεχούσαις   ὑποτασσέσθω
     every soul   to the ordained authorities   should submit
     (major term)   (minor term)

Restated this enthymeme reads:

*   **every soul (a) must submit to God (b)** (*major premise*) (a=b)
*   and God (b) has ordained the authorities (c) (*minor premise*) (b=c),
*   <u>therefore</u>, every soul (a) should submit to the ordained authorities (c) (*conclusion*) (a=c).

Actual discourse seldom presents the sequence of the logic of the syllogism (major premise, minor premise, conclusion). Rather, discourse presents the conclusion first, followed by the minor premise, and the major premise customarily is not explicitly on the surface structure of the text. In Romans 13 the general and self-evident truth that functions as validation for the argument is the maxim *Everyone should submit to God.* No one would argue with this. To this major premise and self-evident truth, the discourse adds a minor premise, in fact, it repeats it twice (2a and 2b): *God ordained authorities.* Twice it is emphasized that God *ordained* the authorities. The conclusion retains this qualification of the minor term: every person should submit to the ὑπερεχούσαις (=ordained) authorities.

---

[11]Those premises not explicitly stated in the text are rendered in Greek in this analysis and are thus my own creations. This is done because the logic of the syllogism is easier to grasp on the basis of three Greek sentences in which the Greek terminology is repeated in the various syllogistic roles. Those conjugations which serve to link different enthymemes are also left out here. Only those connecting the different phrases within a specific enthymeme are retained.

Enthymeme 2:

Major premise:

[(1) ἐξουσίαι	ὑπὸ θεοῦ	τεταγμέναι εἰσίν]
authorities	by God	are ordained
(middle term)	(major term)	

Minor premise:

(2) ὁ ἀντιτασσόμενος	τῇ ἐξουσίᾳ	
the one who resists	the authority	
(minor term)	(middle term)	

Conclusion:

(3) τοῦ θεοῦ διαταγῇ	ἀνθέστηκεν	
an ordination of God	resists	
(major term)	(minor term)	

Restated, this enthymeme reads:

*   **authorities (b) are ordained by God (a)** (*major premise*) (b=a)
*   and the one who resists (c) the authorities (b) (*minor premise*) (c=b)
*   therefore resists (c) an ordination of God (a) (*conclusion*) (c=a).

In this enthymeme the minor premise of the first enthymeme functions as major premise. A new element is brought in as a minor term in the minor premise, namely *the one who resists*. By means of syllogistic logic, the conclusion is reached that to resist the authorities is to resist an ordination of God.

Note that in both enthymemes the guarantee for the validity of the argumentation is given by means of a transfer of values or characteristics to the authorities, values or characteristics that are usually attributed to God.

Enthymeme 3:

Major premise:

[θεὸς κρίνει	τοὺς ἀντιτασσόμενους	τῇ διαταγῇ αὐτοῦ]
God punishes	those who resist	his ordinations
(major term)		(middle term)

Minor premise:

οἱ δὲ ἀνθεστηκότες	(τὰς ἐξουσίας)	
those who resist	the authorities	
(minor term)	(middle term)	

Conclusion:

ἑαυτοῖς	κρίμα λήμψονται	
themselves	will be punished	
(minor term)	(major term)	

Therefore, this enthymeme reads:

* **God punishes (a) those who resist his ordinations (b)** (*major premise*) (a=b)
* and those who resist (c) the authorities (b) (*minor premise*) (c=b)
* therefore, will be punished (a) (by the authorities) (c) (*conclusion*) (a=c).

In this enthymeme 'ordination of God' (διαταγή) and 'authorities' (ἐξουσίαι) serve as middle term as if they are one concept, because their identification was the conclusion of the preceding enthymeme.

Cicero's rhetorical treatise, *De Inventione* (1,67), gives the model for the Hermagorean *epicheireme (ratiocinatio)*, which is an extended syllogism. It consists of five statements: the three statements of the syllogism as well as two statements supporting the premises (Leeman & Braet 88). The model runs like this:

1. All human beings are mortal (*propositio: major premise*)
2. since up till now all human beings have died (*adprobatio*)
3. Socrates is a human being (*adsumptio: minor premise*)
4. since Socrates has all the necessary human qualities (*adprobatio adsumptiones*: confirmation of the *minor premise*)
5. Therefore, Socrates is mortal (*complexio*: conclusion).

The three enthymemes of Romans 13:1-2 fit this model in the following way:

1. Every person should be subject to God
2. since God punishes those who resist him
3. Resistance of the authorities is resistance to an ordination of God
4. since God has ordained authorities
5. Therefore, everyone should submit to the ordained authorities

The fact that Romans 13:1-2 fits the model of Hermagorean school-rhetoric so perfectly points to the gnomic and traditional character of this exhortation. This exhortation is not something newly invented in the rhetorical situation of the letter to the Romans. There is good evidence in Jewish tradition that people were exhorted to believe that authorities are ordained by God and should therefore be obeyed: Josephus, *BJ* ii.8.7 §140 ("Rule does not come from anyone apart from God") and *Sirach* 4:27 ("Do not resist rulers"), cf. Käsemann (1980:345-355). Part of its rhetorical significance, therefore, does not lie in its 'content' as such, but in the fact of its presence.

The use of this well-known exhortation in the form of an *epicheireme* in the first sentence of Romans 13:1-7 is an indication that the *Vertretbarkeitsgrad* (or way of entrance) into the argumentation of Romans 13:1-7 can be identified as ἔνδοξον σχῆμα (*honestum genus*), that is, the issues are agreeable to the readers (Lausberg 1973:57).[12] Clearly, regarding this

---

[12]In contrast to the ἀμφίδοξον σχῆμα (*dubium genus*) = the issue provokes serious questions; the παράδοξον σχῆμα (*turpe genus*) = the issue is shocking to the readers; the

specific issue, the encoded author sets out to meet the audience on familiar ground.

Enthymeme 4:

Major premise:
[τὸ κρίμα	ἐστιν αἴτιος	τοῦ φόβου]
punishment	causes	fear
(middle term)		(major term)

Minor premise:
οἱ ἄρχοντες	κρινοῦσι	τὸν κακὸν ἔργον
the authorities	will punish	the wrong deed
	(middle term)	(minor term)

Conclusion:
οἱ γὰρ ἄρχοντες οὐκ εἰσὶν	φόβος	τῷ ἀγαθῷ ἔργῳ ἀλλὰ τῷ κακῷ
for the authorities are not	a fear	to good conduct but to wrong conduct
(major term)		(minor term)

Restated this enthymeme reads:

* **punishment (b) causes fear (a)** (*major premise*) (b=a)
* and the authorities punish (b) the wrong deed (c) (*minor premise*) (b=c)
* therefore, the authorities are not a terror (fear) (a) to good conduct but to wrong conduct (c) (*conclusion*) (a=c).

Paul repeats the argument of enthymeme 4 in the rest of 13:3 and explicates its positive converse element in the conclusion: authorities do not punish those doing τὸν ἀγαθόν; they praise them. Praise is not added by means of a new enthymeme (with the major premise omitted), but is brought into the argumentation by means of a full syllogism (all three elements are present):

Syllogism 1

Major premise:
θέλεις δὲ μὴ φοβεῖσθαι	τὴν ἐξουσίαν
You do not want to fear	the authorities
(middle term)	(major term)

Minor premise:
τὸ ἀγαθὸν	ποιεῖς
the good	you do
(minor term)	(middle term)

ἄδοξον σχῆμα (*humile genus*) = the issue is uninteresting; or the δυσπαρακολούθητον σχῆμα (*obscurum genus*) = the issue is baffling and obscure (see Lausberg 56–61).

Conclusion:

καὶ ἕξεις	ἔπαινον	ἐξ αὐτῆς
and you will have	praise	from [him]
	(major term)	(major term)

Restated this syllogism reads:

* you do (b) not want to fear the authorities (a) *(major premise)* (b=a)
* and you do (b) good (c) *(minor premise)* (b=c),
* therefore they (a) will praise (c) you *(conclusion)* (a=c).

Note the similar, yet converse, conclusions of syllogism 1 and enthymeme 4.

Enthymeme 5:

Major premise:

[ὁ θεὸς	πάντως ποιεῖ τὸν ἀγαθὸν σοί]
God	always does what is good for you
(middle term)	(major term)

Minor premise:

[ἐξουσία]	θεοῦ γὰρ διάκονός ἐστιν
the authority	is a servant of God
(minor term)	(middle term)

Conclusion:

[ἐξουσίαι]	εἰσίν σοι εἰς τὸ ἀγαθόν
the authorities	[do] good to you
(minor term)	(major term)

Restated, this enthymeme reads:

* **God (b) always does what is good (a) for you** *(major premise)*, (b=a)
* and since the authority (c) is a servant of God (b) *(minor premise)* (c=b),
* therefore the authorities (c) do good (a) to you *(conclusion)* (c=a).

This argument is followed by yet another repetition, explicating the logical consequences of the negative conduct in terms of enthymeme 4. Thus, the conclusion of enthymeme 4 is used as *major premise* in this repetition:

Syllogism 2:

Major premise

οἱ ἄρχοντες οὐκ εἰσὶν	φόβος	τῷ ἀγαθῷ ἔργῳ ἀλλὰ τῷ κακῷ
the authorities are not	a fear	to good conduct but to wrong conduct
	(major term)	(middle term)

Minor premise

ἐὰν δὲ τὸ κακὸν	ποιῆς
but if the wrong	you should do
(middle term)	(minor term)

Conclusion:
φοβοῦ
you should fear
(major term)   (minor term)

Restated, this syllogism reads:

* the authorities are not a terror (fear) (a) to good conduct but to wrong conduct (b) (*major premise*) (a=b)
* and you do (c) wrong (b) (*minor premise*) (c=b),
* therefore you (c) should fear (a) (*conclusion*) (c=a).

The next enthymeme elaborates on this conclusion, once again on the basis of an omitted major premise regarding what God usually does. Every action (positive or negative) of the authorities is thus motivated on the basis on assumptions of what God does and what God wants.

Enthymeme 6:

Major premise:
[ὁ θεὸς πάντως ἐχεὶ ὀργὴν   τῷ τὸ κακὸν πράσσοντι]
God always holds wrath   for the wrongdoer
(middle term)   (major term)

Minor premise:
οὐ εἰκῇ τὴν μάχαιραν φορεῖ·   θεοῦ γὰρ διάκονός ἐστιν
he does not bear the sword in vain   for it is a servant of God
(middle term)   (middle term)

Conclusion:
ἔκδικος εἰς ὀργὴν   τῷ τὸ κακὸν πράσσοντι
one who executes wrath   on the wrongdoer
(minor term)   (major term)

Restated, this enthymeme reads:

* **God (b) always holds wrath for the wrongdoer (a)** (*major premise*) (b=a)
* and as a servant of God (b) the authority (c) carries the sword (*minor premise*) (b=c),
* therefore the authority (c) executes wrath on the wrongdoer (a) (*conclusion*) (c=a).

Again, the action of the authorities is motivated on the basis on assumptions of what God usually does and what God usually wants.

Enthymeme 7:

Major premise
ἡ συνείδησις ἀναγκάζει   δικαίωμα
the conscience compels   right conduct
(middle term)   (major term)

Minor premise
[ἀνάγκη ἐστιν] οὐ μόνον διὰ τὴν ὀργὴν
ἀλλὰ καὶ διὰ   τὴν συνείδησιν
it is compelling not only because of the wrath
but also because of   the conscience
(minor term)   (middle term)

Conclusion:
διὸ ἀνάγκη   ὑποτάσσεσθαι
therefore [it is] compelling   to obey [the authorities]
(minor term)   (major term)

Restated, this enthymeme reads:

*   **conscience (b) compels the right conduct (a)** (*major premise*) (b=a)
*   and it is compelling (c) not only to avoid God's wrath but also (to do right) for the sake of conscience (b) (*minor premise*) (c=b)
*   it is therefore compelling (c) to obey (a) (the authorities) (*conclusion*) (c=a).

In chapter 1 (§8.6) the meaning of συνείδησις was defined as "the psychological faculty which can distinguish between right and wrong." In the argumentation up to this point, it has repeatedly been indicated what the right or what the wrong conduct toward the authorities is. The contrast in the *minor premise* indicates that the role of συνείδησις in the *major premise* in this particular enthymeme is the choice to do the *right* thing. Therefore, this premise should not be understood as a new trait in Pauline theology in terms of which the human conscience always and necessarily compels a choice for the right conduct. That one can choose between right or wrong is the general meaning of συνείδησις. At this particular point in the argumentation in Romans 13:1–7, however, it has been established that the direction of the choice which conscience compels is to choose the right conduct (δικαίωμα). That is why the *major premise* was phrased in enthymeme 7 in this manner.

Syllogism 3:

Minor premise
αἱ ἐξουσίαι λαμβάνουσι   φόρους
the authorities collect   taxes
(middle term)   (minor term)

Major premise
(αἱ ἐξουσίαι)   λειτουργοὶ θεοῦ εἰσιν εἰς αὐτὸ τοῦτο προσκαρτεροῦντες
(the authorities)   are servants of God attending to this very thing constantly
(middle term)   (major term)

Conclusion:
διὰ τοῦτο γὰρ καὶ   φόρους   τελεῖτε   (τοῖς λειτουργοῖς τοῦ θεοῦ)
Because of this also   taxes   you pay   (to the servants of God)
                    (minor term)   (major term)

Restated, this syllogism reads:

* authorities (b) are servants of God (a) (*major premise*) (b=a)
* and authorities (b) collect taxes (c) (*minor premise*) (b=c)
* therefore you must pay taxes (c) (to the servants of God) (a) (*conclusion*) (c=a).

The authorities' status as servants of God is once again the motivation behind their authority, even in such a general fact that authorities collect taxes. An implicit premise underlying the *major premise* of this syllogism is that **everything belongs to God**, which, on its turn builds on the premise **God gives everything**. As giver of everything, God has the right to expect one to pay everything to him.

In verse seven the conclusion of enthymeme 7 is elaborated and applied in a stylistically appealing manner (§7.4) to explicate just how far and wide $\pi\hat{\alpha}\sigma\alpha$ $\psi\nu\chi\acute{\eta}$'s responsibilities to pay everyone their dues in fact stretch.[13]

This analysis has provided us with the premises which underpin the argumentation in Romans 13:1–7. They are:

1. Every soul must submit to God.
2. Authorities are ordained by God.
3. God punishes those who resist God's ordinations.
4. Punishment causes fear.
5. People do not want to fear.
6. God always does what is good.
7. The authorities punish those who do wrong.
8. God always holds wrath for the wrongdoer.
9. Conscience compels the right conduct.
10. Authorities are servants of God.
11. Everything belongs to God.

Seven premises relate to God:

1. Every soul must submit to God.
2. Authorities are ordained by God.
3. God punishes those who resist his ordinations.
6. God always does what is good.
8. God always holds wrath for the wrongdoer.
10. Authorities are servants of God.
11. Everything belongs to God.

Three premises relate to the authorities:

2. Authorities are ordained by God.

---

[13]An allusion to the Jesus-*logion* (Mark 12:17) to pay Caesar what he must get and to pay God what he must get may be a possibility here. This would support the underlying premise of the exhortation to pay taxes to authorities: in actuality, everything belongs to God.

7. The authorities punish those who do wrong.
10. Authorities are servants of God.

Three premises are gnomic statements:

4. Punishment causes fear.
5. People do not want to fear.
9. Conscience compels the right conduct.

These propositions serve as the basis for the meeting of minds in the argumentation in Romans 13:1-7. They are the values which the encoded author presumes to be the ground of accepted values the encoded author and the implied readers share in common. The encoded author argues deductively, using seven enthymemes and three syllogisms. The gnomic nature of these propositions seems to confirm Käsemann's (1980:355) observation that the argument in Romans 13:1-7 has a view towards universally valid realities. These results of an analysis of the enthymemes in Romans 13:1-7 illustrate the value of such a procedure based on classical rhetoric. In order to work out the implications of these results for the interpretation of the passage, however, we need to turn to modern rhetorical theory.

Sillars and Ganer have worked out a matrix in terms of which the values which underpin the process of argumentation can be described systematically. They understand this matrix of values as threefold, namely beliefs, values and attitudes (Sillars & Ganer 186).

* A belief is the smallest unit in a social value system. A belief is any simple proposition, conscious or unconscious, inferred from what a person says or does, capable of being preceded by the phrase, 'I believe that . . . .' The content of a belief may describe the object of belief as true or false, correct or incorrect; evaluate it as good or bad; or advocate a certain course of action or a certain state of existence as desirable or undesirable.
* A value is a type of belief centrally located within one's total belief system, about how one ought or ought not to behave, or about some end state of existence worth or not worth attaining.
* An attitude is a relatively enduring organization of beliefs around an object or situation predisposing one to respond in some preferential manner. As the common ground between arguer and listener, they serve as the backing of statements within the argument. Thus, while they may often remain below the surface of a discourse, they are actually its focal point.

Sillars and Ganer (191) suggest five possible options for the arguer in his or her attempt to modify the value system of the audience by means of argumentation: (i) value acquisition or abandonment, (ii) value redistribution (when a value becomes more or less widely distributed within the society), (iii) value-rescaling (changing the relative importance of one value to another), (iv) value re-employment (changing the range of application for a value), and (v) value-restandardization (raising or lowering what one expects a particular value to mean when converted to specific belief).

In Romans 13:1-7 we have an example of the use of value-restandardization. Those beliefs generally attributed to God (numbers 1, 2, 5, 10) are raised and expanded and made valid also for the authorities (numbers 6 and 9). To accomplish this restandardization, the encoded author uses strategies of association,[14] in particular the form of argumentation which Perelman and Olbrechts-Tyteca (227) call an 'argument by transitivity':

> Transitivity is a formal property of certain relations which makes it possible to infer that because a relation holds between *a* and *b* and between *b* and *c*, it therefore holds between *a* and *c*; the relations of equality, superiority, inclusion, and ancestry are transitive.

By means of transitive argumentation three parties are arranged in order of superiority in Romans 13:1-7: God, the authorities, and πᾶσα ψυχή (including the implied readers). The values attributed to God by the encoded author and, in his perception, shared by the implied readers, are transposed to the authorities. The argument by transitivity is followed with sequential relations linked by a causal chain (Perelman & Olbrechts-Tyteca 266). Values are transferred between the elements by going from cause to effect and from effect to cause. J. N. Vorster (1988:106) has characterized Romans 13:1-7 as a typical example of a pragmatic argument. Perelman and Olbrechts-Tyteca (266) call that argument pragmatic which permits the evaluation of an act or an event in terms of its favorable or unfavorable consequences. The praise of the authorities is the favorable consequence of obedience to the authorities and their wrath and punishment of the unfavorable. The validity of the argumentation in Romans 13:1-7 is established on this fact-consequence scheme. Paul emphasizes that the right conduct towards the authorities necessarily has a positive effect and the wrong conduct a negative effect. The pragmatic thus dominates in this rhetorical unit.

It is clear then that the process of restandardization takes place through the use of argument by transitivity and pragmatic argumentation. The standard to which the authorities are brought to bear is of a very general and gnomic nature. The argument has a view toward universally valid realities, as Käsemann (1980:355) has put it. When understood in isolation from the

---

[14]Perelman and Olbrechts-Tyteca specify three forms of association, namely (i) quasi-logical arguments (they appear to be like formal reasoning in structure but the ambiguity of terms and the possibility of multiple interpretation makes them quasi-logical) (193-195); (ii) arguments based on the structure of reality (either liaisons of succession or liaisons of co-existence) (261-263); and (iii) arguments which establish the structure of reality (by means of an example, an illustration or an analogy; 350-410).

context of the letter and particularly the rhetorical situation of the letter, the very general and gnomic character of these values may tempt one to see Romans 13:1-7 as 'an unequivocal, unrelenting call for blind, unquestioning obedience to the state,' as Boesak (138) objects. It must be clear by now, however, that the rhetorical situation of this passage excludes such a conclusion. It cannot be denied that the argumentation intends to set up a universally valid order, but this is done in a way thoroughly tied to a particular rhetorical situation.

7.3 Identification of the rhetorical disposition

The rhetorical dispositio 'seeks to determine the rhetorically effective composition of speech and mold its elements into a unified structure' (Kennedy 1984:23; see also Lausberg 241-248). A unit within a larger whole has its own disposition and may therefore exhibit some of the features of the exordium and peroratio as they were described in classical rhetoric (see Thurén 75-76). This is also true in the case of Romans 13:1-7. Since the rhetorical disposition of Romans 13:1-7 was analyzed and described in detail in chapter 1 (§9.3 – 9.4), it will not be repeated here in detail. However, a few remarks may be illuminating in this context.

The epicheirema of which Romans 13:1-2 consists serves as additional motivation to see this section as a full and rounded-off argumentative unit (or semantic cluster, see chapter 1, §9.4). This unit is the 'exordium' of Romans 13:1-7 as a rhetorical unit. Building on this exordium, the progression in the passage is carried forward by means of important conjugations, confirming the quasi-logical argumentative strategy of association employed in the passage. The introductory epicheirema is formally linked to the elaborating theoretical section (13:3-5, identified as cluster B in chapter 1, §9.3) by means of the γάρ introducing verse 4. In this unit the basic exhortation of Romans 13:1a is argued or demonstrated *theoretically* by means of a number of techniques and strategies, described above (§7.2.4). Romans 13:6-7 forms the third and final unit (identified as cluster C in chapter 1, §9.3). The unit is formally linked to the preceding two units by means of the conjugation διὰ τοῦτο in verse 6. In this unit the *practical* consequences of the basic exhortation are drawn, and the implied readers are directly addressed.

7.4 Identification of rhetorical techniques or style

The reservations about the misconception of a 'rhetoric restrained' (that is, a reduction of rhetoric to stylistics) expressed earlier (§2.3.1) do not imply that an analysis of stylistic features of a text has become totally obsolete in rhetorical criticism. Snyman (1988a) has written a valuable article in which he explains the role of a stylistic analysis within the framework of an argumentative conception of rhetoric, particularly the concept set out by Perelman and Olbrechts-Tyteca. In order to increase the support of minds in the process of rhetorical interaction, rhetorical figures may play a role: they are manifestations of the functions attributed to certain argumentative procedures or schemes (Snyman 1988a:99).

Stated differently, this means that rhetorical figures are not described in isolation for their own sake in order to point out the 'optional' formal or purely aesthetic niceties in a text (as is often done in 'rhetorical' or 'stylistic' analyses of texts). Such a way of dealing with the figures of style in the text — and doing *only* that — is yet another example of a scientist ethos in biblical scholarship. It is possible to get totally lost in the endeavor to discover all sorts of stylistic figures in a text and to stay only on the level of discovery and description without asking what all these figures actually do in the text and how they serve the argumentation as such. Moving beyond such a context-less description of the formal characteristics detectable in the text implies that the figures of style should be seen as techniques of persuasive discourse and their function should be described in the context of the rhetorical situation of the text.

In an earlier study, Snyman and Cronjé have proposed a classification of the figures based on four principles, namely (i) repetition, (ii) omission, (iii) shift in expectancies, and (iv) measurement of units. This classification is still at a general level, attributing one of only four possible functions to all the figures of speech. Keeping this limitation in mind, their system is nevertheless helpful to describe and classify the figures in Romans 13:1-7. In order to move from these four general functions attributed to the figures toward a more text-specific (or rather, argument-specific) description, the possible functions of the figures are described within the framework of the rhetorical situation of Romans 13:1-7 as it was analyzed above (see §7.2). This type of analysis also gives one an idea of the progression and cohesion at what Nida *et al.* (1983:17) call 'the macrolevel of the rhetorical structure' of the passage. The functions of the figures could be to enhance the progression/cohesion at the macrolevel of the rhetorical structure (namely in the relationship between parts of the text to one another) and/or to cause impact or appeal, enhancing the persuasive effectiveness of the passage.

In Romans 13:1-7 the following figures can be identified:

i)   Repetition:

Six instances of stylistically significant repetitions occur in Romans 13:1-7.

1) The repetition of single items contiguously (*anadiplosis*)[15] is found in verse 7: τὸν φόρον τὸν φόρον . . . τὸ τέλος τὸ τέλος . . . τὸν φόβον τὸν φόβον . . . τὴν τιμὴν τὴν τιμήν.

2) Repetition of items in non-structurally significant positions, referring to the non-linguistic world (*anaphora*)[16] is most notably the word γάρ (in 13:1, 3a, 4a, 4c, 4d, 6a, and 6b, that is, seven times in seven verses. Other examples of this kind of repetition are ὑποτασσέσθω/ὑποτάσσεσθαι in verses 1 and 5 (although in this case it is structurally significant), the repetition of ἐξουσία (in 13:1a, 1b, 2a, and 3b) and the repetition of διάκονος (13:4a and 4d) (related to λειτουργοί in verse 7).

3) An important semantic parallelism is present in verses 3–5 (the second cluster):

οἱ γὰρ ἄρχοντες οὐκ εἰσὶν φόβος

τῷ ἀγαθῷ ἔργῳ	A	GOOD
ἀλλὰ τῷ κακῷ	B	BAD

θέλεις δὲ μὴ φοβεῖσθαι τὴν ἐξουσίαν; τὸ ἀγαθὸν ποίει,
καὶ ἕξεις ἔπαινον ἐξ αὐτῆς. θεοῦ γὰρ διάκονός   A1   GOOD
ἐστιν σοὶ εἰς τὸ ἀγαθόν.

ἐὰν δὲ τὸ κακὸν ποιῇς, φοβοῦ· οὐ γὰρ εἰκῇ τὴν
μάχαιραν φορεῖ· θεοῦ γὰρ διάκονός ἐστιν, ἔκδικος   B1   BAD
εἰς ὀργὴν τῷ τὸ κακὸν πράσσοντι.

διὸ ἀνάγκη ὑποτάσσεσθαι,

οὐ μόνον διὰ τὴν ὀργὴν	B2	BAD
ἀλλὰ καὶ διὰ τὴν συνείδησιν	A2	GOOD

A generic-specific relationship exists at a semantic level between the different legs of the parallelism. However, there is an important difference in the syntactic structure of verses 3 and 4. When the attitude and action of the authorities towards a good/right behavior are stated (verse 3), an indicative (ἕξεις) is used to name the consequence of good behavior. In the case of negative behavior, an imperative (φοβοῦ) is used before the authority's action against bad/wrong behavior is stated — yet it should be noted here that although the future indicative and imperative differ grammatically, as used here they are identical in terms of modality (see Wuellner 1987b for a discussion of modality).

---

[15]Ἀναδίπλωσις is the repetition of one or several words, for example Θῆβαι δέ, Θῆβαι πόλις ἀστυγείτω . . . (see Smyth 673; Lausberg 314–317).

[16]For Snyman and Cronjé (116) *anaphora* is the repetition of single items in non-structurally significant positions referring to the non-linguistic world. This definition differs from those of Smyth (673) and Lausberg (318) who define ἀναφορά as the repetition, with emphasis, of the same word or phrase *at the beginning of* several successive clauses (x/. . . ; x/. . .).

4) The semantic parallelism in 1b and 1c is a *pleonasm,*[17] thus a repetition of different forms with the same meaning:

οὐ γὰρ ἔστιν ἐξουσία εἰ μὴ ὑπὸ θεοῦ
αἱ δὲ οὖσαι ὑπὸ θεοῦ τεταγμέναι εἰσίν

5) A striking example of *paronomasia* (the repetition of similar forms with different meanings) is found in verse 7: τὸν φόρον and τὸν φόβον and τὸ τέλος and τὴν τιμήν.

6) The last four phrases are parallel at two different levels:

a) τὸν φόρον τὸν φόρον
b) τὸ τέλος τὸ τέλος
c) τὸν φόβον τὸν φόβον
d) τὴν τιμὴν τὴν τιμήν.

In (a) and (b) two concrete things due to the authorities are named and in (c) and (d) two abstract things; thus, a semantic parallelism exists between the first two and the last two items. However, between (a) – (c) and (b) – (d) we have a sound parallelism cutting right through the just-mentioned semantic parallelism.

ii) Omission:

Two instances of stylistically significant omissions exist in Romans 13:1-7.

1) An example of *zeugma*[18] (the omission of the same word in analogous positions) can be found in verse 7: the verb ἀπόδοτε is omitted from the last four phrases.

2) Examples of *elleipsis*[19] are the omission of the verbs in 3a and 5b (in each case before the conjunction ἀλλά).

---

[17]Πλεονασμός ('excess' or redundancy) is the admission of a word or words which is not necessary to the complete logical expression of thought. Such words, though logically superfluous, enrich the thought by adding greater definiteness and precision, picturesqueness, vigor and emphasis (Smyth 681; Lausberg 251).

[18]Ζεῦγμα (junction, bond) is a form of brachylogy by means of which two connected substantives are used jointly with the same verb (or adjective), though this is strictly appropriate to only one of them (Smyth 683; Lausberg 346).

[19]Ἔλλειψις (leaving out, defect) is the suppression of a word or of several words of minor importance to the logical expression of thought, but necessary to the construction; ellipse gives brevity, force, and liveliness (Smyth 677–678; Lausberg 346).

iii) Shift in expectancy

One possible example of this process in Romans 13:1–7 is the reversal of the order form positive/negative (A B) positive/negative (A1 B1) to negative/positive (B2 A2) pointed out in the semantic parallelism analyzed above in the third example in the section dealing with repetitions.

In the relationship between the different parts of the text the stylistic figures identified above have the following functions:

* The repetition of γάρ, έξουσία and διάκονος enhances the cohesion in the passage.

* The anaphoric repetition of έξουσία (13:1 and its repetition in 13:5) marks the beginning and end of the first two clusters and the end of the more theoretical part of the argument.

* The parallelism in 13:3–5 and its reversal in 13:5b bind cluster B together as a unity.

* The combination of anadiplosis and paronomasia in verse 7 marks the climactic end of the passage. The two levels of parallelism may be taken as an indication that concrete and abstract things due to the authorities are inseparable. One can also see this as an example of the stylistic figure known as *prepon*: similarity in 'content' and 'form.'

With regard to the possible persuasive functions of these figures (that is, how they function as argumentative procedures to increase the support of minds in the process of rhetorical interaction), a number of observations can be made:

* The pleonasm serves to underscore the minor premise of the first and most important enthymeme in the argument (13:1). There can be no doubt: authorities are established by God.

* The difference in syntactical structure of the parallel phrases in verses 3 and 4, especially the imperative in verse 4 (φοβοῦ), is striking, emphasizing the warning against the consequences of bad/wrong behavior against the authorities.

* The setting of a pattern in the parallelism in verses 3 and 4 and the sudden reversal of it in verse 5 again serve to attract the attention of the reader to the propositional content of verse 5b — which is a repetition of the basic exhortation in 13:1 — as well as a means of (unexpected) backgrounding (and thus emphasizing) of the important concept συνείδησις.

* The concentration of two figures of speech (anadiplosis and zeugma), as well as two kinds of parallelism in verse 7, serves to lead the passage to a climactic end and almost gives it a poetic quality. It has an aesthetic value, which contributes positively towards the intended assent of the reader. This is a typical function traditionally ascribed to the peroratio.

* The repetition of γάρ has a strong persuasive function. It enhances the impression of reasonability of the passage as a whole. A reasonable reader can identify with what is said.[20] It underscores and enhances the impression of reasonableness created by the quasi-logical argumentative technique employed in the passage.

* To start off right at the beginning with the primary exhortation is an example of foregrounding (and thus emphasis). The reader's attention is immediately focused (and with emphasis, see the imperative in 13:1) on the basic point put forward for the implied readers' assent.

* This main thesis is repeated again in a structurally significant position in verse 5. The repetition of a proposition is another important means of emphasizing. There can be no doubt: πᾶσα ψυχή must submit to the authorities.

* Yet no less than three times is it stated that the authorities, themselves, are in a submissive position: they are διάκονοι and λειτουργοί. Again the repetition functions as a means of emphasis.

In classical rhetorics three types of style and four levels of style were usually distinguished (Aristotle *Ars Rhetorica* 3,1 and Cicero *De Oratore* 37–39), namely, ἀδρός/*grave*, μέσος/*medium* and ἰσχνός/*humile* are the basic types, with the ἰσχνότητος (plain), ἡ δεινότητος (forceful), ὁ μεγαλοπρεπός (elaborate) and ὁ γλαφυρὸς λόγος (elegant) as the four possible levels of style (Demetrius, Περὶ ἑρμηνείας 36–304; see also Leeman & Braet 1987: 101). Each style was used in specific circumstances and it was also determined by the content of what was argued. Because of the considerable use of quasi-logical relations and repetition as a means to highlight concern for both the subject matter and the response of readers (Nida *et al.* 1983:52), we could possibly characterize Romans 13:1–7 as an example of the use of forceful style.

7.5 Identification of rhetorical criticism as a synchronic whole

The purpose of this final step in the process of rhetorical criticism is to look back and review the argumentation's success in meeting the rhetorical exigence (Kennedy 1984:38). The question to which Romans 13:1–7 is the response can be phrased as: *What is the right conduct with regard to the governing authorities?* Submission or resistance? The need exists to indicate that a certain line of action would be the correct one to follow. The emphasis is on the quality of the deed, and the *status* of the rhetorical situation of

---

[20]Although this may be the intention of the text, according to Käsemann (1980), at least some statements are not reasonable at all: the idea that the authorities constantly seek to be God's servants is to his mind obviously an exaggeration if not wholly incredible, and he also maintains that the authorities surely are not occupied solely with taxes!

Romans 13:1-7 is therefore identified as *status qualitatis*. The argumentation in this passage is presented in the epideictic genre since the encoded author confirms the existing and well-known Jewish values of his audience — values which were held more or less as self-evident truths in the wider context of the Hellenistic world. Strobel (1956:67-93; 1962:58-62) and Van Unnik (334-343) have collected convincing evidence to demonstrate that the vocabulary used is that of the Hellenistic administration and that the Greek ideals of the just and honorable man (not women, see chapter 4, §5) are manifested in Romans 13:1-7.

A quasi-logical form of association (Perelman & Olbrechts-Tyteca 193ff) — in particular the technique of transitivity — is used as a strategy to transfer the adherence of the implied readers from the general and gnomic values which serve as premises for the basic exhortation (πᾶσα ψυχὴ ἐξουσίαις ὑπερεχούσαις ὑποτασσέσθω, 13:1) to a specific conclusion, spelled out in practical terms in 13:6-7. A number of stylistic figures are used effectively in this process, binding the passage to a unity and enhancing the persuasive impact and appeal of the passage. Perhaps one of the most important factors responsible for the success of this argumentation in meeting the rhetorical exigence lies in its appeal to general and gnomic values.

8. *Summary and conclusions*

The aim of this chapter was to read Romans 13:1-7 from a rhetorical perspective. The field of reference of the concept 'rhetorical,' as it was used in this chapter, was described at the outset (§2). The long history of the practice as well as the study of rhetoric necessitated a rather elaborate discussion of this matter, and a number of misconceptions and distortions of rhetoric had to be treated (§2.3). Furthermore, the rather complicated relationship between literary criticism and rhetorical criticism (§2.4) needed clarification in order to be able to set the focus for what was done later in the chapter (§2.5). Following this, a brief overview of the impact of rhetorical criticism on modern New Testament interpretation was given (§3). It was concluded that rhetorical criticism has emerged in recent times as one of the most important new developments in New Testament interpretation. Four specific characteristics of modern rhetorical critical studies of the New Testament were indicated. After the stage was thus set (in general terms in §2 and in historical terms in §3), it was necessary to discuss two related conceptual issues in some detail before the actual rhetorical critical reading of Romans 13:1-7 as such could be undertaken, namely, the problem of the relationship between rhetoric and epistolography (§4), and the relationship between a historical situation, an epistolary situation and a rhetorical situation (§5). I concluded that:

* Rhetorical criticism differs from literary criticism (or an epistolographical approach) since it studies discourse primarily *as argumentation*, as social interaction, and not only as communication, or the transmission of information. On the one hand, a literary critical perspective is broader than a rhetorical critical perspective since goal-orientated communication is one possible expression or mode of literary communication. On the other hand, a rhetorical critical perspective has a broader perspective, specifically in the case of the interpretation of letters, since all elements of a persuasive letter are rhetorical. Letter writing can be seen as a *species* of the *genus* rhetoric. The concept of 'rhetoric' or 'literary' which one holds in a particular instance is determinative for how one would see this relationship (§4).

* The historical situation and the rhetorical situation are not identical. The rhetorical situation is more specific since it is always an element in/of a human communication situation, in which *language* usually plays the dominant (though not exclusive) role (depending on how broad one defines 'language'). The rhetorical situation is always an element in/of a *specific type* of human communication, namely goal-oriented social interaction, or persuasion. A historical situation, on the other hand, can be conceptualized in a comprehensive manner, encompassing all the events, objects, persons, abstractions, interactions and relations (social, political, personal, cultural, ideological, ecological, or whatever) which constituted a situation which existed in the past (§5.4).

* If the rhetorical situation is understood as an element in/of a specific mode of human discourse, namely goal-oriented human interaction (or persuasion), the epistolary situation is one possible manifestation of a rhetorical situation coming into existence when this interaction takes place by means of a letter. The epistolary situation is primarily a text-internal, literary, phenomenon. It is the situation created by the structural framework which identifies the writing as a letter (§5.5).

In the latter half of this chapter and on the basis of these theoretical considerations, the actual rhetorical critical reading of Romans 13:1-7 was undertaken. This was done in two phases: a number of the modern rhetorical critical studies of the letter to the Romans as a whole were reviewed and the proposal of J. N. Vorster (1991) was taken as the framework (§6) within which the analysis of Romans 13:1-7 was then undertaken (§7). The results and conclusion of this analysis can be summarized in the following points:

* Romans 13:1-7 can be seen as a distinct rhetorical unit, since it displays a discernible beginning and end, connected by some demonstrative argumentation.
* The question to which Romans 13:1-7 is a response was formulated as *What is the right conduct with regard to the governing authorities?* and the *status* of its rhetorical situation was therefore identified as *status qualitatis*: the need exists

to indicate that submission to the governing authorities would be the correct line of action to follow within this particular situation. Compromise rather than confrontation will be to the benefit of both the encoded author and the implied readers.

* The relatively powerful position and role of the implied readers in the letter to the Romans are confirmed and simultaneously limited in Romans 13:1-7: if they do not submit to the authorities they could cause serious problems for themselves and for the encoded author.

* The exhortation in Romans 13:1-7 to submit (and to pay taxes) does not function *primarily* as 'exhortation' in the literal sense of the word within the specific rhetorical situation of the letter aimed at persuading the implied readers to follow a particular way of conduct in the future (although this needs not to be ruled out as the secondary spin-off of the argumentation). The exhortation is primarily one of the strategies employed by the encoded author to enhance his credibility, and it serves as one more way to identify with the implied readers. The encoded author shares the (Jewish) values of the implied readers since he also holds that the right conduct towards the authorities (in the normal course of things) is to submit to them and to pay taxes.

* Since the confirmation of values already shared by the encoded author and implied readers seems to be the intended effect of the argumentation in Romans 13:1-7, its rhetorical genre was identified as epideictic.

* A number of universal values serve as premises for the argumentation in Romans 13:1-7. Of particular importance are those attributed to God:

  — Everyone should submit to God,
  — God punishes those who resist God's ordinations,
  — God always does what is good,
  — Everything belongs to God.

* By means of a quasi-logical form of association, specifically a transitive strategy of argumentation, these values attributed to God are transposed to the authorities. With this pragmatic argumentation strategy, the encoded author associates with his implied readers, confirming their value system in order to succeed in enlisting their cooperation at a number of levels (see §6.2.4.1).

* A number of stylistic features serve as techniques of persuasive discourse to strengthen the progression as well as the cohesion in the argumentation (see §7.4).

* Perhaps one of the most important factors responsible for the success of this argumentation in meeting the rhetorical exigence lies in its appeal to general and gnomic values.

These conclusions give an indication of the nature of the results gained from reading a passage from a rhetorical perspective. A reading from a rhetorical perspective compels the interpreter to reflect consciously and explicitly on the implications of the *rhetoricity* of the text. It is a way of reading 'between the lines.' It brings to the fore the implicit and unspoken/unwritten values which underpin the argumentation. By bringing this to the surface, the act of interpretation moves beyond a mere linguistic or normal literary analysis of the text. With this movement beyond 'reading the lines' or 'describing the forms' towards 'reading between the lines,' the interpreter moves beyond regarding the New Testament (in terms of the scientist ethos) as an abstract 'language-phenomenon' closer towards 'life' — although this 'life' or 'reality' is still a construction made up from textual information and is therefore not to be equated with 'real historical life.' I submit that rhetorical criticism, when liberated from a number of constraints (see §2.3) and when focused on persuasion, or social interaction, particularly with a view to value systems operative in this process, is another necessary aspect of an ethics of responsible reading.   Confined to a mere stylistic analysis in a mode of a rhetoric restrained, a rhetorical reading may be regarded as scientist (and ethically unacceptable), specifically within socio-political circumstances which call for involvement and commitment. A rhetoric 're-invented,' on the other hand, is a particularly powerful mode of reading. It is a mode of reading which begins to bridge the gap between Schüssler Fiorenza's 'ethics of historical reading' and her notion of an 'ethics of public accountability.'

Once the values 'in' the text have been made explicit by means of rhetorical criticism, the interpreter is in a better position to evaluate them in terms of a religious scale of values.   Doing this inevitably brings the interpreter within the realm of the ethics of public accountability. It is therefore obvious why Schüssler Fiorenza and more particularly Wuellner have begun to write so urgently about the ethics of interpretation when they call for a rhetorical study of the biblical texts.   Granted all these very valuable and exciting possibilities created by the practice of a 'reinvented' rhetoric, I want to argue that we may go even one step further.   In order to be able to assess and evaluate social values in a plausible manner — be they the values 'in' the ancient texts or the values of modern societies — the different modes of what has become known as social-scientific interpretation of the New Testament may prove to be of particular value.   In this attempt to outline elements of what I regard as an ethos of responsible biblical interpretation, I finally want to illustrate how a social-scientific mode of reading forms yet another essential aspect of the ethics of reading. This will be the concern in the next chapter.

CHAPTER 4

READING ROMANS 13:1-7 FROM A SOCIAL-SCIENTIFIC PERSPECTIVE

1. Introduction

The aim of this chapter is to propose a reading of Romans 13:1-7 from a social-scientific perspective. In particular it serves to illustrate the value of such a reading for the description and subsequent assessment of some of those social values which underpin the argumentation in Romans 13:1-7 and which were brought to the surface in the rhetorical critical reading of the previous chapter.

The chapter is structured in the following way: first the concept 'reading from a social-scientific perspective,' as it is understood for the purposes of this chapter, is described and demarcated from what has been done in the previous three chapters (§2). This is followed by a brief overview of the impact of modern studies from a social-scientific perspective on New Testament interpretation (§3). This background is necessary to indicate into which mold of the social-scientific approach this reading fits. The actual reading consists of two parts, namely an analysis of the social function of Romans 13:1-7 as Paraenetic Literature (§4) and an analysis of the role of the ancient social value of honor and shame in Romans 13:1-7 (§5).

2. Reading from a 'social-scientific perspective': definitions and foci

In very general terms, sociology can be defined as the scientific study of how human beings live together. The study of a phenomenon as complex, wide-ranging and varied as human society in all its facets necessarily implies a wide variety of perspectives, theories and models in terms of which such a study can be accomplished. Three major theoretical perspectives are usually distinguished in sociology, namely (see Wallace & Wallace 13-21):

* *a conflict perspective*: the dominant process in society is conflict; social arrangements represent the dominance of a powerful establishment or small elite over the masses, and once the masses become aware of their plight, they will overthrow the prevailing order and establish a more just world. Karl Marx and C. Wright Mills are among the earliest and most influential proponents of this perspective;

* *a functional-structural perspective*: order is dominant in society and social arrangements arise and persist because they serve society and their members

well, social patterns serve to stabilize and maintain groups and their members. Although this view was already promoted by Auguste Comte in 1915, Emile Durkheim is generally heralded as the major proponent of this perspective, with Talcott Parsons as the best-known figure during later times;

* *a symbolic interaction perspective*: symbols (namely a word, gesture or sign which conveys meaning) are seen as central to the understanding of social patterns and a person's sense of self; important action in society takes place around the use of symbols. G. H. Mead is generally regarded as the pioneer of this perspective, a perspective which was later elaborated on and developed by, among others, W. I. Meads, E. Goffman and Peter Berger.

The 'social sciences,' however, encompass more than sociology. Psychology, for example, is also a social science, as are many others. This is the reason why J. H. Elliott (1990:5) has changed the sub-title of the second edition of his well-known book, *A Home for the Homeless*, to read '*A Social-Scientific Criticism of 1 Peter, Its Situation and Strategy,*' instead of the original sub-title which read '*A Sociological Exegesis of 1 Peter.*' In the introduction to the new edition, he explains that he wishes to utilize concepts and perspectives from all the related sub-disciplines of the field of the social sciences directly relevant to the study of ancient and modern texts in their social context. Among these related sub-disciplines he specifically mentions sociology (which he narrows down to the study of modern social systems), anthropology (which he takes to be primarily concerned with the study of pre-industrial social systems), economics, sociolinguistics and semiotics (J. H. Elliott 1990:5). For our present purposes the validity of these distinctions is not at issue. We only need to establish in general terms the field of reference of what can be designated as 'social-scientific' disciplines.

In the context of New Testament interpretation, Van Staden (30) has made the following informative remark:

> The bewildering diversity of quantitative and qualitative methods and models that these disciplines [i.e. sociology, anthropology and psychology et cetera] present has led to all kinds of exploratory work within the exegetical sub-discipline that has come to be known as the sociology of the New Testament. Different scholars have opted for different approaches, methods and models in trying to uncover new information on the social background of the New Testament.

This situation necessitates a careful delimitation and clear indication of the specific approach to be used. In this chapter the model proposed by Perdue will be used to describe the social act performed by Romans 13:1-7 as Paraenetic Literature (§4), and the model proposed by Malina (§5) will be used to analyze the role of honor and shame as social values in Romans 13:1-7. It is of course possible to consider other social aspects of Romans 13:1-7 (for example the specific issue of taxation) in terms of many other available social-scientific models (see §3.3.2). For the purposes of this study, however, the discussion is limited to these two issues and the two models indicated here.

Since the social information which will be dealt with in this chapter is available primarily in the form of the *text* of the letter to the Romans, it is necessary to consider its implications carefully. Put otherwise, what are the implications of the *textuality* of Romans 13:1–7 for a reading of this text from a social-scientific perspective? To treat the social 'data' presented by a literary text, such as a letter, as if it were directly accessible for *historical* (re)construction is a simplistic way of handling a text, presupposing a direct and mirror-like representation of the 'real world' in the text. The social data presented in a literary text can not be simplistically translated into 'pure' social data.[1] A social-scientific reading of a literary text, therefore, cannot ignore the textual (literary or rhetorical) nature of its source of information. In this regard, Petersen (1985) works with the concept of a *narrative world*. He understands this concept to refer to the 'world' as it is represented *in the text* (1985:33), maintaining that 'the world of a narrative is a literary construction, and the events that take place in that world have a narrative quality' (1985:33), and that 'the narrative world is that reality which a narrator bestows upon his actors and upon their actions' (1985:7).

'Worlds' are always human constructions; it does not matter whether they are the constructions of societies or the constructions of narrators. 'Narrative worlds are comprised of the same kinds of social facts — symbolic forms and social arrangements — as so called real worlds' (Petersen 1985:ix). Therefore, the 'world' to be analyzed from a social-scientific perspective in the case of a literary text is the world constructed by the narrator, and this world is not to be simplistically equated with the 'real world' — although narrative worlds and social reality are somehow akin in terms of construction and operation. To translate the literary-social data derived from an analysis of a narrative world into 'pure' social data to be used in historical (re)construction, is a rather complex procedure (Van Staden 59) — an endeavor not to be undertaken in this chapter. The work which Peter Lampe has done on the actual historical circumstances of the Christian communities in Rome during the first two centuries C.E., for example, falls outside our purview. Methodologically speaking, this distinction will be maintained consistently. An analysis of the world created by the text should always *precede* any conclusions about the 'real world' which the text may represent. However, this does not imply that such an analysis of the world created by

---

[1]The text/reality issue has been dealt with already a number of times in this study — see chapter 2 (§6.3.1) for a discussion of the issue in the context of the literary nature of the text, and chapter 3 (§5) for a discussion of the issue in the context of the rhetoricity of the text.

the text can be undertaken by an interpreter void of any assumptions and perceptions of the social world from which the text originated, or free of any influence from the interpreters' own social world. Although a methodological distinction can be made, in the actual reading process things tend to be too interwoven and integrated for such clear-cut distinctions. Nevertheless, for the sake of methodological consistency and to stay within the limits of what I understand as the ethics of *reading* — dealing with texts and not primarily with (texts as) historical phenomena — this distinction is presupposed in this chapter.

As I made clear in the Introduction to this book, my idea is not to develop an encompassing model which integrates linguistic, literary, rhetorical and social-scientific considerations in the interpretation of the New Testament into *one* methodological whole. Although the interdisciplinary nature of the interpretational act makes it impossible to cast each of these approaches into neat containers which have nothing to do with each other[2] (since all these, and other considerations, have to be taken into account in interpretation), I nevertheless attempt to work consistently from one perspective at a time. Therefore it is necessary to indicate how what will be done in this chapter differs from what was done in the previous three chapters.

In the reading of Romans 13:1-7 from a linguistic perspective (chapter 1), the linguistic signs of the text, specifically the relationship between the signs and the 'world' (that is, the semantic information) on the level of the word, the sentence and the paragraph, were in focus. In the reading of Romans 13:1-7 from a literary perspective (chapter 2) the literary phenomena of Romans 13:1-7, specifically its literary genre (namely a letter) and form (Paraenetic Literature) and how literary communication takes place by means of or within this genre and form, was in focus. In the reading of Romans 13:1-7 from a rhetorical perspective (chapter 3), the nature of the discourse of Romans 13:1-7 was understood as persuasive or interactional, and the rhetoricity of the text was in focus. In this chapter, reading Romans 13:1-7

---

[2]Regarding the distinctions between the disciplines, Wallace and Wallace (11) have made the following helpful observation: 'A look at the typical college catalog might give us the impression that someone had succeeded in parceling reality into neat compartments called sociology, psychology, anthropology, economics, history, political science, and so forth . . . . But it is an illusion to think that the disciplines logically divide human behavior into exclusive and neat categories so that a particular topic is studied in only one discipline. A discipline is only a convenient organizational unit which serves the purpose of bureaucratic schools, which seem to need such divisions to function smoothly.' This is all the more true of the act of interpretation as one of the most basic human actions, it simply cannot be split up into neat compartments. But, just as colleges need departments to function smoothly, so interpretation needs to be approached from different and distinguishable perspectives to make sense in a systematic way.

from a social-scientific perspective, social phenomena (the symbolic forms and social arrangements) of the narrative world constructed by the narrator of the letter to the Romans, are in focus.

A close affinity between social-scientific criticism and rhetorical criticism is generally recognized, particularly when rhetoric is understood as a specific mode of human interaction (as it was defined in chapter 3, §2.5). So, for instance, J. H. Elliott (1990:24) maintains:

> Although I have not presented *Home* as a sample of rhetorical criticism, the central attention I devote to the "situation and strategy" of 1 Peter . . . indicates how inter-related I consider the tasks and goals of social-scientific criticism and rhetorical criticism. Both criticisms are necessary for the full exposure of any New Testament document. Here, too, I believe the time has come for methodological consolidation on these two fronts also.

Wuellner (1987a:454), on the other hand, holds that a 'reinvented' rhetoric is more comprehensive than what can be labelled 'socio-rhetorical criticism' — that which Robbins (1987) and Petersen (1985) set out to do. In the final instance, how one understands the similarities and differences will depend on how one defines 'rhetoric' and 'social-scientific.' This chapter on social-scientific criticism differs from the previous one on rhetorical criticism in the sense that I will use a specific model developed in modern social sciences to interpret social phenomena of the world created by Romans 13:1–7 as a manifestation of Paraenetic Literature. The social phenomena as such and in a broader social-scientific perspective are in focus, and not the goal-specific interaction (or persuasion) represented by this specific type of discourse. In the last part, the social value of honor and shame and its manifestation and role in Romans 13:1–7 are described. The close link between the discovery of this 'value between the lines' of Romans 13:1–7 (in the rhetorical critical reading of the previous chapter) and its social-scientific description in this chapter is evident.

3. Social-scientific criticism and New Testament interpretation

3.1 A renewed interest in the social aspects of early Christianity

For a number of reasons the utilization of insights, perspectives and methods derived from the social sciences has moved to the center of interest in contemporary New Testament interpretation. In a sense much of this can be attributed to the unspoken but widely-felt need for some form of 'relevance' for biblical studies because of the changing needs and issues of modern society (see Mack 13). This is the tendency which was eventually formulated explicitly by Schüssler Fiorenza with her call for an ethics of public accountability in biblical scholarship. The Bible is used most of all by Christian believers seeking guidance and comfort in their personal lives. The idea that the message of the Bible is a message of salvation for the individual is deeply rooted and the result of centuries of theology and preaching. Yet, it is also clear from history that the Bible was often made applicable to more than the personal life of the individual. So, for instance, the abolition of slavery in the nineteenth century is an important example of how Christians came to understand that the Bible's message of salvation also applies to society and that certain social structures need to be changed in the light of this message (De Villiers 1988:1).

All over the world there is, among Christians from almost all traditions, a growing consciousness and sensitivity for the social problems of the modern world. Among the important issues which concern many Christians today are injustices of all sorts: exploitation, poverty and the suffering it causes (for instance the growing gap between the material welfare of the so-called First and Third Worlds); discrimination in church and society (for example on the basis of race or gender, et cetera) and the plight of the victims of discriminatory practices; physically disabled and mentally retarded people; the homeless; the unemployed; drug abuse; AIDS victims; refugees; teenage pregnancies; the abortion issue; lost youth; the threat of nuclear, chemical and biological weapons; the tremendous ecological crises facing our planet; and so forth (see Lategan [1990:1] for an informative list of the amazing wide spectrum of discourses taking place simultaneously on these and other issues). Against this background it is understandable that more and more study and reflection are devoted to the relation of the biblical texts and the social contexts within which they originated and functioned and the possible implications of that for modern societies.

Another factor contributing to the revival of interest in the social contexts of biblical texts is extensive research being done in recent linguistic and literary studies on communication as a specific form of social interaction (De Villiers 1984:66). It is generally recognized that texts are part of a comprehensive communication process which involves speakers/authors and audience/readers, a communication situation and many social presuppositions and consequences. For example, modern pragmatics has made it clear that the meaning of an utterance is fundamentally determined by the context in which it is used (see Leech). Thus a general shift in focus has taken place in biblical hermeneutics: readers and their contexts have moved to the center of attention (Lategan 1984:10–12; W. S. Vorster 1988:37–38).

The social contexts of today's readers as well as the social context of the original readers of the biblical texts are therefore deemed more and more important. In New Testament studies this interest has been responsible for the use of methods of interpretation which take over insights and methods from contemporary social sciences. It is possible today to talk in this regard about a new approach in New Testament criticism dubbed *social-scientific criticism*. Old problems concerning the understanding and relevance of the New Testament for contemporary society are tackled anew within new paradigms (see Domeris 1988, 1991). This approach has developed in a short time to such an extent that De Villiers (1982) could more than ten years ago justifiedly speak about a *renaissance* in social-scientific study of the New Testament. This development is also a logical and understandable development, given the interdisciplinary approach to the study of the New Testament in recent times (see Combrink 1986).

3.2 Earlier studies focusing on the social aspects of early Christianity

Interest in the social aspects of the New Testament, however, is not something totally new. Since the emergence of a historical consciousness with the *Aufklärung* in the eighteenth century, there has always been an awareness of the exegetical process as something which was called *Zeitgeschichte*. Together with all the other '-geschichten' it formed part of the methodological arsenal of the historical-critical paradigm (see Marshall; Klijn). Although this interest, caused primarily by historical considerations, was for a very long time detectable in New Testament interpretation, the so-called 'décor' or 'background' of the New Testament was mostly treated as a separate section, and such background material was often incorporated in the exegetical process on an *ad hoc* basis. The renewed interest in social phenomena in recent times, in contrast, is characterized by a greater methodological sophistication and a more specific focus — often on a particular book of the New Testament (see §3.3.2).

During the early decades of the twentieth century, with the epitome of the so-called *social gospel* in the USA, a number of scholars addressed social questions to the New Testament. Among the best-known and influential studies which can be named from this period are: Adolf Deissmann's *Licht vom Osten* (published in 1911 in English as *Light from the Ancient East: The New Testament illustrated by Recently Recovered Texts of the Graeco-Roman World*); E. Lohmeyer's *Soziale Fragen im Urchristentum* (1921); S. J. Case's *The Social Origins of Christianity* (1914); S. Matthews's *The Social Teaching of Jesus: An Essay in Christian Sociology* (1897); and F. Grant's *The Economic Background of the Gospels* (1926). With the shift of interest during mid-century in neo-orthodoxy to theology and the Word (Karl Barth), these lines of questioning seemed to have fallen out of fashion, and almost no new research in this regard was done (Scroggs 1980:165).

Since the middle seventies the situation has changed drastically, in part due to the factors sketched briefly in the previous section (§3.1). After many decades of dominance of theological and historical problems, an awareness has arisen that these approaches alone do not address the urgent issues of our time. So, for instance, traditional historical and theological approaches (can) hardly address the problem of the relation between material wealth and faith and the interaction between theological assertions and the social reality in which people live. A general *Unbehagen* has arisen about a discipline which limits the acceptable methods to the historical and theological. As Scroggs (1980:166) has put it:

> To some it has seemed that too often the discipline of theology of the New Testament (the history of *ideas*) operates out of a methodological docetism, as if believers had minds and spirits unconnected with their individual and corporate bodies.

Scroggs (1980:165–166) is careful, however, to warn that the social-scientific study of the New Testament and early Christianity must not reduce the reality of Christianity to a social dynamic. This line of questioning should rather be seen as an effort to guard against a reductionism from the other extreme, namely 'a limitation of the reality of Christianity to an inner-spiritual, or objective-cognitive system' (Scroggs 1980:166).

Although I agree with this sentiment of Scroggs, I think it is important to state explicitly that a 'pure' theological or historical approach to New Testament is everything but void of interaction with the social reality in which it was or is still being practiced. It should rather be understood as a specific way of coping with social reality, namely to limit New Testament interpretation to a study of history and ideas. This kind of limitation is itself a definite ideological position which has been responsible for the creation and maintenance of this kind of methodological docetism which characterized much of mid-century New Testament scholarship. All theological ideas are always socially and culturally determined.

3.3 Modern studies working from a social-scientific perspective

The ever-growing flood of studies working from one or another social-scientific perspective (understood broadly) renders it almost impossible to provide an exhaustive overview of what has been done in this regard in New Testament studies (in 1981 Elliott already listed eighty-one such studies published in the previous decade!). In order to give a glimpse of this type of interpretation, a number of basic approaches within this rather broad perspective will be mentioned briefly as well as some of the representative studies in each case (cf. the surveys done by Scroggs 1980; Gager 1983; Best 1983; De

Villiers 1984; Domeris 1988; Schmeller 1989; Van Staden; J. H. Elliott 1990:1-28; Holmberg 1-20; Joubert). The study of Craffert offers helpful conceptual instruments in terms of which such an overview can be presented. He distinguishes among three different molds of New Testament social-scientific studies, namely those done by (i) historically minded or social-historical scholars, (ii) sociologically minded scholars, and (iii) sociologically informed historians. These different categories are the results of three different views on the relationship between history and the social sciences.

3.3.1 Historically minded or social-historical scholars

Many of the studies which aim to provide social descriptions or social histories of the New Testament documents and/or the early Christian movement proceed from the assumption that the concept *social* is a neutral or innocent concept void of theory and models (see Meeks 1-5; Holmberg 2-3). They assume that texts are read without their being subject to or even implicitly informed by theoretical concepts or social theory. The studies of Hock, Malherbe (1983) and Stambaugh and Balch are exemplary of this mold. So, for example, Hock (27) maintains that

> . . . [T]hese few references, however, will provide a *factual basis* for the following reconstruction of Paul's daily life, using the parallel experiences of contemporary artisans and philosophic missionaries. Only then will Paul's daily life be seen in greater clarity and *truer* perspective [my italics].

From this remark it is clear that he works with a comparative method, reading all possible relevant ancient texts as if they were mirrors directly reflecting actual historical and social reality, assuming that on the basis of the 'facts' collected in this manner, the historical social reality of Paul's ministry could be reconstructed.

Malherbe (1983:20) holds that

> Sociological description of early Christianity can concentrate either on social facts or on social theory as a means of describing the 'sacred cosmos' or 'symbolic universe' of early Christian communities. Even though new historical information may be assimilated within old paradigms, we should strive to know as much as possible about the actual social circumstances of those communities before venturing theoretical descriptions or explanations of them.

These historicist presuppositions are characteristic of a scientist ethos of biblical scholarship. However, as it has been emphatically and convincingly argued by sociologically-minded scholars (see Rohrbaugh 23), it is not possible to know 'as much as possible' of 'actual social circumstances' *without* some theory or model which accompanies one's attempts, since all interpreters use models either explicitly or implicitly (Craffert 129). Part of such a model or theory is the interpreters's conception of the text/reality relation and the implications of the textual nature of the sources for the 'social facts' to be gathered.

One of the most recent studies in this mold is the book of Stambaugh and Balch. No reference to any social theory — or *any* theory — in terms of which they gathered their 'facts' or presented their description of the 'political, religious, economic, and social features of Palestine and of the cities of the Roman empire' (11) is found in their book. Yet, theoretically charged concepts such as class, status, city, cults, society, social context, patterns of economic activity, urbanization, and social interaction are used in abundance. In general they suggest that early Christians shared many of the perceptions and traditions of the 'world around them' (as if they were not part and parcel of that 'world') and consciously rejected certain aspects of it (11). This 'sharing' or 'rejecting,' however, is not explained in terms of a consistent sociological theory. None of these studies can therefore, strictly speaking, be referred to as social-scientific. Craffert (129) justifiedly characterizes these studies as the work of historically minded or social-historical scholars.

In a survey of modern research done in this mold, Scroggs (1980:168–171) pointed out that much attention has been given to the issue of the socio-economic level of the early Christians. The notion, popular since Deissmann, that the early Christians were economically poor and socially deprived has been the dominant perception for many decades. This stock picture, however, was successfully challenged in a seminal study by E. A. Judge, *The Social Pattern of Christian Groups in the First Century*, which was published in 1960, so much so that Malherbe (1983:31) could speak of a 'new consensus' emerging among scholars which places the social level noticeably higher than did Deissmann. Smith (447–455) underscores this 'new consensus' with an informative study of Matthew, First Corinthians and Acts, concluding that 'Matthew and his community do *not* seem to fit the popular picture of unlearned evangelist and unwashed people' (447), that '[t]he congregation at Corinth may have recruited its members not only from the very poor, but also — and perhaps largely — from the well-to-do bourgeois circles, even from the upper classes' (452). Therefore,

> [i]t is a mistake to think that the recruits of earliest Christianity came primarily from the lowest ranks of society . . . . Christianity was not a religion of slaves. The majority of its adherents in the whole period up to Constantine were members of the middle class of antiquity. They were primarily free workmen, craftsmen, small businessmen, and independent farmers; and as time passed more and more members from the upper classes entered the church . . . (Smith 453).

This is also one of the larger conclusions at which Grant arrived in his *Early Christianity and Society*: The Christian movement as a whole in all the years up to Constantine was not 'a proletarian mass movement' but a 'relatively small cluster of more or less intense groups, largely middle class in origin' (Grant 11).

The implications of this 'new consensus' for the interpretation of the New Testament and other documents of the early Christian period are immense. Scroggs (1980:170–171) and Smith (454–455) offer a number of penetrating questions, particularly with regard to the social and economic status of the scholars who studied this issue, the conclusions they arrived at, and the importance they have given to this particular issue. This is all directly relevant for the kind of assessment which an ethos of public account-ability in biblical scholarship necessitates. Middle-class and wealthy white American males (to refer to Patte's and Phillips's group — see the Introduc-tion, p. 6) and poor Third World women will relate differently to the way in which the social class and economic status of the early Christian communities are presented. For the development of an ethics of public accountability in biblical scholarship, therefore, these issues are of utmost importance.

3.3.2 Sociologically minded scholars

The second mold, which Craffert (129) has dubbed *sociologically minded* scholars, is on the one hand a reaction to theologically oriented New Testa-ment research which failed to realize that theological ideas are socially and culturally determined (see §3.2 above). On the other hand, it is also a reac-tion to the 'theory-innocent' assumptions underpinning much of the work done by social-historical scholars. Inspired by the traditional history-sociology antithesis, these scholars explicitly opted for the sociological side. The difference between social description and proper social-scientific studies of the New Testament is usually attributed to the fact that the latter uses explicitly explanatory theories, hypotheses and models of academic dis-ciplines such as sociology, anthropology and psychology (Gager 1982:258; Domeris 1988:379). Because of their explicit use of the tools and techniques of modern social sciences, scholars working in this mold maintain that they move beyond mere social *description* to a second level, namely *explanation* (Best 185). As J. H. Elliott (1990:6) has put it, contrary to social history, social-scientific interpretation 'advances beyond mere social description and inspired hunches concerning social relationships to social-scientific relation-ships and explanation.'

A whole range of sociological models based on different perspectives has been used by sociologically minded scholars of the New Testament, for example, typologies, cognitive dissonance, role analysis, sociology of knowl-edge, Marxist historical materialism, normative dissonance, legitimation,

knowledge, Marxist historical materialism, normative dissonance, legitimation, community values, cultural anthropology, the grid/group model of Mary
Douglas for investigating cultural values, transformation of human experience, and so forth (for more information on each of these models and for
exemplary New Testament studies in each case, see Scroggs 1980:171–177;
J. H. Elliott 1990:7–8; Domeris 1991:220–224).

3.3.3 Sociologically-informed historians

This third mold can be described as that used by the sociologically-informed
historian, or the *new history* which has emerged from the interaction between
history and the social sciences (Craffert 130). The new history was the result
of the upheaval in historical studies in the past few decades. It is a movement
away from the narration and explanation of essentially political events where
the emphasis is mainly on politics, the individual and chronology, to a
problem-oriented analytic approach. With the help of the social sciences it
has become possible not only to describe social phenomena but also to structure and explain historical data (Craffert 127).

One of the most influential modern social-scientific studies of the New
Testament which can best be classified in this mold is the book by Wayne A.
Meeks, *The First Urban Christians: The Social World of the Apostle Paul.*
For Meeks (2) the task of the social historian of early Christianity is to describe the life of the ordinary Christian within the environment in which the
movement was born. To enable him to provide such a description, he has
accumulated a mass of information relevant to the urban context of early
Christianity. On the basis of the people mentioned in the Pauline letters and
their titles or functions in society, Meeks attempts to sketch a profile of the
typical community. In his attempt to understand the motivation of people for
joining the Pauline communities, Meeks moves beyond social description. In
this context he refers to 'status dislocation,' that is, the difference between
achieved and attributed status. Wealth might contribute to a higher achieved
status than the rigid social order which the Roman world allowed. To com-
pensate for this lack of attributed status, such people would be drawn towards
a community which understood their experience of high status inconsistency,
like the Pauline communities (51–75).

It is clear, therefore, that social description in Meeks's view includes the
explicit use of social-scientific models for explanation and understanding.
For Meeks the use of grand theory as in many sociological studies as well as
the neglect of theory as in many socio-historical studies are both
unacceptable. He maintains that 'to collect facts without any theory too often
means to substitute for theory our common sense. Making that substitution

modernizes no less than does the scientist who follows his theory, for our common sense, too, is a cultural artifact' (Meeks 5). Meeks works with a different concept of social description or social history than those working in the historically minded or social-historical mold (discussed in §3.3.1) by allowing an explicit place for theory. On the other hand, his work was criticized by a number of sociologically oriented scholars (discussed in §3.3.2) for not explicating his social-scientific theory sufficiently (Malina 1985:347; Elliott 1985:332). His work, therefore, seems not to fit comfortably within any of those two molds.

3.4 General assessment of modern social-scientific studies of the New Testament

The contribution of modern social-scientific studies of the New Testament is welcomed and positively evaluated over a wide spectrum. So, for example, the feminist scholar Claudia Camp (250) specifically notes how much she — and many others practicing some form of liberationist criticism — has been influenced by the rise of social analysis in Biblical studies. There can be no doubt that J. H. Elliott (1990:16) expresses, to my mind, a valid and generally held sentiment by maintaining that:

> In the last decade the use of the social sciences in exegesis has increased significantly in application and methodological sophistication. The social dimensions and implications of a wide range of New Testament texts have been brought to light; dominant social and cultural scripts of ancient Mediterranean life have been identified; models for analyzing first century social systems have been developed; and the intersection of texts and contexts, of social milieu and conceptual world view, of group interests and religious ideology have been profitably explored. This progress, accompanied by the reciprocal conversation and critique among scholars employing and refining this approach, has established social-scientific criticism as an indispensable feature of the total exegetical and historical enterprise.

In the light of this overview and this assessment of the influence of social-scientific criticism in New Testament interpretation, it is therefore imperative that a special chapter should be devoted to a reading of Romans 13:1-7 from a social-scientific perspective. Excluding such a reading from this study of the ethics of recent New Testament interpretation would leave an unacceptable lacuna. Moreover, as I argued at the end of the previous chapter, a social-scientific reading can form an important bridge between an 'ethics of historical reading' and an 'ethics of public accountability' in biblical scholarship. How this could happen will be illustrated by a social-scientific analysis of the cultural value of honor and shame in Romans 13:1-7. It is also clear, however, that 'social-scientific criticism' has such a wide field of reference that the reading of Romans 13:1-7 to be proposed here can by no means be taken as exhausting the possibilities offered by this approach. The idea is rather to offer a reading exemplary of the kind of work which can be done from this perspective and to illustrate how this kind of reading may form part of an ethos of responsible interpretation.

4. The social function of Romans 13:1-7 as Paraenetic Literature

4.1 Introduction

In a very helpful study, 'The Social Character of Paraenesis and Paraenetic Literature,' Perdue has provided a paradigm for the description and interpretation of the social character of paraenesis in the cultural worlds of the Eastern Mediterranean from the early Bronze Age through the beginnings of Christianity. This programmatic essay will be used here to analyze the social character of Romans 13:1-7 as Paraenetic Literature.

In chapter 2 (§5.3.2) I indicated that — strictly on formalistic grounds — Romans 13:1-7 qualifies as protreptic literature rather than paraenesis. Both categories, however, are included in the broader category which Gammie has called 'Paraenetic Literature.' Perdue (23), in turn, holds that paraenesis[b] (which he defines primarily as *confirmation*) and protrepsis (which he defines primarily as *conversion*) are two possible social functions of paraenesis[a]. He defines paraenesis[a] as 'general and practical guidance for human behavior within a previously shaped comprehensive understanding of social reality' (6). Although I maintain that the literary form of Romans 13:1-7 can (on the formalistic grounds proposed in Gammie's [47] morphology of the taxonomy of Paraenetic Literature) accurately be described as protreptic, its general social function can still adequately be labelled with the term 'paraenesis' in terms of this broader understanding of the nature of paraenesis: namely paraenesis[a]. Therefore, in this chapter, the term *paraenesis* will be used to indicate the general character of Romans 13:1-7, since this does not run counter to its more precise formal-literary characterization as protreptic.

4.2 A social model for interpreting the paraenesis in Romans

Perdue (9-11) proposes that the structure--anti-structure model developed by Victor Turner can be used fruitfully to describe the social function of Paraenetic Literature, since this type of literature reflects both a paradigm of order and of conflict. The assumption that paraenesis was sometimes used to maintain a particular social order and sometimes to undermine a particular social order has been argued convincingly by Perdue (6-9).

4.2.1 A paradigm of order

Mention has already been made of the paradigm of order, represented by modern sociologists such as Emile Dürkheim, Robert K. Merton and Talcott Parsons (see §2). This social model, in its ideal form, projects a world order as originating at creation and continuing to categorize all existing elements into a harmonious whole (Wallace & Wallace 17–18). Everything has its place, norms, time, and function. A divine council or natural law maintains this order, often through a system of retribution which sustains life and grants well-being to those who live in harmony with cosmic norms, but brings punishment and destruction to violators (Perdue 6–7).

Perdue takes over the distinction between *Gesellschaft* and *Gemeinschaft* proposed by Toennies. Society in its broad sweep, conceived as a microcosm with its basic institutions, classes, and laws grounded in and reflective of the structure of the cosmos, is a *Gesellschaft*, while a smaller more personal type of society (family, kinship groups, clubs, and religious groups based on personal piety) is a *Gemeinschaft*.

In the *Gesellschaft* (such as the broad Greco-Roman *Umwelt* in which the letter to the Romans originated), social inequities based on class, gender, and position were projected as part of the natural order or due to the will of the gods. Individuals were to accept their fate, normally determined at birth, and to behave according to their 'predestined' place and norms (Perdue 7). The following remarks of Perdue (7) are directly relevant for the interpretation of the social act performed by Romans 13:1–7 as paraenesis, and are therefore quoted here in full:

> Grounded in the order of creation and enforced by the power of the state, laws . . . were authoritative and required obedience. State religion legitimated social institutions, patterns and laws, and its festivals and rituals were designed through mythic enactment to sustain the natural and social order. Conformity to social rules and obligations of the *Gesellschaft* was required, while variance from the laws and customs of the prevailing order was considered deviant behavior, threatening the well-being of both the individual and the society. Change was viewed as disruptive and consequently was resisted by both political power and custom.

Perdue (1990:8) argues that paraenesis which reflects this type of model has the tendency to control powerless groups by means of an ideology. The appeal to nature, the gods, and tradition may well be used to support the privileged status and position of those who possess power and wealth. Moral exhortation became a powerful means of ideological control in the process of social formation. This is exactly what the former South African State President, P. W. Botha, did with his reference to Romans 13:1–7 in his speech to the Zionist Christian Church at Pietersburg in April 1985 — only weeks before the first State of Emergency was announced (see the Introduction). He

used the moral exhortation of Romans 13:1-7 as a powerful means of ideological control in order to enforce submission to his authoritarian rule and his
conception of 'law and order.'

In the *Gemeinschaft* (such as the Pauline Christian communities), social
custom and religious precepts defined responsibilities and obligations for
group and individual behavior. Authority was more personal and was usually
grounded in the recognizable leaders of such communities. Motivations for
ethical action were based on intimacy, honor, compassion, and the will of the
personal gods of these smaller groups and associations (Perdue 8).

The observation of natural laws and divine revelation was the primary
source for social knowledge. Natural and divine law tended to be equated
and were authoritative, requiring unquestioning submission from community
members. As a type of social knowledge, traditional paraenesis encompassed
the projected cosmic, social and anthropological order of the *Gesellschaft*,
and it exhorted the members of the community on the basis of duty and self-
interest to follow and conform to its expectations. The obligations and
behavior for the more personal social existence (the *Gemeinschaft*) were also
reflected in paraenesis. This paraenesis appealed more to personal relationships (e.g., the authority of the parent) and feelings of intimacy. Perdue (8)
concludes his exposition of the paradigm of order by pointing out that:

> Ethical action produced well-being within nature, the larger society, the community,
> and the individual, sustaining their ongoing existence. Immoral behavior produced
> chaos in every sphere and was viewed as a threat to communal and individual life.

Read in isolation from its co-text (particularly Romans 12:1 - 15:13) and
in isolation from the rhetorical situation of the letter to the Romans, Romans
13:1-7 may be seen as a model example of paraenesis presupposing a
paradigm of order and legitimizing the *status quo*.

A number of the most important elements of the paradigm of order can
be found in Romans 13:1-7. The argumentation in Romans 13:1-7 is
underpinned by premises appealing to divine characteristics, such as 'Every
person should submit to God,' 'God punishes those who resist his ordinations,' 'God always does what is good' and 'Everything belongs to God' (see
chapter 3, §7.2.4). Through a strategy of transitive argumentation, these
values are transposed to the authorities — primarily to warrant the claim that
authorities are ordinations of God and should therefore be obeyed by
everyone. Accordingly, authorities have a specific place, norms and functions within the *Gesellschaft*. Their function and authority form part of the
cosmic order. The authorities are instrumental in maintaining this order
through a system of retribution and punishment.

Those who live in harmony with this order, that is, in this specific context, those who submit to the authorities, are characterized as people who 'do

good' (13:3). To 'do good' is conduct in accordance with the divine characteristic, 'God always does what is good.' Those who 'do good' are retributed; they receive the authorities' approval/praise (καὶ ἕξεις ἔπαινον ἐξ αὐτῆς, 13:3), and their life and well-being are assured. This approval or bestowing of praise from the authorities is specifically grounded with a reference to the function of the authorities in terms of their divine ordination: θεοῦ γὰρ διάκονός ἐστιν σοὶ εἰς τὸ ἀγαθόν (the authority is a servant of God for your good, 13:4). Note that what 'good' consists of is not explicated. The unspoken assumption is that everyone *knows* what is good (and what is bad). This general and unspoken assumption is a reflection of the idea of a cosmic order consisting of a harmonious whole.

Those who violate the cosmic norms, in this case by resisting the authorities, will be punished: they will incur judgment (οἱ δὲ ἀνθεστηκότες ἑαυτοῖς κρίμα λήμψονται, 13:1). The punishment is explicated with the reference to the 'sword' being carried and used by the authorities (οὐ γὰρ εἰκῇ τὴν μάχαιραν φορεῖ, 13:4). The implication of this reference is clear, namely, the punishment consists of the fact that the authorities will execute those who do 'bad.' This may also be taken as an assumption presupposing a cosmic order of harmony and order. Everyone knows what is bad. To resist the authorities is one specific example of 'bad' conduct. To resist the authorities, therefore, endangers the harmony of the divinely ordained cosmic order sustained by the divinely ordained authorities. Therefore 'bad' behavior should be rooted out to ensure the continued harmonious existence of the cosmic order.

Nothing is said about the possibility that authorities themselves might do bad. To consider such a possibility would be out of line within this line of argumentation since it would presuppose that divine ordinations might do bad, which would put in question the values and characteristics attributed to God. That is unthinkable. The conduct of the authorities (whether to praise or to punish) is justified with appeals to characteristics of God as well as by repeating that they act in this particular way *as servants* of God. This enhances the idea that the role and function of the authorities are a reflection of the cosmos as created and sustained by divine council. The social rules and obligations of the *Gesellschaft* with regard to the authorities are submission and conformity. As one of the major instruments for the enforcement of the laws for sustaining the harmonious cosmic order, the state acts authoritatively and requires obedience. A challenge to the state would be disruptive of the social order at a very basic level, and its consequences to the detriment of both the individual and the society.

This analysis would hold true if Romans 13:1–7 were read in isolation from its co-text and its context or when the analysis is limited to the

Gesellschaft. Such an isolationist reading, however, is not satisfactory, since there are elements in the co-text of Romans 13:1–7 on the basis of which it can be argued that the paraenesis in the letter to the Romans presupposes a paradigm of conflict.

4.2.2 A paradigm of conflict

This social model (with Marcuse, Marx and Habermas among its best-known modern theorists), in its ideal expression, projects a world which is not a harmonious order but rather an arena of opposing forces which struggle for domination (Wallace & Wallace 17–18). Forces of order and chaos or the gods themselves are in conflict, vying for control. The social life of the *Gesellschaft* is characterized by struggle, not harmony. Within the powerless groups (who experience the ruling group as coercive and oppressive, denying them access to power and status), 'paraenesis took on the significant role of undermining traditional teaching in order to destabilize the oppressive institutions controlled and ordered by the power elite' (Perdue 1990:9). Since some of the powerless groups concluded that substantial social change would be impossible, they found meaningful existence in a variety of more intimate communities, such as families, clubs, friendships and religious groups. Others, such as apocalyptic seers, considered social change at the level of the *Gesellschaft* possible, but then only in the form of radical divine intervention, supplemented perhaps by non-conformist human behavior. According to Perdue (9) there are two senses in which paraenesis within communities adhering to a model of conflict could be subversive, namely, (i) by assuming the forms of traditional paraenesis, but giving it new content and thus bringing its legitimacy into question, or (ii) by positing a new, though not fully realized, social order which calls for its own code of behavior (for example the 'Kingdom of God' in Luke).

Two strong arguments can be derived from the co-text of Romans 13:1–7 to support an order of conflict as the underlying vision of the cosmos and society of the paraenesis in this letter. The whole paraenetic section in Romans is overturned in Romans 12:1–2 (see the detailed analysis of the co-text of Romans 13:1–7 in chapter 1, §9.5):

1 Παρακαλῶ οὖν ὑμᾶς, ἀδελφοί, διὰ τῶν οἰκτιρμῶν τοῦ θεοῦ, παραστῆσαι τὰ σώματα ὑμῶν θυσίαν ζῶσαν ἁγίαν εὐάρεστον τῷ θεῷ, τὴν λογικὴν λατρείαν ὑμῶν· 2 καὶ μὴ συσχηματίζεσθε τῷ αἰῶνι τούτῳ, ἀλλὰ μεταμορφοῦσθε τῇ ἀνακαινώσει τοῦ νοός, εἰς τὸ δοκιμάζειν ὑμᾶς τί τὸ θέλημα τοῦ θεοῦ, τὸ ἀγαθὸν καὶ εὐάρεστον καὶ τέλειον.

I appeal to you therefore, brethren, by the mercies of God to present your bodies as living sacrifice, holy and acceptable to God, which is your spiritual worship. Do not be conformed to this world but be transformed by the renewal of your mind, that you may prove what is the will of God, what is good and acceptable and perfect.

The non-conformist character of the whole paraenetic section is marked explicitly, first negatively — μὴ συσχηματίζεσθε τῷ αἰῶνι τούτῳ (do not be conformed to this world) — and then positively — ἀλλὰ μεταμορφοῦσθε (but be transformed). The τῷ αἰῶνι τούτῳ is clearly a reference to the *Gesellschaft* within which the implied readers are pictured. In the rest of the paraenetic section, the non-conformist conduct to which the readers are exhorted is spelled out at different levels, namely, the conduct of members of the *Gemeinschaft* within the *Gesellschaft* (12:9 – 13:10) and the conduct of members of the *Gemeinschaft* among themselves (14:1 – 13:13).

The apocalyptic interjection (13:11–14) in the middle of the exposition of the non-conformist behavior to which the readers are exhorted is the second strong argument which can be derived from the co-text of Romans 13:1–7 in favor of a conflict model of society presupposed in the paraenesis of the letter to the Romans. Non-conformist human behavior is exhorted and emphasized in typical apocalyptic terminology: ἀποθώμεθα οὖν τὰ ἔργα τοῦ σκότους ('let us cast off the works of darkness') and ἐνδυσώμεθα δὲ τὰ ὅπλα τοῦ φωτός ('let us put on the armor of light') (13:13). Radical action in the form of divine intervention will bring the value-system and conduct of the *Gesellschaft* in accordance with what is pictured as the ideal for the *Gemeinschaft* is at hand: ἡ νὺξ προέκοψεν, ἡ δὲ ἡμέρα ἤγγικεν ('the night is far gone, the day is at hand' 13:12).

It is true that the non-conformist 'heading' of Romans 13:1–7 (namely 12:1–2) and the apocalyptic interjection almost directly subsequent to this passage are strong arguments in favor of a model of conflict to explain the social act of the paraenesis in Romans. This alone, however, does not provide a satisfactory explanation specifically for Romans 13:1–7, since, as it was argued above (§4.1.1), the conformational language of this passage perfectly fits the paradigm of order. Therefore, we have to look for a model which would integrate these two contrastive perspectives at a higher level of abstraction.

4.2.3 Structure--anti-structure

Since paraenesis may reflect both a paradigm of order and a paradigm of conflict, Perdue (10) maintains that Victor Turner's structure--anti-structure model, which accounts for both forms of social organization, provides adequate conceptual tools for dealing with the social function of paraenesis. Turner (1969) has developed a dynamic, bipolar, processual model in which society represents the continuing movement back and forth between structure (*societas*) and anti-structure (*communitas*). These two poles operate within both the larger society (*Gesellschaft*) and the smaller communities (*Gemein-schaften*).

Basic to Turner's model is a distinction among three temporal and spatial phases contained by the rites which accompany every change of place, state, social position, and age in society, namely: (i) separation, (ii) margin (*limen*, threshold), and (iii) aggregation (reincorporation). In the first phase individuals or groups are detached from a fixed place in the social structure and they leave behind all prior cultural conditions. In the second phase, liminality, they are in a state of 'betwixt and between,' devoid of structure's laws, customs and ceremonies. Two phases of ritual actions and symbols can be distinguished during liminal situations. In the first phase of liminality the novices experience the death of their previous social identity and its norms. Their situation is metaphorically described as death, the tomb, the womb, wilderness, darkness, eclipse, et cetera (Perdue 10). Paraenesis in this phase is subversive, aiming to undercut the validity of the prior social world and to produce anomy. The rituals and symbols associated with the second phase of liminality imitate the experiences of birth (with light, fertility, new creation, et cetera, as typical metaphors). Now ritual leaders construct a new social reality for the novices and instruct them in their roles and responsibilities which they will have to assume once aggregation takes place. During the liminal experience the initiates are reduced to *prima materia* out of which new beings are created who are capable of living transformed lives with different patterns of behavior. Once recreated, they re-enter society, completing the cycle with the third stage (Perdue 10-11).

In the context of status elevation during liminality (the novice moving to a higher social position), much traditional paraenesis can be found. Some social groups of marginals may develop their own alternative social structure and hierarchy within which they become the chosen who are to rule over their unrepentant oppressors. A feature of social groups in such a 'permanent' state of liminality is anti-traditional paraenesis, designed to subvert the existing social structure and produce a new social reality. On the other hand, traditional paraenesis can function within such liminal periods as a means by which proponents of the existing social order may attempt to lessen the danger of egalitarianism (*communitas*) and to stabilize the social order by preventing such new social realities from developing. Turner (1974:83) argues that the great religions are those which harmonize structure (*societas*) and anti-structure (*communitas*) or hold them in a field of legitimate tension. The great religions recognize that a human being 'is both a structural and an anti-structural entity' who *grows* through anti-structure and *conserves* through structure' (Turner 1974:80).

Since its formative beginnings, of which the letter to the Romans is one testimony, Christianity has aimed at holding structure and anti-structure in tension. The explicit exhortation to the readers of Romans *not* to conform (μὴ συσχηματίζεσθε τῷ αἰῶνι τούτῳ, 12:2) and the apocalyptic language in 13:11–14 are clear indications that the encoded author, Paul, perceives himself and the adherents of his gospel to be in a liminal state. In fact, one of the most characteristic rituals of liminality, as well as its accompanying metaphors, is explicitly mentioned in the letter (Romans 6:3–4):

ἢ ἀγνοεῖτε ὅτι ὅσοι ἐβαπτίσθημεν εἰς Χριστὸν Ἰησοῦν εἰς τὸν θάνατον αὐτοῦ ἐβαπτίσθημεν; συνετάφημεν οὖν αὐτῷ διὰ τοῦ βαπτίσματος εἰς τὸν θάνατον, ἵνα ὥσπερ ἠγέρθη Χριστὸς ἐκ νεκρῶν διὰ τῆς δόξης τοῦ πατρός, οὕτως καὶ ἡμεῖς ἐν καινότητι ζωῆς περιπατήσωμεν.

Do you not know that all of us who have been baptized into Jesus Christ were baptized into his death? We are buried therefore with him by baptism into death, so that as Christ was raised from death by the glory of the Father, we too might walk in newness of life.

In terms of the communicative axis of the letter (see chapter 2, §6.3.3.2) the personal deictic 'we' includes both the encoded author and the implied readers. They 'have died' and they 'have been buried.' They have left behind their previous social identity (ὁ αἰῶνος τούτος) and its governing norms. Having gone through this phase of separation, and having been reduced to *prima materia*, they are now perceived to be in the second phase of liminality, and they are portrayed with the characteristic metaphor 'new life' (καινὴ ζωή, Romans 6:4). The paraenesis in this phase is designed to create them anew, capable of living transformed lives with different behavior patterns. A number of the exhortations in Romans 12:9–21 are characteristic of anti-structural paraenesis, for example, εὐλογεῖτε τοὺς διώκοντας ('bless those who persecute you,' 12:14), μηδενὶ κακὸν ἀντὶ κακοῦ ἀποδιδόντες ('repay no one evil for evil,' 12:17), μὴ ἑαυτοὺς ἐκδικοῦντες ('never avenge yourselves,' 12:19). These are exhortations to highly a-typical behavior, since it is in contrast to what would generally be expected from normal human behavior. The new *communitas* is therefore anti-structural. Amongst the members of the *communitas* harmony is emphasized. The brief exhortation, τὸ αὐτὸ εἰς ἀλλήλους φρονοῦντες ('live in harmony with one another,' 12:16), is elaborated and argued extensively with reference to a number of specific issues in Romans 14:1 – 15:13 (for example, the significance of religious days and food purity customs).

Although the paraenesis in Romans is characteristic of a second stage of liminality (that is, creating a new social reality), in the encoded author's perception this ideal can be realized best through a strategy of conformity. Although highly a-typical, all the exhortations in Romans 12:9–21 have a conformationist orientation. This orientation must be understood within the rhetorical situation of the letter to the Romans. This is of utmost importance. If this paraenesis had been part of, for instance, a letter from a Roman emperor to his subjects, it would have functioned as a means to lessen the danger of a new *communitas* to develop and to stabilize the social order. For example, from the point of view of an emperor, an exhortation to his subjects to conform to existing social structures and to live in harmony would have had a totally different pragmatic effect than the same exhortation would have had if it had come from a religious leader with no official status or power within the *Gesellschaft*. If the emperor urges his subjects to pay taxes, it is a totally different matter than when a religious leader urges members of his *Gemeinschaft* to pay taxes in order to secure their ongoing existence.

The fact that the conformationist oriented paraenesis of Romans 13:1–7 *forms part of the letter to the Christians in Rome* is an indication that the *Gemeinschaft*, within their situation as envisioned by the encoded author, condones and confirms obedience to the authorities within their own line of conduct. The norms of the *Gesellschaft* are taken over, not to maintain the *societas* but rather to benefit the *communitas* in its process of creation. The personal authority of the apostle as leader within the *Gemeinschaft* functions in the role of the authority of the parent, which is characteristic of the intimate and personal nature of the *Gemeinschaft*. The inclusion of the traditional paraenesis of Romans 13:1–7 aims at the benefit of the *Gemeinschaft*. The features of the cosmic order regulating the *Gesellschaft* are encompassed within this traditional paraenesis. The *Gemeinschaft* is exhorted on the basis of self-interest and duty to conform to the expectations of the *Gesellschaft*. This would result in their well-being and ensure their ongoing existence as Christian communities in Rome, which, in its turn, is to the benefit of the encoded author of the letter. Since the Christian communities were religious groups, the appeals to God and the characteristics ascribed to God to warrant this line of conduct towards the authorities have an even greater power than they might have had in the more general *Gesellschaft* — religion, after all, is about God. The natural law (to submit to the authorities) is equated with the divine law: to submit to the authorities is to submit to (an institution of) God. The *communitas* operates with a new understanding of the concept 'God' (as explicated by Paul in this letter to the Romans). In terms of this new understanding, some of the traditional characteristics ascribed to God (by the *Gesellschaft*) are sustained by the *Gemeinschaft*. For example, the belief that God is authoritative and requires obedience is gnomic and held by a greater circle than only the Christian communities. The exhortation to submit to the authorities was therefore also authoritative, and it required submission from community members. To resist the authorities would be immoral behavior (since it would mean to resist God), and that would produce chaos in every sphere, which would be a threat to the life and well-being of the community.

We may summarize the argument in this section as follows: read in isolation from its co-text, Romans 13:1-7 reflects a paradigm of order. Within the rhetorical situation of the letter to the Romans, it forms part of the paraenesis of a liminal experience in the second phase, namely, the creation of new beings with new behavior patterns which are non-conformist to the previous social order (the ὁ αἰῶνος οὗτος). In order to succeed with the creation of the new *communitas* and in order to further its aims (by means of the establishment of an operational base for Paul in Rome and his envisioned missionary activities in Spain), it is for pragmatic reasons necessary for the Christian *Gemeinschaft* to conform to *some of* the values of the *Gesellschaft*, in particular those regarding conduct towards state authorities. The social function of the paraenesis in Romans is to transform and replace the social values of the Christian *Gemeinschaft* on the basis of a newly envisioned view of God and human society. On the point of the conduct to authorities, however, the existing values operating within a paradigm of order converge with those envisioned by the encoded author for the new *communitas* as they are constructed within the rhetorical situation of the letter to the Romans.

This social-scientific reading confirms the point that I made at the end of the previous chapter (see chapter 3, §8): this type of reading begins to bridge the gap between an 'ethics of historical reading' and 'an ethics of public accountability.' Such explicit consideration of the social forces and functions created by the 'world of the text' brings the interpreter closer to reflection on his or her world. The differences and possible parallels are easier to recognize. Of course, this is still only one half of the job. An ethics of public accountability requires the interpreter also to reflect responsibly on the current twentieth century context in which the act of interpretation takes place. But I submit once again that a social-scientific reading of the world created by the text (which is something different from the historical world from which the text originated) has to precede any subsequent claims about possible implications of the text for the historical world of the text and the current world of the interpreter. Although such a social-scientific reading of the text is only one half of the job, it 'must' be the *first* half of the job — otherwise it can no longer be a responsible act of interpretation. At the same time, however, it is obvious that with only half of the job done, the job itself is not done — and that would be another manifestation of an irresponsible act of interpretation. One other qualification which is of utmost importance must be added here: the context or society of the interpreter plays a determining role throughout this whole process. It is not as if the interpreter can do — in a positivistic sense — the 'first half' of this job and after that — in a temporal sense — the 'second half' of the job. As one manifestation of the intertext, the intertextuality of the subject is inevitably part of the whole process of reading. In order to bring this theoretical claim closer to the ground, one concrete example of a social-scientific description of a value operative in the world created by the text will now be discussed and assessed.

5. *Romans 13:1-7 and the ancient social value of 'honor' and 'shame'*

In an informative anthropological study published in 1981, Bruce Malina (1981:25) dubbed honor and shame as 'pivotal values' of the first-century Mediterranean world. The important role of these values is evident in the letter to the Romans. In fact, the thesis of the letter explicitly reflects this value: Οὐ γὰρ ἐπαισχύνομαι τὸ εὐαγγέλιον ('I am not ashamed of the Gospel,' Romans 1:16). Malina's discussion of the importance of these values is therefore relevant for an interpretation of the letter to Romans as they form major elements of the cultural code which the letter presupposes.

The main characteristics of an honor-and-shame society can be summarized in the following points (see Malina 1981:25-50 and Moxnes 208):

* The group is more important than the individual
* The individual receives status from the group
* Recognition and approval from others are important
* Interaction between people is characterized by the competition for recognition and the defense of one's own status and honor
* To refuse a person's claim for honor is to put the person to shame

The basic notion in honor-and-shame societies is that these values represent the value of a person not only in her or his own eyes but also in the eyes of his or her society. We may perhaps say that the quest for honor and concurrently, the avoidance of shame, makes a person, or rather the person-within-the-group, as well as the society as a whole 'tick.' The order of society is kept together by this common quest for honor and praise. The individual and the group are constantly confronted with the obligation to seek value (honor) in the eyes of a 'significant other.' This 'significant other' can be the greater *Gesellschaft*, or other members of the *Gemeinschaft*, or other individuals within the patron-client relationship, or even more than one of these simultaneously. Malina (1981:47) explains the role of these values in terms of the two of the three major theoretical perspectives are usually distinguished in sociology (see §2). From a symbolic point of view honor 'stands for a person's rightful place in society, his social standing' and from a structural-functionalist point of view honor 'is the value of a person in his or her own eyes plus the value of that person in the eyes of his or her social group.' Malina writes (1981:47):

> Honor is a claim to worth along with the social acknowledgement of worth. The purpose of honor is to serve as a sort of social rating which entitles a person to interact in specific ways with his or her equals, superiors, and subordinates, according to the prescribed cultural cues of the society.

Malina (1981:48) and Wikan (648) distinguish between the male and female component of honor. In terms of this distinction, honor is primarily a male value since it is intimately related to power and might — the power to assert one's honor in public. Shame, on the other hand, is predominantly a female value. Usually women are subordinate and limited to a small public role within honor-and-shame societies.[3]

My analysis of the *topoi* operative in the rhetorical situation of Romans 13:1-7 (see chapter 3, §7.2.4) has revealed how intricately the argumentation in this passage is interwoven with the 'praise' (honor) or 'punishment' (shame) which authorities — in their capacity as servants of God — can bestow on people. To interpret the role of these values within the social-scientific model proposed by Malina, I have found a study by Moxnes very helpful (although he does not work with a consistent *textual* approach as I have been attempting to do in this study).

Moxnes (210–212) argues that Romans 13:1-7 provides an excellent reflection of a society which holds honor as its most prominent value. Characteristically honor is linked to *power*,[4] as can be seen in the frequent occurrence of the term ἐξουσία (13:1, 2, 3) and other words related to 'might' and 'power' (κρίμα 13:2; μάχαιρα 13:4; ὀργή 13:4). The historical-critical studies of Strobel (1956:67–93) and Käsemann (1980:353–354) have illustrated that the terminology used in Romans 13:1-7 may *refer* to[5] representatives of Hellenistic administration, Roman officials or municipal authorities (ἐξουσία 13:1; ἄρχων 13:3; λειτουργός 13:6). My analysis of the *lexical sense* of these terms has indicated that these words or terms do not have the meaning of abstract 'institutions' or 'systems.' Rather, their lexical sense is specifically related to personal relationships (see chapter 1, §8.2 and §8.3). Therefore, Moxnes (1988:211) makes a valid observation by indicating that these officials do not correspond to the modern Western-democratic notion of 'civil servants' who perform their duties on behalf of the citizenry and are in that sense 'servants' of the citizens. Rather, they are presented in

---

[3]For more recent treatments of honor and shame in ancient Mediterranean cultures see, for example, Malina and Neyrey 25–65; Gowler 16–17, 77–296, 359–376.

[4]For an instructive comparison of the power structures operative in Romans 13:1-7 and the power structures which characterized the Botha-government in South Africa at its height during 1987 and 1988, see Draper.

[5]See chapter 2, §4.4 and §4.6, for the distinction between 'reference' and 'sense.'

the text as 'bearers of power with whom the common man may come into contact' and behind whom the regional or central administration could be seen (Käsemann 1980:354). Therefore, the relationship between authorities and subjects as presented in Romans 13:1–7 is not a relationship between the citizenry and an abstract 'institution.' It is a relationship between *people*, with the subordinates vying for honor or praise from the authorities. Such a relationship is characteristic of a society in which the patron-client relationship plays such an important role (see Elliott 1987).

I have already indicated that, for strategic reasons, Paul confirms this value as characteristic of the paradigm of order of the Greco-Roman *Gesellschaft* in his letter to the Romans (see §4.2.1 and §4.2.3 above). Although he is active as leader during a period of liminality for the Christian communities, on the matter of authorities and their subjects he presupposes the existing order of the society and exhorts the implied readers to recognize that order. He exhorts them to be subject and thereby underscores their dependent and subordinate position. The authorities and the implied readers are not equals. They have a relationship characterized by the common bond in the quest for honor. The common bond has implications for the authorities as well as for the subordinates. Moxnes (1988:211) maintains that one half of this quest is implied in the admonition to the readers to accept their role as subjects: ἀπόδοτε πᾶσιν τὰς ὀφειλάς, τῷ τὸν φόρον τὸν φόρον, τῷ τὸ τέλος τὸ τέλος, τῷ τὸν φόβον τὸν φόβον, τῷ τὴν τιμὴν τὴν τιμήν (13:7) — 'Pay all of them their dues, taxes to whom taxes are due, revenue to whom revenue is due, respect to whom respect is due, honor to whom honor is due.' Moxnes writes:

> The phrase "Pay all . . . their dues [*opheilas*]" was widely used to describe the relations between rulers and subjects, patrons and clients. Likewise, to "give honor [*timen*]" was the obligation of subjects, who thereby accepted their position. Taxes and dues, beyond their economic importance, had a symbolic significance by granting precedence and honor. In fact, honor was more important than economy. Thus, the economic, ritual, and social aspects came together to form a symbolic and practical reality, a world order (1988:211).

Perhaps Moxnes overstates his case by making economic considerations hierarchically subordinate to the symbolic importance of honor. Nevertheless, the very important role of the quest for honor in creating and sustaining the particular world order created by this text cannot be denied. The remarkable accumulation of stylistic figures of speech in Romans 13:7 may be seen as an additional motivation to attribute this important significance to this verse (see the analysis in chapter 3, §7.4). It may therefore also not be incidental that the τιμή is put at the end of this list of things due. In fact, it is a remarkable example of the literary phenomenon of emphasis by means of postponement: the most important element is deferred to the very end of a sequence.

Equally significant for the upholding of the social order was praise (ἔπαινος 13:3): οἱ γὰρ ἄρχοντες οὐκ εἰσὶν φόβος τῷ ἀγαθῷ ἔργῳ ἀλλὰ τῷ κακῷ. θέλεις δὲ μὴ φοβεῖσθαι τὴν ἐξουσίαν; τὸ ἀγαθὸν ποίει, καὶ ἕξεις ἔπαινον ἐξ αὐτῆς ('For rulers are not a terror to good conduct, but to bad. Would you have no fear of him who is in authority? Then do what is good and you will receive his approval/praise,' Romans 13:3)). Van Unnik (334–343) has illustrated by means of a long list of parallel or related expressions from a wide range of Hellenistic-Roman writings that this was a well-known expression in Hellenistic society. The 'good acts' refers to the ideal of the good man (ἀνὴρ καλὸς κἀγαθός) who knows his place and acts accordingly. The reward for 'good' behavior is praise (ἔπαινος). This was a technical term used to refer to specific forms of recognition granted by rulers to clients, cities, or citizens who had contributed to the common good (Van Unnik 342). In the honor-and-shame society from which this letter originates it was an important goal of a citizen to lead a life that was honored and made memorable through such praise.

The 'dues to the authorities' and the 'honor to the citizens' therefore constituted a mutually reinforcing system. Persons who wielded power were accorded respect and honor. In turn they distributed praise and approval as favors to obedient clients. Of particular importance for the interpretation of Romans 13:1–7 is that this distribution of praise by the authorities was done in their capacity as 'servants of God.' I have indicated how a transitive strategy of argumentation was used to apply to the authorities values usually attributed to God (see chapter 3, §7.2.4). Ultimately then, the 'significant other' in whose eyes the citizens are exhorted to seek honor is God. Moxnes (212) holds that Paul's exhortation in Romans 13:1–7 serves to strengthen the integration of Christians into the Hellenistic symbolic universe. In terms of the multifaceted character of the paraenesis in Romans (see §4.2.3) this integration as such is perhaps not an explanation of the whole picture, and it is also too generalizing. Regarding the specific issue of conduct to the authorities the values characteristic of the Hellenistic symbolic universe are confirmed. This is done for specific strategic reasons, namely the confirmation of Paul's ethos in order to enlist the cooperation of the implied readers for a number of reasons (see chapter 3, §7.5).

Interestingly enough 'shame' does not seem to be at issue in this context. Moxnes (212) makes this observation and argues:

There was no possibility that subjects could put the authorities to shame by refusing to give them their due honor: the status difference was too great to pose such a challenge. Thus, the subjects were faced with only one alternative: either praise for the good deed, or punishment for the bad. The lines of authority were clear. This was the public sphere, that is, the men's world, in which the quest for honor and praise reigned.

Moxnes (213–216) has illustrated that 'shame' plays an important role in other sections of the letter to the Romans, for example the discussions of sex roles and sex behavior in Romans 1 and Romans 6. He concludes that Paul accepted the system of honor operating in the public arena of Hellenistic society, but that Paul rejected this society as shameful in the area of sex roles and sexual life. The private world of the *Gemeinschaft* was concerned with the shame area. Regarding this world, Paul exhorts his implied readers to non-conformist behavior (μὴ συσχηματίζεσθε τῷ αἰῶνι τούτῳ: 'do not conform with this world,' Romans 12:1). Regarding the conduct of members of the *Gemeinschaft* within and as part of the greater Greco-Roman *Gesellschaft* the honor-area of public life is confirmed and the implied readers are exhorted to a conformational attitude. Regarding the conduct of members of the *Gemeinschaft* among themselves, particularly on matters such as the significance of religious days and food purity customs (dealt with in Romans 14), the implied readers are also exhorted to a conformational attitude.

I have argued that a social-scientific study such as this may serve as a way in terms of which the modern interpreter can begin to bridge the gap between the 'world created by the text' and the current world of the interpreter (see §4.2.3). A few remarks will illustrate this practically. The differences between the role which honor and shame play in the world of the text and (certain so-called First World) sections of the modern world are obvious. No one would argue, for instance, that the contemporary relationship of the United States' government and its citizenry presupposes a mutual bond of a quest for honor and praise. Honor and praise (or punishment) may play a role in today's society in the United States, but definitely not in the same way as it does in the world of the text. Furthermore, it is simply not plausible to claim any longer that the public sphere of authorities and subjects is exclusively a world of males. The quest for honor and the avoidance of shame are no longer the dominant factors that make contemporary American society 'tick.' There are a host of other factors. What exactly they are, though, is a subject for another study. Responsible reflection and comparison on this matter necessitate a careful sociological study of the values of the modern society in which the interpreter of the New Testament lives. Only on the basis of such a study and on an explicitly worked-out scale of modern religious values can the values operative in the text be critically assessed and possible implications for a modern society be inferred.

Such a social analysis of the modern society in which the interpreter of the New Testament lives does not form part of this study. Enough has been said, however, to indicate the direction and some of the demands of an 'ethics of public accountability.' What I want to argue for is that in an 'ethics of reading' a social-scientific reading of 'the world of the text' has preference over these additional responsibilities of an 'ethics of public accountability.' It must also be emphasized again that, of course, such a study of the 'world of the text' does not and cannot happen in a positivistic sense in isolation from the world of the interpreter since the interpreter as reading subject is inevitably part of the whole process of intertextuality which characterizes the reading process.

6. *Summary and conclusion*

The aim of this chapter was to read Romans 13:1–7 from a social-scientific perspective. The concept 'reading from a social-scientific perspective,' as it was understood for the purposes of this chapter, was described in §2. This was followed by a brief overview of the impact of modern studies from a social-scientific perspective on New Testament interpretation (§3) in order to indicate into which mold of the social-scientific approach this reading fits. The model proposed by Perdue was then used for a social-scientific analysis of the social function of Romans 13:1–7 as Paraenetic Literature. I have concluded that if Romans 13:1–7 is read in isolation from its co-text, it reflects a paradigm of order. Within the rhetorical situation of the letter to the Romans, however, it forms part of a type of paraenesis which is characteristic of a society going through a liminal experience in the second phase, namely, the creation of new beings with new behavior patterns which are non-conformist to the previous social order (ὁ αἰῶνος οὖτος). In order to succeed with the creation of this new *communitas* and in order to further its aims (by means of the establishment of an operational base for Paul in Rome and his envisioned missionary activities in Spain), it is for pragmatic reasons necessary for the Christian *Gemeinschaft* to conform to *some* of the values of the *Gesellschaft*, in particular those regarding conduct towards the people in positions of authority. The social function of the paraenesis in Romans is to transform and replace the social values of the Christian *Gemeinschaft* on the basis of a newly-envisioned view of God and human society. On the point of the conduct towards authorities, however, the existing values operating within a paradigm of order converge with those envisioned by the encoded author for the new *communitas* as they are constructed within the rhetorical situation of the letter to the Romans.

Preference for such a social-scientific analysis of the 'world of the text' is a necessary aspect of an ethics of reading. It has to precede any inferences about the relation of the 'world of the text' to the 'historical world which produced the text.' It also has to precede inferences about the relation of the 'world of the text' and the world of the modern interpreter. An ethics of *reading* compels the interpreter to give such preference to the 'world created by the text.' An ethics of reading obliges the interpreter to take the reading of the text seriously. Such a reading has to include *and move beyond* serious attention to the linguisticality, literariness and rhetoricity of the text as textual phenomenon. By moving beyond the rhetoricity of the text, or rather, because of taking rhetoricity of the text seriously, the interpreter is put in a position to reflect explicitly on the values operative in the 'world created by the text.' This process may serve as the beginning of a responsible interaction between, on the one hand, 'an ethics of reading' and 'an ethics of historical reading' (which was not part of what was done in this chapter), and, on the other hand, 'an ethics of reading' and 'an ethics of public accountability' in biblical scholarship. To illustrate this interaction by means of one concrete example, the role of the values of honor and shame operative in Romans 13:1-7 was analyzed and an indication was given of the direction into which an 'ethics of public accountability' may lead the interpreter in this specific instance.

CHAPTER 5

GENERAL SUMMARY AND CONCLUSIONS

The thrust of the argument in this book can be summarized as follows: a responsible and serious *reading* of the text of Romans 13:1-7 must take place *before* any study of the possible extrinsic relations (or ethical inferences drawn from this text) can be undertaken with confidence. Such a reading, however, has to be qualified or modified in three important respects:

* A responsible reading of Romans 13:1-7 cannot remain oblivious to text-external (social, ecclesiastical, personal) matters — as often happens in a scientist ethos of biblical scholarship. At one point or another the New Testament scholar shares the responsibility to address text-external matters (in particular issues of the contemporary world of the interpreter). Nevertheless, without a preceding reading of the text — allowing for and trying to understand its nature, how it works or what it can do — we cannot understand the role that New Testament literature may have in society, history, the church and individual life.

* A responsible reading of Romans 13:1-7 cannot treat the text in isolation from its original historical context. However, a responsible reading of the New Testament cannot treat the text as if it were a simplistic mirror-like representation of first century 'historical reality.' This would violate the textual nature of the text in all its different facets, and thus it would not be ethically responsible with regard to the nature of the material with which we are dealing.

* Any interpreter involved in a responsible act of interpretation has to be consistently aware of and allow for the decisive role of his or her own context and of herself or himself as a composition of intertexts during the process of reading. This appeal for serious reading is *not* a call for a positivistic-type of 'close-reading' in terms of the simplistic conception of Bodoh that '. . . the first law of criticism is to obey the text' (see Swanepoel 1989:366). On the contrary, the complexity of the reading process as it was illustrated in this book illustrates to what an extent the *reader* is continually making choices during this process. In fact, the first half of each chapter in this study was devoted to the motivation and explanation of *choices* on a whole range of issues. None of those choices are innocent. They are inevitably always determined by the theoretical framework and ideological preferences of *the reader* and her or his interpretive community. They are choices made *by the interpreter.*

This book theoretically developed and illustrated this understanding of an ethics of responsible reading by reading Romans 13:1-7 consecutively from a linguistic, a literary, a rhetorical and a social-scientific perspective.

In the linguistic reading of Romans 13:1-7 (chapter 1) the lexical sense of five important words in Romans 13:1-7 was defined in terms of a structuralist view on the nature of meaning (ἐξουσία, ἄρχων, ὑποτάσσεσθαι, ἀντιτάσσομαι and συνείδησις). At a higher level the lexical sense of the nuclear structures of Romans 13:1-2 and their interrelationships were described. This was followed by a discourse analysis of Romans 13:1-7 as a whole. Finally, the place of Romans 13:1-7 within its linguistic co-text (in particular Romans 12:1-15:13) was described. I have argued that such a linguistic analysis (whether in terms of a structuralist paradigm or not) forms an essential aspect of responsible reading. Such a systematic attempt to describe the lexical sense of words, phrases, and bigger parts of the text is a necessary aspect of reading and as such it has to precede any confident study of text-external relations. An ethics of responsible reading compels the interpreter to take the linguistic phenomena of the text seriously. Since some of the best available 'tools' for the description of linguistic phenomena of the New Testament are presented within a structuralist paradigm, they were used extensively in chapter one. But precisely because a structuralist view of the language may seduce an interpreter to hide safely from current realities in the ivory tower of an abstract structuralist textual world, I have argued that a responsible act of interpretation should not end with a structuralist-linguistic description of the lexical sense of words and sentences. In terms of an ethos of responsible reading, the interpreter has to move beyond taking the text seriously as a linguistic phenomenon.

The literary reading of Romans 13:1-7 (chapter 2) consisted of two parts. The first part contained a formalist reading of Romans as a letter, and it presented a formal analysis of Romans 13:1-7 as a manifestation of Paraenetic Literature. This part indicates the formal epistolary characteristics of the letter to the Romans — its conventional letter-opening, its thanksgiving, self-recommendation, letter-body, paraenetic section and the different sections of the letter-closing. The analysis made it clear where and how Romans 13:1-7 (as part of the paraenetic section) fits into the letter as a whole. Then this part contained an analysis of the paraenetic section in more detail. I have concluded that, in terms of formal considerations alone, Romans 13:1-7 is an example of Paraenetic Literature, which can be more closely identified as protreptic in nature and in which three different sub-genres of Paraenetic Literature are intermingled — namely Admonition, Exhortation and Precept. As motivation for this formal analysis, I have indicated that the form (or genre) of literature is an important determining factor for its meaning. For this reason a formal analysis should somehow form part of the reading process as a whole. On the other hand, just as a 'pure' linguistic approach may lure an interpreter to hide in an abstract 'world' of textual forms and formulae, the same problem arises when a literary reading of the text begins and ends with a formal analysis. To do so would be a manifestation of a scientist ethos of biblical scholarship.

The second part of the literary reading uses a communicative approach — in particular since such an approach beyond formalism toward communication may serve to bring the interpreter closer to the 'life' *in* the text. This 'in' is a very important qualification. The description of the communicative axis which can be identified in the letter to the Romans is a description of an *intra*-textual phenomenon. It should not be equated simplistically with the real historical author and the real historical addressees of the letter. I have argued that a study of the 'textual world' (with all its consequences and complications) has *priority* over any inferences or conclusions about either the first century historical world or the historical world of the modern interpreter which are made on the basis of this text. Careful consideration of the literary features of the text is a necessary aspect of the respect due to the text. Although this distinction should be heeded consistently, the interpreter also has the responsibility to go further. Working *only* with or in the fictive literary or textual worlds without drawing any implications for the 'real world' or the context in which interpreters live is a specific reflection of the interpreter's ideology and stance regarding contextual matters. It may therefore also be a specific manifestation of an irresponsible act of reading. Although this is a necessary characteristic of an ethics of *reading*, an ethics of *historical* reading and in particular an ethics of *public accountability* in interpretation compel the interpreter not to end the act of interpretation prematurely. While I have underscored all these issues as necessary aspects of the ethics of New Testament interpretation, the important point in this book is that none of this can or should happen before or (worse) without a careful literary reading of the text in all its complexity.

This insight, namely the priority of the 'world created by the text,' is one of the most important implications for an ethics of interpretation which takes the text as literary phenomenon seriously. From the analysis of the communicative axis in Romans, I have concluded that

* The exhortation given to the recipients in Romans 13:1–7 has to be understood against the background of a relationship that exhibits a duality. The one who exhorts (the narrator, identified in the text as 'Paul') is in a delicate situation. On the one hand he is the disadvantaged in the relationship: he does not know the narratees personally, and he is the one who wants their cooperation for his personal plans. Therefore, the influence of this particular situation in which the exhortations were given must be taken into account in the interpretation of the tone of the commands given in Romans 13:1–7. On the other hand, because of the way in which Paul envisioned the religious nature of their relationship and because of the status which he ascribed to himself in terms of these religious convictions, he is in a position of authority over the narratees. Therefore, he is in a position to issue 'commands.' To give recognition to this dual situation and its influence on the nature and tone of the 'commands,' it is

better to use the term 'exhortation' rather than 'command' for the utterances in Romans 13:1–7.

*   Romans 13:1–7 should be read in terms of the decidedly *religious* nature of the basis of the to-be-established relationship between narrator and narratees. The exhortations to submit to the authorities and to pay taxes are not given by some or other 'secular' governmental institution which could itself benefit from such a submission and the payment of taxes. Therefore these exhortations have a 'friendly' and 'advisory' character rather than being clinical, official and enforceable commands given by someone/somebody in a formal, secular position of authority.

*   The personal deixis in Romans 13:1–7 presents a picture of diminishing distance between the interlocutors. From general gnomic statements, the narrator narrows the focus of his narratees by invoking them directly in the last section of the passage.

*   The attitude towards authorities advocated by Romans 13:1–7 serves as 'credential' for the narrator: in his perception the narratees would find it acceptable to identify themselves with such an attitude towards governing authorities. Because they can identify with him on these (and all the others issues he raised, specifically in the paraenetic section of the letter), they will respond favorably and co-operate with him in his future plans. In doing so the desired reciprocity of the letter is fulfilled.

*   The vagueness in time deixis in Romans 13:1–7 can be understood as an indication that it is not a new action which the narrator expects from his narratees in reaction to his letter. Nor is it explicitly marked as an action in which the narratees were engaged prior to the situations of utterance and reception, or, whether or not they were still doing so at the time of reception. This provides additional motivation for the observation that the letter to the Romans, and thus also Romans 13:1–7, is concerned with enlisting the cooperation of the narratees for the (future) personal plans of the narrator.

*   None of the explicit space deictics in other places in the letter (Rome, Jerusalem, Spain), has any particular relevance for the interpretation of Romans 13:1–7 from a literary perspective, except that it provides a general locus for the 'world' created by the text.

This description of aspects of the intra-textual communicative axis in Romans may not be satisfactorily concluded without explicit and serious attention to the rhetoricity of the text.

Because of its long tradition and because of a number of misconceptions often held about rhetoric, considerable attention was given in chapter 3 to an explicit formulation of the notion of rhetoric with which I have been working. To take the rhetoricity of the text seriously is *not* merely a study of the stylistic figures which may be found in a text. Neither is it a description of the text as a form of 'content-less' flattery aimed exclusively at the aesthetic enjoyment of the audience. To limit a rhetorical study of the text to such a notion of a 'rhetoric restrained' is often yet another manifestation of a scientist ethos of interpretation. Rather, doing justice to the rhetoricity of the text implies that the phenomenon of intra-textual *social interaction* which may be described in the text must be studied. As continuation of the line of argumentation of the thesis as a whole, it is of particular importance to demarcate the differences between (i) literary criticism and rhetorical criticism, and (ii) the historical situation and the rhetorical situation. I have argued that

*   Rhetorical criticism differs from literary criticism (or an epistolographical approach) since it studies discourse primarily *as argumentation*, as social inter-action, and not only as communication, or the transmission of information. Letter-writing is a *species* of the *genus* rhetoric.

*   The historical situation and the rhetorical situation are not identical. The rhetorical situation is more specific since it is always an element in/of a human communication situation, in which *language* usually plays the dominant (though not exclusive) role (depending on how broadly one defines 'language'). The rhetorical situation is always an element in/of a *specific type* of human communication, namely a goal-oriented social interaction. A historical situation, on the other hand, refers to a comprehensive concept, encompassing all the events, objects, persons, abstractions, interactions and relations (social, political, personal, cultural, ideological, ecological, or whatever) constitutive of a situation which existed in the past.

In an ethics of interpretation which takes the rhetoricity of the text seriously this distinction between the historical situation which produced the text and the rhetorical situation as text-internal concept is of utmost importance. Preference for the rhetorical situation is a particular manifestation of an ethics of reading which avoids reading texts as simplistic mirror-like representations of their historical situations. The rhetorical analysis of Romans 13:1-7 in terms of such a *textual* conception of rhetoric as goal-oriented interaction has yielded the following results:

*   Romans 13:1-7 can be seen as a distinct rhetorical unit, since it displays a dis-cernible beginning and ending, connected by some demonstrative argumenta-tion.

*   The question to which Romans 13:1-7 is a response can be formulated as fol-lows: *What is the right conduct with regard to the governing authorities?* The *status* of its rhetorical situation has therefore been identified as *status qualitatis*: the need exists to indicate that submission to the governing authorities would be the correct line of action to follow within this particular situation. Compromise rather than confrontation will be to the benefit of both the encoded author and the implied readers.

*   The relatively powerful position and role of the implied readers in the letter to the Romans is confirmed and simultaneously curtailed in Romans 13:1-7: if they do not submit to the authorities they could cause serious problems for themselves and for the future plans of the encoded author.

*   The exhortation in Romans 13:1-7 to submit (and to pay taxes) does not function *primarily* as 'exhortation' in the literal sense of the word within the
specific rhetorical situation of the letter aimed at persuading the implied
readers to follow a particular way of conduct in the future (although this needs
not be ruled out as a secondary consequence of the argumentation). The
exhortation is primarily one of the strategies employed by the encoded author
to enhance his credibility, and it serves as one more way to identify with the
implied readers. The encoded author shares the (Jewish) values of the implied
readers since he also holds that the right conduct towards the authorities (in the
normal course of things) is to submit to them and to pay taxes.

*   Since the confirmation of values already shared by the encoded author and
implied readers seems to be the intended effect of the argumentation in
Romans 13:1-7, its rhetorical genre was identified as epideictic.

*   A number of universal values serve as premises for the argumentation in
Romans 13:1-7. Of particular importance are those attributed to God:

  – Everyone should submit to God
  – God punishes those who resist God's ordinations
  – God always does what is good
  – Everything belongs to God

*   By means of a quasi-logical form of association, specifically a transitive
strategy of argumentation, these values attributed to God are transposed to the
authorities. With this pragmatic argumentation strategy, the encoded author
associates with his implied readers, confirming their value system in order to
succeed in enlisting their cooperation at a number of levels.

*   A number of stylistic features serve as techniques of persuasive discourse to
strengthen the progression as well as the cohesion in the argumentation.

*   Perhaps one of the most important factors responsible for the success of this
argumentation in meeting the rhetorical exigence lies in its appeal to general
and gnomic values.

Such a rhetorical reading compels the interpreter to reflect consciously
and explicitly on the implications of the *rhetoricity* of the text. It is a way of
reading 'between the lines.' It brings to the fore the implicit and
unspoken/unwritten values which underpin the argumentation. By bringing
those to the surface, the act of interpretation moves beyond a mere linguistic
or formal-literary analysis of the text. It also moves beyond a general communicative approach to the reading of the letter *as letter* toward a specific
reading of the goal-oriented, social interaction in the world created by the
text. With this movement beyond 'reading the lines' or 'describing the
forms' towards 'reading between the lines,' the interpreter moves from
regarding the New Testament (in terms of the scientist ethos) as an abstract
'language-phenomenon' closer toward 'life' — although this 'life' or 'reality'
is still a construction based on *textual considerations* and can therefore not be

equated with 'real historical life.' Such respect for the rhetoricity of the text is yet another necessary aspect of the ethics of reading. A rhetoric 'reinvented' is a particularly powerful mode of reading. It is a mode of reading which begins to bridge the gap between Schüssler Fiorenza's 'ethics of historical reading' and her notion of an 'ethics of public accountability.' Once the values 'in' the text have been made explicit by means of rhetorical criticism, the interpreter is in a better position to evaluate them in terms of a religious scale of values. Doing that inevitably brings the interpreter within the realm of an ethics of public accountability.

In the final chapter (chapter 4) the 'bridging' function of a rhetorical reading was illustrated practically by means of a social-scientific reading of Romans 13:1-7. The social model proposed by Perdue for the description of the social function of Paraenetic Literature was used to analyze the social phenomena of the 'world created by the text.' Consistent with the particular notion of an ethics of reading for which I have been arguing throughout this study, it was indicated that the social phenomena to be analyzed were not 'pure' social phenomena, but rather the social phenomena of the 'world created by the text.' Even with regard to this seemingly pure contextual phenomena, the study of the *text* and textual phenomena has to precede any text-extrinsic conclusions or inferences.

On the basis of the social-scientific analysis in terms of Perdue's model I have concluded that if Romans 13:1-7 is read in isolation from its co-text, it reflects a paradigm of order. Within the rhetorical situation of the letter to the Romans, however, it forms part of a type of paraenesis which is characteristic of a society going through a liminal experience in the second phase, namely, the development of new patterns of behavior no longer compatible with the previous social order (ὁ αἰῶνος οὗτος). In order to succeed with the establishment of this new *communitas* and in order to further its aims (by means of the establishment of an operational base for Paul in Rome and his envisioned missionary activities in Spain), it is for pragmatic reasons necessary for the Christian *Gemeinschaft* to conform to *some* of the values of the *Gesellschaft*, in particular those regarding conduct towards the people in positions of authority. The social function of the paraenesis in Romans is to transform and replace the social values of the Christian *Gemeinschaft* on the basis of a newly-envisioned view of God and human society. Regarding the specific issue of the right conduct with regard to authorities, however, the existing values operating within a paradigm of order converge with those envisioned by the encoded author for the new *communitas* as they are constructed within the rhetorical situation of the letter to the Romans.

In order to indicate a way in which these results of a responsible ethics of social-scientific reading may be utilized to bridge the gap between an 'ethics of historical reading' and 'an ethics of public accountability' in New

Testament scholarship, I have referred briefly to the pivotal role of the values of honor and shame operative in the 'world' created by the text of Romans. It was also indicated, however, that these values — in so far as they are still operative at all — in, say, contemporary American society, play a totally different role. Contemporary Americans simply do not submit to their government or pay taxes primarily because they seek honor and praise from the government. Neither does it make sense to hold that the contemporary public sphere of politics is exclusively the world of 'males.' The vast differences between the values operative in the 'world' created by the text and the modern world are thus obvious. On the other hand, in some present-day African communities, there is a much closer affinity with these values. The interpreter has to be very careful about simplistic generalizations.

Elizabeth Schüssler Fiorenza (1988:15) claims that an 'ethics of accountability' makes the biblical interpreter responsible not only for the choice of theoretical interpretive models but also for the ethical consequences of the biblical text and its meanings, in particular to evaluate the construction of the historical worlds and symbolic universes of the text in terms of a religious scale of values. In order to take up this responsibility in a plausible manner, I believe that the New Testament scholar must rely on (scientific) studies of the particular context within which he or she works. An 'ethics of accountability,' therefore, inevitably compels the interpreter to move far beyond the traditional 'boundaries' of the discipline of biblical scholarship. It is obvious that this is a formidable task. Formidable in its own right, however, is the preceding task to *read* the New Testament responsibly.

POSTSCRIPT

Exactly how language and "reality" — or texts and text-external phenomena — are related continues to be an intriguing and tremendously complex issue. Reflection on this issue formed an important aspect of this study even though the focus of the book was on the textuality of New Testament texts. I maintain that reflection on *textuality* necessitates reflection on *reality*: both the reality of the original social and historical contexts in which New Testament texts originated and the reality of today's interpreters and reading communities. The nature of the New Testament — the issues it deals with and the reading communities within which it continues to function authoritatively — makes it vital for interpreters to grapple both with textuality and with reality.

Paul's letter to the Romans, including chapter 13:1-7, is part and parcel of the New Testament — whether we like it or not. How can interpreters come to terms with the authority of such a possibly authoritarian text? Of course, it is not the text itself that is authoritarian, but given the nature of the issue with which it deals it is possible to *use* this text in an authoritarian manner. I have given an example of how this was in fact done during the apartheid years in South Africa. In that case there was, of course, no regard for the complexities and the nuances of its textuality: the text was directly and brutally used and abused in a very real reality. This kind of interpretation of Romans 13:1-7 has prompted others to search for clues to read the text differently and to indicate that, in fact, Romans 13:1-7 can be used for a call to resist authorities who do not act "for the good" of its subjects (Romans 13:4). In both cases, whether conformation or confrontation is exhorted, readers find clues in Romans 13:1-7 (and other New Testament texts) in terms of which they interact with today's concrete text-external phenomena. Readers' concrete experiences of their social reality play a significant role in the textual clues they emphasize and more fundamentally, in the approaches to the reading process they choose. And readers explicitly appeal to or implicitly presuppose the authority of New Testament texts in their acts of readings and in their use of the text in their (i.e. the *readers'*) current rhetorical situations. Subject to whose authority can such readings be authoritative?

This book argues for an authority derived from ethically responsible readings of New Testament texts, readings to be undertaken by the various interpretative communities of the New Testament. Legitimate and acceptable authority is not possible without morality. Thus the act of reading of New Testament texts has to be ethically responsible and publicly accountable. This means, inter alia, that the textuality and, concomitantly, the otherness of the text has to be respected. This respect calls for a conscious effort to honor its textuality in all its complexity.

BIBLIOGRAPHY

Achtemeier, P. J.
1985 *Romans.* Atlanta: John Knox.

Alter, R.
1981 *The Art of Biblical Narrative.* New York: Basic.

Altman, J. G.
1982 *Epistolarity. Approaches to a Form.* Columbus: Ohio State University Press.

Aristotle
1947 Τέχνη ῥητορική. Loeb Classical Library. Cambridge, MA: Harvard University Press.

Attridge, H. W.
1990 "Paraenesis in a Homily (λόγος παρακλήσεως): The Possible Location of, and Socialization in, the 'Epistle to the Hebrews.'" *Semeia* 50:211–26.

Aune, D. E.
1981 Review of Betz, H.-D., *Galatians. A Commentary on Paul's Letter to the Churches in Galatia.* Philadelphia: Fortress. *Religious Studies Review* 7:323–24.
1987 *The New Testament in its Literary Environment.* Philadelphia: Westminster.

Barr, J.
1961 *The Semantics of Biblical Language.* Oxford: University Press.
1973 "Reading the Bible as Literature." *Bulletin of the John Rylands University Library* 56:10–33.

Barraclough, R.
1985 "Romans 13:1–7: Application in Context." *Colloquium* 17(2):16–21.

Barrett, C. K.
1957 *A Commentary on the Epistle to the Romans.* London: Maxwell.

Barth, K.
1968 *The Epistle to the Romans.* Trans. E. C. Hoskyns. Oxford: University Press.

Bartsch, R.
1975 "Linguistics." In *Linguistics and Neighboring Disciplines.* Ed. R. Bartsch and T. Vennemann. Amsterdam: North Holland Publishing. Pp. 1–11.

Bassnett-McGuire, S.
1980 *Translation Studies.* London: Methuen.

Beardslee, W. A.
1990 "Ethics and Hermeneutics." In *The Humanistic Interpretation of the New Testament.* Ed. T. W. Jennings. Atlanta: Scholars. Pp. 15–32.

Beekman, J. and J. Callow
1974 *Translating the Word of God.* Grand Rapids: Zondervan.

Berger, K.
1984a *Formgeschichte des Neuen Testaments.* Heidelberg: Quelle & Meyer.
1984b "Hellenistische Gattungen im Neuen Testament." *Aufstieg und Niedergang der römischen Welt* 2.25(2):1031–432.

Best, T. F.
1983 "The Sociological Study of the New Testament: Promise and Peril of a New Discipline." *Scottish Journal of Theology* 36:181–94.

Betz, H. D.
1974   "The Literary Composition and Function of Paul's Letter to the Galatians."
          New Testament Studies 21:353-79.
1979   *Galatians. A Commentary on Paul's Letter to the Churches in Galatia.*
          Philadelphia: Fortress.
1987   "The Problem of Rhetoric and Theology according to the Apostle Paul."
          In *L'Apôtre Paul: Personalité, style et conception du Ministère.* Ed. A.
          Vanhoye. Bibliotheca Ephemeridum Theologicarum Lovaniensium 73.
          Leuven: Peeters. Pp. 6-48.

Bitzer, L. F.
1968   "The Rhetorical Situation." *Philosophy and Rhetoric* 1:1-14.
1980   "Functional Communication: A Situational Perspective." In *Rhetoric in
          Transition. Studies in the Nature and Uses of Rhetoric.* Ed. E. E. White.
          University Park: Pennsylvania State University Press. Pp. 21-38.

Bjerkelund, C. J.
1967   *Parakalo: Form, Funktion und Sinn der parakalo-Sätze in den paulinischen
          Briefen.* Oslo: Universitetsforlaget.

Black, D. A.
1988   *Linguistics for Students of New Testament Greek. A Survey of Basic Con-
          cepts and Applications.* Grand Rapids: Baker.

Bleicher, J.
1980   *Contemporary Hermeneutics: Hermeneutics as Method, Philosophy and
          Critique.* London: Routledge & Kegan Paul.

Boers, H.
1989   Review of *Greek-English Lexicon of the New Testament based on Semantic
          Domains.* 2 vols. Ed. Johannes P. Louw and Eugene A. Nida. New
          York: UBS. *Journal of Biblical Literature* 108:705-707.

Boesak, A. A.
1986   "What belongs to Caesar? Once again Romans 13." In *When Prayer
          makes News.* Ed. A. A. Boesak and C. Villa-Vicencio. Philadelphia:
          Westminster. Pp. 138-157.

Boman, T.
1968   *Sprache und Denken: Eine Auseinandersetzung.* Göttingen: Vandenhoeck
          & Ruprecht.

Borg, M.
1973   "A New Context for Romans XIII." *New Testament Studies* 19:205-18.

Bornkamm, G.
1977   "The Letter to the Romans as Paul's Last Will and Testament." In Don-
          fried (ed.) 1977:17-31.

Botha, J.
1992   "The Ethics of New Testament Interpretation." *Neotestamentica* 26/1:169-
          194.

Botha, J. E.
1989   "A Study in Johannine Style: History, Theory and Practice." DTh thesis,
          University of South Africa, Pretoria.

Botha, P. W.
1985   Address by President P. W. Botha on the occasion of the award of the free-
          dom of Moria, 7 April 1985. Cape Town: Office of the State President.

Braet, A. C.
1987   "The Classical Doctrine of Status and the Rhetorical Theory of Argumenta-
          tion." *Philosophy and Rhetoric* 20:79-93.

Brinton, A.
1981   "Situation in the Theory of Rhetoric." *Philosophy and Rhetoric* 14:234–
             48.

Brown, G. and G. Yule
1983   *Discourse Analysis.* Cambridge: University Press.

Bruce, F. F.
1984   "Paul and 'The Powers That Be.'" *Bulletin of the John Rylands University
             Library* 66:79–96.

Bultmann, R.
1910   *Der Stil der paulinischen Predigt und die kynisch-stoische Diatribe.*
             Göttingen: Vandenhoeck & Ruprecht.

Burgess, T. C.
1902   "Epideictic Literature." *Studies in Classical Philology* 3:86–261.

Burke, K.
1962   *A Grammar of Motives and a Rhetoric of Motives.* Cleveland: World Pub-
             lishing Company.

Camp, C. V.
1990   "Paraenesis: A Feminist Response." *Semeia* 50:243–60.

Classen, Carl J.
1991   "Paulus und die antike Rhetorik." *Zeitschrift für die neutestamentliche
             Wissenschaft* 82:1–33.

Combrink, H. J. B.
1985   "Op die breuklyn met die Skrif." In *Op die breuklyn. 'n Feesbundel saam-
             gestel ter herdenking van die 125–jarige bestaan van die Teologiese Semi-
             narium Stellenbosch.* Ed. D. J. Louw. Kaapstad: N G Kerk-Uitgewers.
             Pp. 153–168.
1986   "The Changing Scene of Biblical Interpretation." In Petzer & Hartin (eds.)
             1986:9–17.
1988   "Readings, Readers and Authors: An Orientation." *Neotestamentica*
             22:189-204.

Consigny, S.
1974   "Rhetoric and its Situations." *Philosophy and Rhetoric* 7:175–86.

Corbett, E. P. J.
1965   *Classical Rhetoric for the Modern Student.* New York: New York
             University Press.

Cornelius, E. M.
1991   "Die funksie van die 'danksegging(s)' in 1 Tessalonisense." MA thesis,
             Potchefstroom University for Christian Higher Education.

Cotterell, P. and M. Turner
1989   *Linguistics and Biblical Interpretation.* London: SPCK.

Cox, J. R. and C. A. Willard, eds.
1982   *Advances in Argumentation Theory and Research.* Carbondale and
             Edwardsville: Southern Illinois University Press.

Craffert, P. F.
1991   "Towards an Interdisciplinary Definition of the Social-Scientific Interpreta-
             tion of the New Testament." *Neotestamentica* 25(1):123–44.

Cranfield, C. E. B.
1975   *A Critical and Exegetical Commentary on the Epistle to the Romans. Vol I.*
             International Critical Commentary. Edinburgh: T & T Clark.

1979   *A Critical and Exegetical Commentary on the Epistle to the Romans. Vol II.* International Critical Commentary. Edinburgh: T & T Clark.

Cronjé, J. van W.
1985   "Defamiliarization in the letter to the Galatians." In *A South African Perspective on the New Testament.* FS Bruce M. Metzger. Ed. J. H. Petzer and P. J. Hartin. Leiden: Brill. Pp. 214–227.

Cruse, D. A.
1986   *Lexical Semantics.* Cambridge: University Press.

Cullmann, O.
1962   *Christ and Time: The Primitive Christian Conception of Time and History.* Trans. F. V. Filson. London: SCM Press. <1951>.

Culpepper, A.
1983   *Anatomy of the Fourth Gospel: A Study in Literary Design.* Philadelphia: Fortress.

Danker, F. W.
1988   *A Century of Greco-Roman Philology. Featuring the American Philological Association and the Society of Biblical Literature.* Atlanta: Scholars Press.

De Groot, A.
1968   *Inleiding tot de algemene taalwetenschap.* Groningen: Wolters-Noordhoff.

De Kruijf, T. C.
1987   "The Literary Unity of Rom 12,16–13,8a. A Network of Inclusions." *Bijdragen* 48(3):319–26.

De Saussure, F.
1966   *Course in General Linguistics.* Ed. C. Bally and A. Sechehaye, in collaboration with Albert Reidlinger. Trans. by W. Baskin. New York: McGraw-Hill. <New York: The Philosophical Library, 1959>.

De Villiers, P. G. R.
1982   "Renaissance van die sosiologiese eksegese." *Theologia Evangelica* 15(3):19–33.
1984   "The Interpretation of a Text in the Light of its Socio-cultural Setting." *Neotestamentica* 18:66–79.
1988   "Inleiding: Bybel, Kerk en konteks." In Breytenbach (ed.) 1988:1–10.
1989   "New Testament Scholarship in South Africa." *Neotestamentica* 23(1):119–24.

Deissmann, Adolf
1924   *Licht vom Osten.* Tübingen: Mohr/Siebeck.

Deist, F. E.
1978   "Ope vrae aan die diskoersanalise." *Nederuits gereformeerde teologiese Tydskrif* 19:260–71.

Den Heyer, C. J.
1978   *Exegetische methoden in diskussie. Een analyse van Markus 10,46–13,37.* Kampen: Kok.
1979   "Struktuur analyse." *Geformeerde Teologische Tijdschrift* 2:86–110.

Dippenaar, M. C.
1988   "Prayer in the Letters and Theology of Paul." DTh thesis, University of Stellenbosch.

Domeris, W. R.
1988   "Social-scientific Study of the Early Christian Churches: New Paradigms and Old Questions." In Mouton et al. (eds.) 1988:378–93.

1991   "Sociology and Socio-history: Sociological and Social Historical Investigations." In Hartin & Petzer (eds.) 1991:215–34.

Donfried, K. P., ed.
1977   *The Romans Debate.* Minneapolis: Augsburg. (See now *The Romans Debate.* Revised edition. Peabody, MA: Hendrickson, 1991.)

Donfried, K. P.
1977a   "False Presuppositions in the Study of Romans." In Donfried (ed.) 1977:120–48.
1977b   "The Nature and Scope of the Romans Debate." In Donfried (ed.) 1977:ix–xvii.

Dormeyer, D.
1986   "Das Verhältnis von 'wilder' und historisch-kritischer Exegese als methodologisches und didaktisches Problem." *Jahrbuch der Religionspädogogik* 3:111–126.

Doty, W. G.
1966   "The Epistle in Late Hellenism and Early Christianity: Development, Influences, and Literary Form." PhD thesis, Drew University.
1973   *Letters in Primitive Christianity.* Philadelphia: Fortress.

Draper, J. A.
1988   "'Humble Submission to Almighty God' and its Biblical Foundation." *Journal of Theology in Southern Africa* 63:30–38.

Du Plessis, I. J.
1990   *'n Kykie in die hart van God.* Pretoria: N. G. Kerkboekhandel.

Du Plessis, J. G.
1988   "Why did Peter ask his Question and how did Jesus answer Him? or: Implicature in Luke 12:35–48." *Neotestamentica* 22:311–24.

Du Plooy, Heilna
1990   "Die polifoniese gesprek — intertekstualiteit as leesmodus." *Stilet* 2(2):1–14.

Du Toit, A. B.
1981   "Strukturele teksanalise en die Suid-Afrikaanse redevoeringsanalise — enkele opmerkings aan die hand van Van Iersel se analise van die Emmausverhaal." *Skrif en Kerk* 2:3–1.
1989   "Persuasion in Romans 1:1–17." *Biblische Zeitschrift* 33:192–209.

Du Toit, H. C.
1977   "What is a Colon?" *Neotestamentica* (Addendum) 11:1–10.

Elliott, J. H.
1981   *A Home for the Homeless: A Sociological Exegesis of 1 Peter, Its Situation and Strategy.* Philadelphia: Fortress Press.
1985   Review of W. A. Meeks, *The First Urban Christians. The Social World of the Apostle Paul.* New Haven: Yale University Press. *Religious Studies Review* 11:329–35.
1987   "Patronage and Clientism in Early Christian Society." *Foundations and Facets Forum* 3(4):39–48.
1990   *A Home for the Homeless. A Social-Scientific Criticism of 1 Peter, Its Situation and Strategy.* Second edition, with introduction. Minneapolis: Augsburg-Fortress.

Elliott, N.
1990   *The Rhetoric of Romans. Argumentative Constraint and Strategy and Paul's Dialogue with Judaism.* Journal for the Study of the New Testament Supplement Series 45. Sheffield: JSOT Press.

Erickson, R. J.
1980 "Biblical Semantics, Semantic Structure, and Biblical Lexicology: A Study of Methods, with Special Reference to the Pauline Lexical Field of 'Cognition.'" PhD thesis, Fuller Theological Seminary.

Exler, F. X. J.
1923 "The Form of the Ancient Greek Letter: A Study in Greek Epistolography." PhD thesis, Catholic University of America, Washington. D.C.

Fillmore, C. J.
1971 *Santa Cruz Lectures on Deixis.* Indiana: Indiana Linguistics Club.

Fokkema, D. W. and E. Kunne-Ibsch
1977 *Theories of Literature in the Twentieth Century.* London: C. Hurst.

Forbes, C.
1986 "Comparison, Self-praise and Irony: Paul's Boasting and the Conventions of Hellenistic Rhetoric." *New Testament Studies* 32:1–30.

Fowler, A.
1982 *Kinds of Literature: An Introduction to the Theory of Genres and Modes.* Cambridge, MA: Harvard University Press.

Fowler, R. M.
1988 "'Wriggling off the Hook': Strategies of Resisting Authoritarian Readings of Romans 13:1–7." Paper read at Studiorum Novi Testamenti Societas Seminar on "The Role of the Reader." Cambridge, England.

Fraiken, D.
1986 "The Rhetorical Function of the Jews in Romans." In *Anti-Judaism in Early Christianity. Volume 1. Paul and the Gospels.* Ed. P. Richardson. Studies in Christianity and Judaism Number 2. Waterloo, Ontario: Wilfrid University Press. Pp. 91–106.

Friedrich, G.
1969 "Semasiologie und Lexicologie." *Theologische Literaturzeitung* 90:801–16.

Friedrich, J., W. Pöhlmannn, and P. Stuhlmacher
1976 "Zur historischen Situation und Intention von Rom 13,1–7." *Zeitschrift für Theologie und Kirche* 73:131–166.

Frye, N.
1983 *The Great Code: The Bible and Literature.* San Diego: Harcourt Brace Jovanovich.

Funk, R. W.
1967 "The Apostolic Parousia: Form and Significance." In *Christian History and Interpretation: Studies Presented to John Knox.* Ed. W. R. Farmer, C. F. D. Moule, and R. Niebuhr. Cambridge: University Press.

Furnish, V. P.
1985 *The Moral Teaching of Paul.* Nashville: Abingdon.
1989 "Pauline Studies." In *The New Testament and its Modern Interpreters.* Ed. E. J. Epp and G. W. MacRae. Philadelphia/Atlanta: Fortress/Scholars. Pp. 321–350.

Gager, J. G.
1982 "Shall We Marry our Enemies? Sociology and the New Testament." *Interpretation* 37(3):256–65.
1983 "Social Description and Sociological Explanation in the Study of Early Christianity." In *The Bible and Liberation. Political and Social Hermeneutics.* Ed. N. K. Gottwald. New York: Orbis Books. Pp. 428–40.

Gamble, H. A.
1977   *The Textual History of the Letter to the Romans: A Study in Textual and Literary Criticism.* Grand Rapids: Eerdmans.

Gammie, J. G.
1990   "Paraenetic Literature: Toward the Morphology of a Secondary Genre." *Semeia* 50:41-80.

Godet, F.
1881   *Commentary on St. Paul's Epistle to the Romans.* Edinburgh: T & T Clark.

Gowler, D. B.
1991   *Host, Guest, Enemy, and Friend: Portraits of the Pharisees in Luke and Acts.* Emory Studies in Early Christianity, vol. 1. New York, Bern, Frankfurt am Main: Peter Lang Press.

Grant, R. M.
1977   *Early Christianity and Society: Seven Studies.* San Francisco: Harper & Row.

Greijdanus, S.
1933   *De brief van den apostel Paulus aan de gemeente te Rome.* Kommentaar op het Nieuwe Testament. Kampen: Kok.

Güttgemanns, E.
1969   "Sprache des Glaubens — Sprache der Menschen: Probleme einer thologischen Linguistik." *Verkündigung und Forschung* 14:86-114.

1970   *Offene Frage zur Formgeschichte des Evangeliums. Eine methodologische Skizze der Grundlagenproblematik der Form- und Redaktionsgeschichte.* München: Kaiser.

1971   *Studia linguistica neotestamentica: Gesammelte Aufsätze zur linguistischen Grundlage einer neutestamentlichen Theologie.* Beiträge zur evangelischen Theologie 60. München: Kaiser.

Hartin, P. J.
1991   "Methodological Principles in Interpreting the Relevance of the New Testament in South Africa." *Scriptura* (37):1-16.

Hartin, P. J. and J. H. Petzer, eds.
1991   *Text & Interpretation. New Approaches in the Criticism of the New Testament.* New Testament Tools and Studies 12. Leiden: Brill.

Hartman, L.
1986   "On Reading Others' Letters." In *Christians among Jews and Gentiles.* Ed. G. W. E. Nickelsburg. FS Krister Stehndahl. Philadelphia: Fortress. Pp. 137-146.

Hayes, J. H. and C. A. Holladay
1987   *Biblical Exegesis. A Beginner's Handbook.* Revised Edition. Atlanta: John Knox.

Hendriksen, W.
1980   *Romans. Volume I. Chapters 1-8.* Edinburgh: Banner of Truth Trust.

Hester, J. D.
1986   "The Use and Influence of Rhetoric in Galatians 2:1-14." *Theologische Zeitschrift* 42:386-408.

1991   "Maxims in Paul." Paper prepared for the SBL Annual Meeting, Kansas City.

Hill, D.
1967   *Greek Words and Hebrew Meanings: Studies in the Semantics of Soteriological Terms.* Cambridge: University Press.

Hirsch, E. D., Jr.
1967   *Validity in Interpretation.* New Haven: Yale University Press.
Hock, R. F.
1980   *The Social Context of Paul's Ministry: Tentmaking and Apostleship.*
            Philadelphia: Fortress.
Hodge, C.
1950   *A Commentary on the Epistle to the Romans.* Grand Rapids: Eerdmans.
            <1886>.
Hofmann, T. R.
1976   "Varieties of Meaning." *Language Sciences* 39:6–18.
Holmberg, B.
1990   *Sociology and the New Testament.* Minneapolis: Fortress.
Hübner, H.
1984   "Der Galaterbrief und das Verhältnis von antiker Rhetorik und
            Epistolographie." *Theologische Literaturzeitung* 109:241–50.
Hughes, F. W.
1989   *Early Christian Rhetoric and 2 Thessalonians.* Journal for the Study of the
            New Testament Supplement Series 30. Sheffield: JSOT Press.
Hutchinson, S.
1971   "The Political Implications of Romans 13:1–7." *Biblical Theology*
            21(3):49–59.
Ivič, M.
1970   *Trends in Liguistics.* The Hague: Mouton.
Jacobson, R.
1986   "The Structuralists and the Bible." In McKim (ed.) 1986:280–96.
Jakobson, R.
1964   "Closing Statement: Linguistics and Poetics." In *Style in Language.* Ed.
            T. A. Sebeok. Cambridge, MA: Technology Press. Pp. 350–77.
Jefferson, A. and D. Robey, eds.
1986   *Modern Literary Theory. A Comparative Introduction.* Second edition.
            London: Batsford Academic and Educational.
Jervell, J.
1977   "The Letter to Jerusalem." In Donfried (ed.) 1977:61–74.
Jewett, R.
1982   "Romans as Ambassadorial Letter." *Interpretation* 36:5–20.
1986   "Following the Argument of Romans." *Word and World* 6(4):382–89.
Johanson, B. C.
1987   *To All the Brethern. A Text-linguistic and Rhetorical Approach to 1 Thes-
            salonians.* Coniectanea Biblica. New Testament Series 16. Uppsala:
            Almqvist & Wiksell International.
Josipovici, G.
1988   "Interpretation versus Reading: From Meaning to Trust." *Salmagundi. A
            Quarterly for the Humanities & Social Sciences* 78–79:228–254.
Joubert, S. J.
1991   "'n Verruimende invalshoek tot die verlede? Die sosiaal-wetenskaplike
            benadering tot die Nuwe Testament." *Hervormde Teologiese Studies*
            47(1):39–54.
Judge, E. A.
1960   *The Social Patterns of Christian Groups in the First Century.* London:
            Tyndale.

Jüngel, E.

1986   "'Jedermann sei Untertan der Obrigkeit . . .' Eine Bibelarbeit über Römer 13:1-7." In *Evangelische Christen in unserer Demokratie*. Ed. E. Jüngel, R. Herzog, and H. Simon. Gütersloh: Gütersloher Verlaghaus. Pp. 8–37.

Kallas, J.

1965   "Romans xiii,1-7: An Interpolation." *New Testament Studies* 11:365-374.

Karris, R. J.

1977   "Romans 14:1 – 15:13 and the Occasion of Romans." In Donfried (ed.) 1977:75-99.

Käsemann, E.

1969   "Principles of the Interpretation of Romans 13." In *New Testament Questions of Today*. Philadelphia: Fortress Press. Pp. 196-216.

1980   *Commentary on Romans*. Trans. and ed. G. W. Bromiley. Grand Rapids: Eerdmans.

Keck, L. and V. P. Furnish

1984   *The Pauline Letters*. Nashville: Abingdon.

Kennedy, G. A.

1963   *The Art of Persuasion in Greece*. Princeton: Princeton University Press.

1980   *Classical Rhetoric and its Christian and Secular Tradition from Ancient to Modern Times*. Chapel Hill: University of North Carolina Press.

1984   *New Testament Interpretation through Rhetorical Criticism*. Chapel Hill: University of North Carolina Press.

Kim, C. H.

1972   *The Familiar Letter of Recommendation*. Missoula: Scholars Press.

Klein, G.

1977   "Paul's Purpose in Writing the Epistle to the Romans." In Donfried (ed.) 1977:32-49.

Klijn, A. F. J., ed.

1983   *Inleiding tot de studie van het Nieuwe Testament*. Kampen: Kok.

Koester, H.

1982   *Introduction to the New Testament. Vol. 1. History, Culture, and Religion of the Hellenistic Age*. Philadelphia: Fortress Press.

Koskenniemi, H.

1956   *Studien zur Idee und Phraseologie des griechischen Briefes bid 400 n. Chr.* Helsinki: Akateeminen Kirjakauppa.

Kraftchick, S. J.

1985   "Ethos and Pathos Appeals in Galatians Five and Six: A Rhetorical Analysis." PhD thesis, Emory University, Atlanta.

1990   "Why do the Rhetoricians Rage?" In *Text and Logos. The Humanistic Interpretation of the New Testament*. Ed. T. W. Jennings. Atlanta: Scholars. Pp. 55-79.

Krentz, E.

1975   *The Historical-critical Method*. Philadelphia: Fortress.

Kuhn, T. S.

1961   *The Structure of Scientific Revolutions*. Second edition. Chicago: University of Chicago Press.

Lampe, P.

1987   *Die stadtrömische Christen in der ersten beiden Jahrhunderten*. Tübingen: J. C. Mohr [Paul Siebeck].

Larson, R. L.
1970   "Lloyd Bitzer's 'Rhetorical Situation' and the Classification of Discourse:
          Problems and Implications." *Philosophy and Rhetoric* 3:165–68.
Lategan, B. C.
1978   "Directions in Contemporary Exegesis. Between Historicism and Struc-
          turalism." *Journal of Theology for South Africa* 25:18–30.
1982   "Inleiding tot de uitlegging van het Nieuwe Testament." In Klijn (ed.)
          1982:47–70.
1984   "Current Issues in the Hermeneutical Debate." *Neotestamentica* 18:1–17.
1985a   "Reference: Reception, Rediscription, and Reality." In Lategan and Vor-
          ster 1985:67–94.
1985b   "Some Unresolved Methodological Issues in New Testament
          Hermeneutics." In Lategan and Vorster 1985:3–25.
1988   "Why so Few Converts to New Paradigms in Theology?" In Mouton et al.
          (eds.) 1988:65–78.
1990   "Introducing a Research Project on Contextual Hermeneutics." *Scriptura*
          33:1–5.
1991a   "Formulas in the Language of Paul. A Study of Presuppositional Phrases
          in Galatians." *Neotestamentica* 25(1):75–88.
1991b   "Reception: Theory and Practice in Reading Romans 13." In Hartin &
          Petzer (eds.) 1991:145–70.
Lategan, B. C. and W. S. Vorster
1985   *Text and Reality. Aspects of Reference in Biblical Texts.* Philadelphia:
          Fortress.
Lausberg, H.
1960   *Handbuch der literarischen Rhetorik (2 vols).* München: Max Hüber. 2nd
          revised edition, 1973.
Leech, G.
1983   *Principles of Pragmatics.* London: Longman.
Leeman, A. D. and A. C. Braet
1987   *Klassieke retorika. Haar inhoud, functie en betekenis.* Groningen:
          Wolters-Noordhoff/Forsten.
Leenhardt, F. J.
1961   *The Epistle to the Romans.* London: SCM.
Lekkerkerker, A. F. N.
1980   *De Brief van Paulus aan de Romeinen II.* De Prediking van het Nieuwe
          Testament. Nijkerk: Callenbach.
Levinson, S. C.
1983   *Pragmatics.* Cambridge: University Press.
Longmann T., III
1987   *Literary Approaches to Biblical Interpretation.* Foundations of Con-
          temporary Interpretation, vol 3. Grand Rapids: Academie Books.
Lotman, J. and B. A. Uspenski
1978   "On the Semiotic Mechanism of Culture." *New Literary History* 9(2):211–
          32.
Louw, J. P.
1967   "Klassieke filologie en moderne linguistiek." *Taalfasette* 3:9–19.
1979   *A Semantic Discourse Analysis of Romans. Vol 1 Text, Vol 2 Commentary.*
          Pretoria: Beta.
1982   *Semantics of New Testament Greek.* Philadelphia: Fortress.

1985a	*Lexicography and Translation, with Special Reference to Bible Translation.* Cape Town: BSS.
1985b	"A Semantic Domain Approach to Lexicography." In Louw 1985a:157–97.
1990	"New Testament Greek — The Present State of the Art." *Neotestamentica* (24).

Louw, J. P. and E. A. Nida, eds.
1988	*Greek-English Lexicon of the New Testament based on Semantic Domains (2 vols).* New York: United Bible Societies.

Lundin, R., A. C. Thiselton, and C. Walhout
1985	*The Responsibility of Hermeneutics.* Grand Rapids: Eerdmans.

Lyons, G.
1985	*Pauline Autobiography. Toward a New Understanding.* Society of Biblical Literature Dissertation Series 73. Atlanta: Scholars.

Lyons, J.
1972	*Introduction to Theoretical Linguistics.* London: Cambridge University Press.
1977	*Semantics I/II.* Cambridge: Cambridge University Press.
1981a	*Language and Linguistics. An Introduction.* Cambridge: University Press.
1981b	*Language, Meaning & Context.* Suffolk: Fontana.

McDonald, J. I. H.
1989	"Romans 13:1–7: A Test Case for New Testament Interpretation." *New Testament Studies* 35:540–49.

Mack, B. L.
1990	*Rhetoric and the New Testament.* Minneapolis: Fortress.

Macky, P. W.
1986	"The Coming Revolution: The New Literary Approach to New Testament Interpretation." In D. K. Mckim (ed.) 1986:263–279.

Malherbe, A. J.
1983	*Social Aspects of Early Christianity.* Second edition. Philadelphia: Fortress.
1986	*Moral Exhortation, a Greco-Roman Source Book.* Library of Early Christianity, vol 4. Philadelphia: Westminster.
1988	*Ancient Epistolary Theorists.* Atlanta: Scholars Press.

Malina, B. J.
1981	*The New Testament World. Insights from Cultural Anthropology.* Atlanta: John Knox Press.
1985	Review of W. A. Meeks (1983). *Journal of Biblical Literature* 104:346–49.

Manson, T. W.
1977	"St. Paul's Letter to the Romans — and Others." In Donfried (ed.) 1977:1–16.

Marshall, I. H., ed.
1979	*New Testament Interpretation. Essays on Principles and Methods.* Exeter: Paternoster.

Martin, J. P.
1987	"Toward a Post-critical Paradigm." *New Testament Studies* 33:370–85.

McKim, D. K., ed.
1986	*A Guide to Contemporary Hermeneutics. Major Trends in Biblical Interpretation.* Grand Rapids: Eerdmans.

McKnight, E. V.
1985   *The Bible and the Reader. An Introduction to Literary Criticism.* Philadelphia: Fortress.
1990   *Postmodern Use of the Bible. The Emergence of Reader-oriented Criticism.* Nashville: Abingdon.

Meecham, H. G.
1923   *Light from Ancient Letters: Private Correspondence in the Non-literary Papyri of Oxyrynchus of the First Four Centuries, and its Bearing on NT Language and Thought.* London: George Allen & Unwin.

Meeks, W. A.
1983   *The First Urban Christians: The Social World of the Apostle Paul.* New Haven: Yale University Press.

Michel, O.
1966   *Der Brief an die Römer.* Göttingen: Vandenhoeck & Ruprecht.

Miller, J. H.
1987   "The Triumph of Theory, the Resistance of Reading, and the Question of the Material Base." *Publications of the Modern Language Association of America* 102:281–91.
1989   "Is There an Ethics of Reading?" In *Reading Narrative: Form, Ethics, Ideology.* Ed. J. Phelan. Columbus: Ohio State University Press. Pp. 78–101.

Minear, P.
1971   *The Obedience of Faith. The Purpose of Paul in the Epistle to the Romans.* London: SCM.

Moiser, J.
1990   "Rethinking Romans 12–15." *New Testament Studies* 36:571–82.

Moule, H. G. C.
1894   *The Epistle of Paul to the Romans.* London: Expository Bible.

Mouton, J., A. G. Van Aarde, and W. S. Vorster, eds.
1988   *Paradigms and Progress in Theology.* Pretoria: HSRC.

Moxnes, H.
1988   "Honor, Shame, and the Outside World in Paul's Letter to the Romans." In Neusner 1988:207–18.

Muilenberg, J.
1969   "Form Criticism and Beyond." *Journal of Biblical Literature* 88(1):1–18.

Mullins, T. Y.
1962   "Petition as Literary Form." *Novum Testamentum* 5:46–54.
1968   "Greetings as a New Testament Form." *Journal of Biblical Literature* 87:418–26.
1972   "Ascription as a Literary Form." *New Testament Studies* 19:194–205.
1973   "Visit Talk in the New Testament Letters." *Catholic Biblical Quarterly* 35:350–58.
1980   "Topos as a New Testament Form." *Journal of Biblical Literature* 42:541–47.
1984   "The Thanksgiving of Philemon and Colossians." *New Testament Studies* 30:288–93.

Nations, A.
1983   "Historical Criticism and the Current Methodological Crisis." *Scottish Journal of Theology* 36:59–71.

Neusner, J., ed.
1988   *The Social World of Formative Christianity and Judaism: Essays in Tribute to Howard Clark Kee.* Philadelphia: Fortress.

Nida, E. A.
1972   "Implications of Contemporary Linguistics for Biblical Scholarship." *Journal of Biblical Literature* 91:73–89.
1975a   *Exploring Semantic Structures.* München: Fink.
1975b   *Language Structure and Translation.* Selected and introduced by A. S. Dil. Stanford: Stanford University Press.
1979   *Componential Analysis of Meaning. An Introduction to Semantic Structures.* The Hague: Mouton.

Nida, E. A. and C. R. Taber
1974   *The Theory and Practice of Translation.* Leiden: Brill.

Nida, E. A., J. P. Louw, A. H. Snyman, and J. v. W. Cronjé
1983   *Style and Discourse. With Special Reference to the Text of the Greek New Testament.* Cape Town: BSSA.

Nygren, A.
1978   *Commentary on Romans.* (Trans of *Pauli Brev till Romarna*). London: SCM. < 1944 >.

O'Brien, P. T.
1977   *Introductory Thanksgivings in the Letters of Paul.* Leiden: Brill.

Ogden, C. K. and I. A. Richards
1949   *The Meaning of Meaning: A Study of Influence of Language upon Thought and of the Science of Symbolism.* Harvest. New York: Harcourt, Brace & World. < 1923 >.

Ohlhoff, H.
1985   "Hoofbenaderings in die literatuurstudie en -kritiek." In *Gids by die literatuurstudie.* Ed. T. T. Cloete, E. Botha, and C. Malan. Pretoria: HAUM-Literêr Uitgewers. Pp. 31–63.

Palmer, F. R.
1981   *Semantics.* Second edition. Cambridge: University Press.

Palmer, R. E.
1969   *Hermeneutics: Interpretation Theory in Schleiermacher, Dilthey, Heidegger, and Gadamer.* Evanston: Northwestern University Press.

Patrick, D. and A. Scult
1990   *Rhetoric and Biblical Interpretation.* Sheffield: Almond Press.

Patte, D.
1979   *What is Structural Exegesis?* Philadelphia: Fortress.
1983   *Paul's Faith and the Power of the Gospel.* Philadelphia: Fortress.
1991   "A Fundamental Condition for the Ethical Accountability in the Teaching of the Bible by White Male Exegetes." *Scriptura* 37:7–28.

Patte, D. and G. Phillips
1991   "Ethical Responsibilities and Practices in Biblical Criticism. A Planning Grant Proposal to the Lilly Endowment." Unpublished.

Pelser, G. M. M.
1984   "Die brief aan die Romeine." In *Handleiding by die Nuwe Testament Vol 5.* Ed. A. B. Du Toit. Pretoria: N. G. Kerkboekhandel. Pp. 41–56.

Perdue, L. G.
1990   "The Social Character of Paraenesis and Paraenetic Literature." *Semeia* 50:5–39.

Perelman, C.
1982   *The Realm of Rhetoric.* Notre Dame: University Press.
Perelman, C. and L. Olbrechts-Tyteca
1969   *The New Rhetoric: A Treatise on Argumentation.* Trans. John Wilkinson
         and Purcell Weaver. Notre Dame: University Press.
Petersen, N. R.
1978   *Literary Criticism for New Testament Critics.* Philadelphia: Fortress.
1985   *Rediscovering Paul: Philemon and the Sociology of Paul's Narrative
         World.* Philadelphia: Fortress Press.
1987   "Prolegomena to a Reader-oriented Study of Paul's Letter to Rome."
         Unpublished Paper read at Studiorum Novi Testamenti Societas Seminar on
         "The Role of the Reader," Trondheim.
Petzer, J. H. and P. J. Hartin, eds.
1986   *A South African Perspective on the New Testament. Essays by South
         African New Testament Scholars presented to Bruce M. Metzger during his
         Visit to South Africa in 1985.* Leiden: Brill.
Plank, K. A.
1987   *Paul and the Irony of Affliction.* Atlanta: Scholars Press.
Poland, L. M.
1985   *Literary Criticism and Biblical Hermeneutics: A Critique of Formalist
         Approaches.* Chico: Scholars Press.
Quintilianus
1920-2   *Institutio Oratoria.* Ed. H. E. Butler. Loeb Classical Library. Cam-
         bridge, MA: Harvard University Press.
Reese, J. M.
1988   Review of Louw and Nida 1988. *Biblical Theology Bulletin* 18:150–51.
Reese, T. J.
1973   "Pauline Politics: Rom 13:1–7." *Biblical Theology Bulletin* 3:323–31.
Rhoads, D. and D. Michie
1982   *Mark as Story. An Introduction to the Narrative of a Gospel.* Philadelphia:
         Fortress.
Ridderbos, H.
1977   *Aan de Romeinen.* Commentaar op het Nieuwe Testament. Kampen:
         Kok. < 1959 >.
Robbins, V. K.
1987   "The Woman Who Touched Jesus' Garment: Socio-Rhetorical Analysis of
         the Synoptic Accounts." *New Testament Studies* 33:502–15. Also found in
         Robbins 1994:184–199.
1990   "A Socio-Rhetorical Response: Contexts of Interaction and Forms of
         Exhortation." *Semeia* 50:261–71.
1992a   *Jesus the Teacher: A Socio-Rhetorical Interpretation of Mark.* Paperback
         edition with new introduction and additional indexes. Minneapolis:
         Fortress Press.
1992b   "A Male Reads a Feminist Reading: The Dialogical Nature of Pippin's
         Power." *Semeia* 59:211–217.
1992c   "Using a Socio-Rhetorical Poetics to Develop a Unified Method: The
         Woman who Anointed Jesus as a Test Case." *1992 SBL Seminar Papers.*
         Ed. Eugene H. Lovering, Jr. Atlanta: Scholars Press. Pp. 302–319.

1993   "Rhetoric and Culture: Exploring Types of Cultural Rhetoric in a Text." In *Rhetoric and the New Testament: Essays from the Heidelberg Conference*. Ed. Stanley E. Porter and Thomas H. Olbrecht. Sheffield: JSOT Press. Pp. 443–463.

1994a   *New Boundaries in Old Territory: Forms and Social Rhetoric in Mark*. Ed. David B. Gowler. Emory Studies in Early Christianity, vol. 3. New York, Bern, Frankfurt am Main: Peter Lang Press.

1994b   "Socio-Rhetorical Criticism: Mary, Elizabeth, and the Magnificat as a Test Case." Ed. Edgar V. McKnight and Elizabeth Struthers Malbon. Valley Forge: Trinity Press International.

Rohrbaugh, R. L.
1987   "'Social Location of Thought' as a Heuristic Construct in New Testament Study." *Journal for the Study of the New Testament* 30:103–19.

Ryan, R. and S. Van Zyl, eds.
1982   *An Introduction to Contemporary Literary Theory*. Johannesburg: A. D. Donker.

Sanday, W. and A. C. Headlam
1902   *A Critical and Exegetical Commentary on the Epistle to the Romans*. International Critical Commentary. Edinburgh: T & T Clark.

Sanders, J. T.
1962   "The Transition from Opening Epistolary Thanksgiving to the Body in the Pauline Letter Corpus." *Journal of Biblical Literature* 81:384–62.

Sapir, E.
1956   *Culture, Language and Personality*. Ed. D. G. Mandelbaum. Berkeley: University of California Press. <1949>.

Schlier, H.
1979   *Der Römerbrief*. Freiburg: Herder.

Schmeller, T.
1987   *Paulus und die "Diatribe."* *Eine vergleichende Stilinterpretation.* Münster: Aschendorff.

1989   "Sociologisch orientierte Exegese des Neuen Testaments." *Bibel und Kirche* 44:103–10.

Schmidt, H. W.
1962   *Der Brief des Paulus an die Römer*. Berlin: De Gruyter.

Schmidt, K. L.
1923   "Die Stellung der Evangelien in der allgemeinen Literaturgeschichte." In *Eucharisterion. Studien zur Religion und Literatur des Alten und Neuen Testaments*. Göttingen: VandenHoeck & Ruprecht. Pp. 50–134.

Schnider, F. and W. Stenger
1987   *Studien zum neutestamentlichen Briefformular*. Leiden: Brill.

Schubert, P.
1939   *Form and Function of the Pauline Thanksgivings*. BZNW 20. Berlin: Töpelmann.

Schüssler Fiorenza, E.
1987   "Rhetorical Situation and Historical Reconstruction in 1 Corinthians." *New Testament Studies* 33:386–403.

1988   "The Ethics of Interpretation: De-centering Biblical Scholarship." *Journal of Biblical Literature* 107(1):3–17.

Scroggs, R.
1976   "Paul as Rhetorician: Two Homilies in Romans 1-11." In *Jews, Greeks and Christians: Essays in Honour of W. D. Davies*. R. Hamerton-Kelly and R. Scroggs, eds. Leiden: Brill. Pp. 271-98.
1980   "The Sociological Interpretation of the New Testament." *New Testament Studies* 26:164-79.

Siegert, F.
1985   *Argumentation bei Paulus gezeigt an Rom 9-11*. WUNT 34. Tübingen: Mohr.

Siertsema, B.
1969   "Language and World View." *The Bible Translator* 20(1):3-21.

Sillars, O. and P. Ganer
1982   "Values and Beliefs: A Systematic Basis for Argumentation." In *Advances in Argumentation Theory and Research*. Ed. J. R. Cox and C. A. Willard. Carbondale and Edwardsville: Southern Illinois University Press. Pp. 184-204.

Silva, M.
1983   *Biblical Words and Their Meaning. An Introduction to Lexical Semantics.* Grand Rapids: Academie.
1988   Review of Louw and Nida 1988. In *Westminster Theological Journal* 51(1):163-67.
1990   *God, Language, and Scripture. Reading the Bible in the Light of General Linguistics*. Grand Rapids: Zondervan.

Sloane, T. O.
1975   "Rhetoric: Rhetoric in Literature." *The New Encyclopedia Brittanica* (15th ed.), 802-810.

Smit, D. J.
1988   "Responsible Hermeneutics: A Systematic Theologian's Response to the Readings and Readers of Luke 12:35-48." *Neotestamentica* 22:441-84.
1990a   "The Ethics of Interpretation — New Voices from the U.S.A." *Scriptura* 33:16-28.
1990b   "The Ethics of Interpretation — and South Africa." *Scriptura* 33:29-43.
1991   "The Bible and Ethos in a New South Africa." *Scriptura* 37:51-67.

Smith, R. H.
1983   "Were the Early Christians Middle-class? A Sociological Analysis of the New Testament." In *The Bible and Liberation. Political and Social Hermeneutics*. Ed. N. K. Gottwald. New York: Orbis. Pp. 441-57.

Smyth, H. W.
1976   *Greek Grammar*. Cambridge, MA: Harvard University Press. < 1920 >.

Snyman, A. H.
1986   "Retoriese kritiek en die Nuwe Testament. Die bydraes van en verband tussen Kennedy en Perelman." *Acta Academica* 6:1-18.
1988a   "On Studying the Figures (Schemata) in the New Testament." *Biblica* 69:93-107.
1988b   "Style and the Rhetorical Situation of Romans 8:31-39." *New Testament Studies* 34:218-31.
1989   "'n Retoriese indeling van die brief aan Filemon." *Acta Academica* 21(2):130-44.
1991   "A Semantic Discourse Analysis of the Letter to Philemon." In Hartin & Petzer (eds.) 1991:83-99.

Snyman, A. H. and J. v. W. Cronjé
1986   "Toward a New Classification of the Figures (σχήματα) in the Greek New Testament." *New Testament Studies* 32:113–21.

Stambaugh, J. E. and D. L. Balch
1986   *The New Testament in its Social Environment.* Library of Early Christianity 2. Philadelphia: Westminster.

Stirewalt, M. L.
1977   "The Form and Function of the Greek Letter-essay." In Donfried (ed.) 1977:175–206.

Stowers, S. K.
1981   *The Diatribe in Paul's Letter to the Romans.* Society of Biblical Literature Dissertation Series 57. Chico: Scholars.
1986   *Letter Writing in Greco-Roman Antiquity.* Library of Early Christianity 5. Philadelphia: Westminster.
1988   "Social Typification and the Classification of Ancient Letters." In J. Neusner (ed.) 1988:78–90.

Strobel, A.
1956   "Zum Verständnis von Röm 13." *Zeitschrift für die neutestamentliche Wissenschaft* 47(56):67–93.
1962   "Furcht, wem Furcht gebührt. Zum profangriechischen Hintergrund von Röm 13,1–7." *Zeitschrift für die neutestamentliche Wissenschaft* 55:58–62.

Suleiman, S. R.
1980   "Introduction: Varieties of Audience-oriented Criticism." In *The Reader in the Text. Essays on Audience and Interpretation.* Ed. S. R. Suleiman and I. Crosman. Princeton: University Press. Pp. 3–45.

Swanepoel, J.
1986   "Literêre analise van die New Testament." *Koers* 51(3):298–327.
1989   "Gebed in die carmina minora van Catullus: 'n Literêre en metodologiese studie, toegespits op enkele probleme in verband met literêre interpretasie." DLitt thesis, Potchefstroom University for CHE.

Tångberg, K. A.
1973   "Linguistics and Theology: An Attempt to Analyse and Evaluate James Barr's Argumentation in *The Semantics of Biblical Language and Biblical Words for Time.*" *Journal of Biblical Literature* 24:301–10.

Tannehill, R. C.
1986   *The Narrative Unity of Luke-Acts.* Philadelphia: Fortress.

Thiselton, A. C.
1979   "Semantics and New Testament Interpretation." In *New Testament Interpretation. Essays on Principles and Methods.* Ed. I. H. Marshall. Exeter: Paternoster. Pp. 75–104.
1985   "Reader-response Hermeneutics, Action Models, and the Parables of Jesus." In Lundin, Thiselton & Walhout 1985:79–114.

Thurén, L.
1990   *The Rhetorical Strategy of 1 Peter. With Special Regard to Ambiguous Expressions.* Åbo: Åbo Akademis Förlag.

Toennies, F.
1963   *Community and Society.* New York: Harper & Row.

Tolbert, M. A.
1989   *Sowing the Gospel. Mark's World in Literary-historical Perspective.* Minneapolis: Fortress.

Toulmin, S. E.
1964   *The Uses of Argument.* Cambridge: University Press.

Tracy, D.
1991   "God, Dialogue and Solidarity: A Theologian's Refrain." In *How My Mind has Changed.* Ed. J. Wall and D. Heim. Grand Rapids: Eerdmans. Pp. 88–99.

Turner, E. G.
1967   *Greek Papyri. An Introduction.* Oxford: Clarendon Press.

Turner, V.
1969   *The Ritual Process: Structure and Anti-Structure.* Ithaca: Cornell University Press.
1974   "Metaphors of Anti-Structure in Religious Culture." In *Changing Perspectives in the Scientific Study of Religion.* Ed. A. W. Eister. New York: John Wiley & Sons. Pp. 63–84.

Van Aarde, A. G.
1988   "Historical Criticism and Holism: Heading towards a New Paradigm?" In Mouton et al. (eds.) 1988:49–64.

Van Eemeren, F. H., R. Grootendorst, and T. Kruiger
1987   *Handbook of Argumentation Theory.* Dordrecht-Holland/Providence-USA: Floris Publications.

Van Iersel, B.
1986   *Marcus.* Boxtel: Katholieke Bijbelstichting.

Van Rensburg, J. J.
1990   "The Use of Intersentence Relational Particles and Asyndeton in First Peter." *Neotestamentica* 24(2):283–300.

Van Staden, P.
1990   "Compassion — The Essence of Life: A Social-Scientific Study of the Religious Symbolic Universe reflected in the Ideology/Theology of Luke." DD thesis, University of Pretoria.

Van Tilborg, S.
1986   *The Sermon on the Mount as an Ideological Intervention.* Assen/Maastricht: Van Gorcum.
1991   "Uitstel van betekenis. Het dekonstruktie-projekt in de literatuurwetenschappen." *Bijdragen* 52:273–292.

Van Unnik, W. C.
1975   "Lob und Strafe durch die Obrigkeit." In *Jesus und Paulus.* Ed. E. E. Ellis et al. FS for W. G. Kümmel. Göttingen: Vandenhoeck & Ruprecht. Pp. 334–43.

Vatz, R. E.
1973   "The Myth of the Rhetorical Situation." *Philosophy and Rhetoric* 6:154–61.

Venter, C. J. H.
1985   "Die Pauliniese paranese in Romeine 12–15 — 'n eksegetiese studie." ThD thesis, Potchefstroom University for CHE.

Violi, P.
1985   "Letters." In *Discourse and Literature.* Ed. T. A. Van Dijk. Amsterdam: John Benjamins. Pp. 149–68.

Visser, N. W.
1982   "Russian Formalism." In Ryan and Van Zyl (eds.) 1982:15–23.

Vorster, J. N.
1988   "Die vroeë Christene en die politiek." In Breytenbach (ed.) 1988:104–22.
1990   "Toward an Interactional Model for the Analysis of Letters."
    Neotestamentica 24(1):107–30.
1991   "The Rhetorical Situation of the Letter to the Romans — An Interactional
    Approach." DD Thesis, University of Pretoria.

Vorster, W. S.
1971   "Moderne linguistiek en Bybelnavorsing." *Theologia Evangelica* 4(2):139–
    48.
1982   "Het structuuranalyse." In Klijn (ed.) 1982:127–52.
1983   "The Bible and Apartheid." In *Apartheid is a Heresy.* Ed. J. W. De
    Gruchy and C. Villa-Vicencio. Cape Town: David Philip. Pp. 94–111.
1984a   "The Historical Paradigm — Its Possibilities and Limitations."
    Neotestamentica 18:104–23.
1984b   "The Use of Scripture and the N. G. Kerk: A Shift of Paradigm or of
    Values?" In *New Faces of Africa. Essays in Honour of Ben Marais.* Ed.
    J. W. Hofmeyer and W. S. Vorster. Miscellanea 45. Pretoria: UNISA.
    Pp. 204–219.
1988   "Towards a Post-critical Paradigm: Progress in New Testament Scholar-
    ship?" In Mouton et al. (eds.) 1988:31–48.

Wallace, R. C. and W. D. Wallace
1985   *Sociology.* Boston: Allyn & Bacon.

Watson, D. F.
1988   "The New Testament and Greco-Roman Rhetoric: A Bibliography."
    Journal of the Evangelical Theological Society 31:465–72.
1990   "The New Testament and Greco-Roman Rhetoric: A Bibliographic
    Update." *Journal of the Evangelical Theological Society* 33:513–24.

Watson, D. F., ed.
1991   *Persuasive Artistry. Studies in New Testament Rhetoric in Honour of
    George A. Kennedy.* Journal for the Study of the New Testament Supple-
    ment Series 50. Sheffield: Sheffield Academic Press.

Webster, A. F. C.
1981   "St. Paul's Political Advice to the Haughty Gentile Christians in Rome:
    An Exegesis of Romans 13:1–7." *St. Vladimir's Theological Quarterly*
    25(4):259–82.

Wedderburn, A. J. M.
1989   *The Reasons for Romans.* Edinburgh: T & T Clark.

Weifel, W.
1977   "The Jewish Community in Ancient Rome and the Origins of Roman
    Christianity." In Donfried (ed.) 1977:100–19.

Weiss, J.
1959   *Earliest Christianity: A History of the Period A.D. 30–150.* Harper Tor-
    chbooks. New York: Harper & Brothers.

Wendland, E. R.
1985   *Language, Society and Bible Translation.* Cape Town: BSSA.

Wendland, E. R.
1990   "What is Truth? Semantic Density and the Language of the Johannine
    Epistles (With Special Reference to 2 John)." *Neotestamentica* 24(2):301–
    334.

White, J. L.
1972   *The Body of the Greek Letter.* Missoula: Scholars Press.

1978   "Epistolary Formulas and Clichés in Greek Papyrus Letters." *SBL Seminar Papers.* Missoula, MT: Scholars. Pp. 289–320.

1986   *Light from Ancient Letters.* Philadelphia: Fortress Press.

Whorf, B. L.

1973   *Language, Thought, and Reality.* Ed. J. B. Carroll. Cambridge, MA: M.I.T. Press. <1956>.

Wikan, U.

1984   "Shame and Honour: A Contestable Pair." *Man* 19:635–52.

Wilckens, U.

1978   *Der Brief and die Römer (Röm 1–5).* Evangelisch-Katholischer Kommentar zum Neuen Testament VI/1. Zürich, Einsiedeln, Köln: Benziger.

1980   *Der Brief and die Römer (Röm 6–11).* Evangelisch-Katholischer Kommentar zum Neuen Testament VI/2. Zürich, Einsiedeln, Köln: Benziger.

1982   *Der Brief and die Römer (Röm 12–16).* Evangelisch-Katholischer Kommentar zum Neuen Testament VI/3. Zürich, Einsiedeln, Köln: Benziger.

Wilder, A. N.

1956   "Scholars, Theologians and Ancient Rhetoric." *Journal of Biblical Literature* 75:1–11.

1971   *Early Christian Rhetoric: The Language of the Gospel.* Cambridge, MA: Harvard University Press.

Wuellner, W.

1976   "Paul's Rhetoric of Argumentation in Romans: An Alternative to the Donfried-Karris Debate over Romans." *Catholic Biblical Quarterly* 38:330–51.

1978   "Toposforschung und Torahinterpretation bei Paulus und Jesus." *New Testament Studies* 24:463–83.

1979   "Greek Rhetoric and Pauline Argumentation." In *Early Christian Literature and the Classical Intellectual Tradition.* Ed. W. R. Schoedel and R. L. Wilken. Paris: Editions Beauchesne. Pp. 177–88.

1987a   "Where Is Rhetorical Criticism Taking Us?" *Catholic Biblical Quarterly* 49:448–63.

1987b   "Reading Romans in Context." Paper read at the Studiorum Novi Testamenti Societas Seminar on "The Role of the Reader," Göttingen.

1988   "Epistolography and Rhetoric in 1 Corinthians." Paper read at the Studiorum Novi Testamenti Societas Seminar on "The Role of the Reader," Cambridge, England.

1989   "Hermeneutics and Rhetorics: From 'Truth and Method' to 'Truth and Power.'" *Scriptura* 35:1–54.

1991   "Rhetorical Criticism and Its Theory in Culture-Critical Perspective: The Narrative Rhetoric of John 11." In Hartin and Petzer (eds.) 1991:171–86.

INDEX OF ANCIENT AND MODERN AUTHORS

EMORY STUDIES IN EARLY CHRISTIANITY

*The first three volumes were published by and are available from Peter Lang Publishing, Inc., 62 West 45th Street, New York, NY 10036-4202; (212) 302-6740; FAX (212) 302-7574.

The fourth and subsequent volumes will be published by Scholars Press.